Short-Form Creative Writing

BLOOMSBURY WRITERS' GUIDES AND ANTHOLOGIES

Bloomsbury Writers' Guides and Anthologies offer established and aspiring creative writers an introduction to the art and craft of writing in a variety of forms, from poetry to environmental and nature writing. Each books is part craft-guide with writing prompts and exercises, and part anthology, with relevant works by major authors.

Series Editors:

Sean Prentiss, Vermont College of Fine Arts, USA
Joe Wilkins, Linfield College, USA

Titles in the Series:

Environmental and Nature Writing, Sean Prentiss and Joe Wilkins
Poetry, Amorak Huey and W. Todd Kaneko

Forthcoming Titles:

Advanced Creative Nonfiction, Sean Prentiss and Jessica Hendry Nelson

Short-Form Creative Writing

A Writer's Guide and Anthology

By

**H. K. Hummel and
Stephanie Lenox**

BLOOMSBURY ACADEMIC

LONDON · NEW YORK · OXFORD · NEW DELHI · SYDNEY

BLOOMSBURY ACADEMIC
Bloomsbury Publishing Plc
50 Bedford Square, London, WC1B 3DP, UK
1385 Broadway, New York, NY 10018, USA

BLOOMSBURY, BLOOMSBURY ACADEMIC and the Diana logo are trademarks of
Bloomsbury Publishing Plc

First published in Great Britain 2019
Reprinted 2019

Cover design: Eleanor Rose
Cover image © Getty images

A catalogue record for this book is available from the British Library.

Library of Congress Cataloging-in-Publication Data
Names: Hummel, H. K. (Heather K.), author. | Lenox, Stephanie, author.
Title: Short-form creative writing : a writer's guide and anthology /
by H. K. Hummel and Stephanie Lenox.
Description: London : Bloomsbury Academic, 2019. |
Series: Bloomsbury writers' guides and anthologies |
Includes bibliographical references and index. |
Identifiers: LCCN 2018019121 (print) | LCCN 2018034175 (ebook) |
ISBN 9781350019904 (ePub) | ISBN 9781350019911 (ePDF) |
ISBN 9781350019898 | ISBN 9781350019898 (hardback) |
ISBN 9781350019881 (paperback) | ISBN 9781350019911 (ePDF) |
ISBN 9781350019904 (eBook)
Subjects: LCSH: Short story–Authorship. |
Creative writing. Classification: LCC PN3373 (ebook) |
LCC PN3373 .H76 2019 (print) | DDC 808.02–dc23
LC record available at https://lccn.loc.gov/2018019121

ISBN: HB: 978-1-3500-1989-8
PB: 978-1-3500-1988-1
ePDF: 978-1-3500-1991-1
eBook: 978-1-3500-1990-4

Series: Bloomsbury Writers' Guides and Anthologies

Typeset by Newgen KnowledgeWorks Pvt. Ltd., Chennai, India
Printed and bound in Great Britain

To find out more about our authors and books visit www.bloomsbury.com
and sign up for our newsletters.

Contents

Part I An Introduction to Short-Form Creative Writing

1 A Long History of the Short Form 3

Part II The Craft of Short-Form Creative Writing

2 Picture This 27

Conclusion: The Beautiful Lightning

Part III Short-Form Creative Writing Anthology

Figures

Preface

What do you get when you cross a zebra with a donkey? No, this is not a joke. During our work on this book, we've come to think of short-form writing—a form of writing that embraces extreme compression—as a literary hybrid akin to the animal kingdom's zebroid. This stunning creature is the crossbreed of a zebra and a member of the equine family, alternately known as a zedonk, zorse, zebra mule, zonkey, zebmule, and more. Since the nineteenth century, zebroids have been bred to combine the most desirable traits of each. With the stripes of a zebra but the shape and temperament of a horse, the zebroid made for a better (and pretty cool-looking) pack animal. It turns out, when you blend the characteristics of two species, the results can be wildly strange and unpredictably beautiful (Figure P.1).

Like the zebroid, short-form writing represents a similar attempt to combine the best of both worlds. It merges the familiar inventiveness of prose and the lyrical intensity of poetry. An abundance of terms attempts to capture the many variations of this unique form. Short forms are free ranging in their subject matter but often confined to a single page. Short forms frequently lean on tradition or convention to propel the reader into uncharted territory. They play with time, space, pattern, and expectation while distilling the literary impulse to its essential elements.

Writer Molly Giles compares short-form literature not to a hybrid creature but to the lightning bug. In her correspondence with us, she explains her theory of extremely short works of fiction:

> I once called flash stories the fireflies of fiction, little sparkles in the dark that wink, go out, and wink again, but that was just fancy writing on my part, for at the time I knew nothing about fireflies. I have since done my homework. I now know that fireflies glow even as eggs, deep underground, that the larvae hibernate for years, that some emerge as flesh-eating cannibals, while others never eat once in their lifetime, that some are so toxic they can poison an owl, that males use their bioluminescence for mating, that females use their bioluminescence to murder their mates, and that somewhere in the Smoky Mountains a thousand of them are blinking in unison right now though no one knows why. Armed with this new information, I will say it

Figure P.1 The Zebroid. Courtesy of Savannah Adams.

again: flash fictions are fireflies, little sparkles in the dark, quick to incubate, slow to develop, omnivorous, amorous, dangerous, mysterious, and, always, illuminating.

This book is devoted to the exploration of the odd species of the short form—prose poems, flash fiction, and flash nonfiction—that startle and please, as much as a firefly, as much as a zorse. We agree with editors Margot Singer and Nicole Walker, who state in *Bending Genre: Essays on Creative Nonfiction* that "there is no such thing as a non-hybrid form." Once you start looking, you will see hybrids everywhere.

Short-form writing, at its best, transgresses. Hybrid work evolves when writers borrow from different genres. They push the boundaries and bend the rules to create a poem that has a taste of fiction, or a story that has an element of the investigative essay, or an essay that is built out of sharp, glittering fragments of ideas. Writers might go even further and write a poem that mimics the FAQs found on the back of a bottle of bleach or a political humor piece that adopts the voice of a Sesame Street character. You can find examples of both approaches in our anthology.

In this textbook, we introduce you to a wide range of writers from around the world and share what they say through a series of flash interviews. In each chapter, you'll explore characteristics and craft elements commonly found in compressed forms, and then you'll get the chance to try out the ideas in your own writing. By examining how these pieces bend or break the rules, you can learn a lot about literary conventions, which in the end will help you define and refine your approach to whatever kind of writing you choose to do.

Why write short?

So, you want to write the next Great American Novel? Go for it. We think the novel has proven time and again that it's a damn good form. Although this book focuses on short-form creative writing, we believe the techniques you'll learn in here will make an impact on any kind of writing you do, whether you eventually gravitate toward writing epic novels, speculative fiction, long-form creative nonfiction, or flash.

When we say **form**, what we mean is the shape that a text takes on the page. There are as many reasons to write as there are forms to write in. The comic Scott McCloud illustrates form as a glass pitcher and content as the liquid that is poured in and shaped by its container. For instance, when we want to express love to someone in writing, we choose a form. The sonnet, a fourteen-line poem written with a defined rhyme scheme and meter, is a form shaped by tradition and associated through the centuries with the expression of love. A text message is also a form, a much more recent one shaped by technology and social conventions. Depending on your audience, one form may be better received than another. In short-form writing, the content is poured into something as tiny as, say, a shot glass. The form makes it easily consumable, but the content is potent, distilled, and might burn a little on the way down.

We call **short-form writing** any type of writing that prioritizes brevity over page count, compression over expansion, and distillation of image and voice over development of plot and character. The works that we explore in this book can all fit onto a few pages, and most can fit on a single page. The short form wears various disguises and flies under the radar, so you might find it hard to pin down at first. Short-form writing is known by different names, and writers and editors frequently disagree about the maximum number of words a piece might contain and still be called "short." In this textbook, we define the short form as creative prose that relies on compression. It can be found in all genres, and it straddles the fence between genres as well. You'll notice we don't dictate a word limit; instead, we provide word counts for each piece so that you can see how a text looks and acts differently, whether it uses 300 words or 1,300 words.

You might have doubts: Is it possible to tell a satisfying story in one hundred words? What about fifty? How exactly do you write with brevity? How much can you leave unsaid? Does constraint inhibit creative freedom? We explore these questions and more.

Despite what some critics say, we argue that the short form is not just for those with short attention spans. Short doesn't mean easy, and it certainly doesn't mean quick—for the writer, that is. Short-form writing concentrates the reader's attention to magnify details, images, and moments. These small texts are microcosms that suggest the existence of macrocosms. Short-form works ask the reader to lean over the microscope. The view is captivating and sometimes weirdly magnificent.

In this book we argue that short-form writing accomplishes the following:

- Distills narrative to its most concentrated form.
- Creates a liminal space that blends, challenges, circumvents, or rejects the norms and expectations of literary convention.
- Fuels innovation and ingenuity through the contained energy of constraint.
- Flirts with the ephemeral and embraces brevity.
- Delights in the irreverent, subversive, and contrarian nature of language.
- Remains aware of the ticking clock, the limits of time and attention, the approaching end of the page.
- Combines the spaciousness of prose with the lyricism of poetry.
- Slips past barriers, boundaries, and borderlines.
- Invites the reader to collaborate in the making of meaning through evocative images and figurative language.

- Insists on silence, white space, and subtext.
- Asserts that less can be more.
- Leverages the power of the small, the overlooked, the underrated.

How we've organized each chapter

We invite you to take a look at what you'll find in each chapter. Along the way, we'll offer advice on how you might use each section to get the most out of the textbook.

Relevant readings

For each chapter, we provide a list of recommended readings from the anthology that illustrate the chapter's concepts. The anthology is designed to give you a wide range of styles and voices so that you can get a feel for the rich diversity of short-form writing being produced by writers from Bosnia, Canada, Chile, France, Greece, Iceland, Italy, the United States, and beyond. You'll notice that the relevant readings recur throughout the book as they are used to illustrate a variety of short-form techniques. This repetition is intentional and designed to deepen your reading practice as you get acquainted with this innovative and challenging form.

Take a few minutes to browse through the anthology. Here are a few ways to approach the texts:

- Read the first sentence of each piece from the anthology. Notice which of the following literary elements are immediately present: character, setting, conflict, time, action. Do you see any common strategies within these opening sentences?
- Each anthology piece is followed by the exact word count. Notice the variations in length. Find the shortest piece. Find the longest piece. Notice the different arrangements of paragraphs and sections within a piece. Hazard a guess: How might a writer approach a 50-word story compared with a 500-word story?
- Consider the organization of the anthology. We have chosen to organize the anthology alphabetically by the author's last name and to identify the genre categories in a separate index. What happens to the way you read a text if you don't know right away how it "should" be categorized?

Flash interviews

Each chapter includes a brief interview with a writer from the anthology. We use these interviews to introduce you to a variety of theories and perspectives on short-form writing. If you enjoy what the featured writers say in their interviews, look for their work so you can see how they put their theories into action on the page.

Free dives

Each chapter opens with an exercise we call a free dive. In the sport of freediving, divers take a breath, dive as far below the surface as possible, immerse in a strange and otherworldly environment, and then resurface, all in the span of one breath. It's an artful kind of sport that requires a sense of adventure and endurance: freedivers might glimpse a whale shark, a hammerhead, a shipwreck, a whirling school of anchovies ... who knows? As divers get better at holding their breath, they build lung capacity and can stay submerged longer. But, no matter how strong their lungs get, the adventure is always brief, and it always relies on a careful regulation of compression as their bodies cope with the intense pressure of being underwater.

In these brief writing exercises, we want to see how deep you can go. Dive in and submerge yourself in another world. Head straight down. Look for surprises. Explore. Study the intensity of this deep, brief adventure, then surface and take a breath. We want you to have the freedom to respond creatively to the prompt in any way that works for you. You have only three rules:

1. Write in prose. That means write in paragraphs and sentences, not lineated verse.
2. Keep it short. If you write five pages you've gone too far.
3. Immerse yourself and your reader in the moment you describe. Make your language as lively and descriptive as you can.

This kind of free-form exploration is meant to be approached as play. It might feel a little risky at first, but practice and keep practicing: your endurance will improve.

Vignettes

As the editors of this textbook, we want to share our own exploration of the short form. We take turns responding to the free dive exercises so that you can see how we put our own spin on it. As teachers we often write alongside our students in the classroom. So we write with you here, too. We're not just talking at you: we're immersed in the process of experimentation with you. We try to offer you a glimpse of what our writing process looks like in action, so you can see what happens as you develop a piece of writing from a journal entry into something more. You might use these free dives and vignettes as a way to think about how these brief moments translate into self-contained works. How might you make your writing look and act more distinctly like something that belongs to the short-form species?

Exercises

Each chapter contains a set of exercises that can be done individually or in the classroom. The activities are designed to get you critically thinking about the ideas discussed in the chapter.

Prompts

The prompts at the end of each chapter are designed to get you writing. Not every writing prompt will lead to a well-developed flash text, but each one provides the chance to try out the craft ideas we talk about in the chapter. If you experiment with applying these moves in your own writing, you'll learn about them in a more tangible way.

One-sentence workshops

These final exercises give you practice working on brevity at the sentence level. Think of them as quick intensives in writing and editing so that each sentence you use can be as clear, concise, and effective as possible. What creates a tight compact sentence that sings and moves in just the right way? Roll up your sleeves: this is where you get your hands dirty as you learn to think like a writer while making the calculated decisions of an editor.

Getting started

Perhaps the most important thing to remember as you begin exploring the anthology in this book is that some of the pieces will challenge everything you believe you know about what writing can and should do with characters, narrative, setting, image, and conflict. Prose poems, flash fictions, sudden fictions, micro-stories, and flash essays are slightly wild beasts. Each one is a scrappy little animal. It has sharp teeth, evades traps, and pounces. And, undoubtedly, these short-form works employ a slow-woo technique; long after you think you're done with a piece, you'll realize you haven't been able to stop thinking about it.

Ask yourself these questions as you read your own work, the work of your classmates, and the work of writers in the anthology:

- What makes it feel unfamiliar or strange? Conversely, what makes it feel familiar and inviting?
- How does it tease, reveal, telescope, or constrict?
- What do you assume, wonder about, or imagine?
- When does it spring open with surprise?

Test out those questions on this prose poem by Russell Edson:

The Prose Poem as a Beautiful Animal
He had been writing a prose poem, and had succeeded in mating a giraffe with an elephant. Scientists from all over the world came to see the product: The body looked like an elephant's, but it had the neck of a giraffe with a small elephant's head and a short trunk that wiggled like a wet noodle.
You have created a beautiful new animal, said one of the scientists. Do you really like it?
Like it? cried the scientist, I adore it, and would love to have sex with it that I might create another beautiful animal …

Edson's definition of prose poetry is purposefully shocking. He uses a range of paradoxical images, merging the scientist's laboratory with the writer's studio and the gangly giraffe with the hefty elephant. The effusive conversation between writer and scientist circumvents conventions of punctuation and politeness. It breaks taboos with talk of sex and animals, leaving the reader with a sketchy narrative in the same way a stand-up comedian might. Edson provokes readers into a moment of uncomfortable surprise to expand their understanding of the prose poem. Then he promptly exits the scene with a lingering sensation of odd delight.

This lingering sensation is accentuated by Edson's use of the ellipsis, those three dots that bring this strange encounter to an unsettling close. The conversation isn't finished. In fact, we suspect that this is only the beginning. The creation of one strange animal leads to the next, and the next, and the next. Readers are left to drift back to a reality that is more malleable and prolific than they at first imagined.

For now, throw your preconceived rules out the door and see what happens when you experiment in your own writing. Ask, *What if?* Why not blend the best of what you know about prose and poetry and see what happens? Can you keep it short and still go deep? Let those questions lead you. Ultimately, we believe that it is at the crossroads of tame and wild where most writers discover their best ideas.

Part I

An Introduction to Short-Form Creative Writing

1

A Long History of the Short Form

Relevant readings

"A Story Possibly Heard in Some Bar at Three in the Morning" by Pía Barros

"Be Drunken" by Charles Baudelaire

"The Man Who Hated Us and Then Forgot" by Karen E. Bender
"Thin Cities 5" by Italo Calvino
"The Dinosaur" by Augusto Monterroso
"Cannibals and Explorers" by Ana María Shua
"Icelandic Hurricane" by Tomas Tranströmer

Flash interview with Pía Barros

Pía Barros is a Chilean fiction writer known for her work as a human rights activist against gender violence. We chose "A Story Possibly Heard in Some Bar at Three in the Morning" for the anthology because of the way she plays with a story within a story to create a never-ending loop of a narrative that captures readers and won't let them go. Here's what she has to say about writing short.

How do you define the kind of short-form writing that you do?
    I define it the old-fashioned way: flash fiction maximizes the "signified" with the fewest number of "signifiers."

How does your approach to writing in short forms differ from the other kinds of writing that you do?
    I have published a few novels and short story collections, but flash fiction, it seems to me, is a challenge that matches our times. If in the past, we traveled by boat for almost two months, we needed books that were more than a thousand pages. Plane rides give us time to read a 100-page novel. But the subway gives us two minutes between every station. In a world characterized by immediacy, flash fiction is here to stay. The very short novel, the very short movie, and short theater pieces all form part of a contemporary reality where quick responses are necessary. In a lot of ways literature and life are tied up in a knot that cannot be untangled.

What demands does the short form make of its writers or readers?
    From its beginnings, literature, and art in general, has been about synthesis. Synthesizing requires intelligence. Flash fiction challenges participatory readers because they are part of the writing itself. All human beings are creative, there is no doubt about that, no matter what they say. To dare to create flash fiction is to dare to survive.

Translated by Resha Cardone

Free dive

Once upon a time, there was a book you loved more than any other. Imagine the book in your hands. How heavy is it? What is the texture of its cover? Are the pages crisp or worn with repeated turning? If a book doesn't come immediately to mind, consider if another art form such as music, dance, photography, or film has changed the way you think and move in the world. Maybe it was Prince, in kohl-black eyeliner and a mermaid green suit during the Super Bowl half-time show singing "Purple Rain." Or Lady Gaga stepping onstage in a meat dress. What place and mindset were you in when you encountered this new idea, and how did it change your thinking? Focus on both the internal change and external details of the experience by incorporating language that refers to the senses. Spend some time reflecting on this pivotal experience, then take ten minutes to write about it. Trade or discuss your free write with a partner. Do your reflections share any common elements? What conclusions can you draw about how art invites us to experience the world in new ways?

Vignette: Urgency and the short form

The summer before my senior year in college, I donned a hairnet, apron, and ergonomic shoes to work fulltime in the kitchen of my hometown's Olive Garden. I'd applied to be a waitress, but a personality test administered during the interview determined that kitchen work best suited my introverted nature. I had answered the questionnaire truthfully: yes, I did "prefer a small group of close friends to large, noisy parties." Once hired, my closest companions became the cooks with whom I communicated using a shorthand of eye rolls, winks, and shrugs over the crash of dishes, the grill's sizzle, and the chirpy waitresses cussing about customers as they loaded their serving trays. For eight hours, I assembled salads, doling out handfuls of shredded iceberg lettuce, four thin bands of onion, three wheel-shaped tomato slices, two black olives, one pepperoncini, and a humble scattering of croutons.

While my coworkers took their fifteen-minute breaks to smoke in an adjacent parking lot, I sat on a curb and consumed, little by little, Micro Fiction: An Anthology of Fifty Really Short Stories edited by Jerome Stern.

During those breaks, I immersed myself in another world. The dishes in my head stopped rattling. The constant loop of faux Italian ballads—"When the moon hits your eye like a big pizza pie"—momentarily paused as I read Molly Giles's "The Poet's Husband," which describes a broken relationship in a single, heart-breaking sentence. I bought the book because of its size; it fit neatly into my apron's pocket, and I could read an entire story from beginning to end and still have enough time to look up, squint into the sun, and take a few deep breaths before heading back into the kitchen.

Pinned to my apron a button advertised, "Hot food fast," the industry's ultimate command under which kitchen staff and servers labored. Day after day, I hurried breadsticks into baskets, poured bags of soup into heating pans, and drizzled chocolate onto flash-frozen tiramisu under the watchful eye of the store manager who, a month into my employment, told me that I too might be management material if I applied myself. The manager was the mouthpiece for the chain's rules and regulations, and because of that the kitchen staff took every opportunity to thwart him. When I could, I treated the customers to a few extra olives atop their salads. When his back turned to the register, a server would grab a breadstick, wag it like a giant cigar, and then eat it in two bites.

One afternoon while the manager was at lunch, I "accidentally" shoved my elbow into a box of tiramisu, and the entire kitchen staff huddled around it with forks to take care of the damaged goods. We had impromptu, minute-long feasts gorging on fettuccini alfredo, skirt steak, and whatever else was mistakenly prepared and bound for the garbage can. There was urgency both to the work and to the many ways we secretly revolted. During my short reprieves from the kitchen's humid din, I found that same urgency reflected and somehow assuaged by the tiny stories in my apron pocket.

I'm telling you all this because me and flash, we go way back. I am drawn to the short form not because I have a short attention span but because of the way it artfully concentrates what little attention I have. Short-form writing is urgent, portable, rebellious, and it refuses to conform to any requirements other than the limits of the page itself. It is a reprieve from the cacophony of contemporary life—its constant barrage of texts, tweets, updates, and alerts—and presents the reader with a solitude that speaks volumes. In this book, we present you with a form that is not novel (and not a novel) but as old as storytelling itself, as deep as your imagination, and as exciting as eating an entire box of tiramisu in two minutes flat.

—Stephanie
Word count: 653 words

In the beginning

What were those Paleolithic cave-dwellers thinking when they first picked up a burnt stick and began sketching images of bison on stone walls over 30,000 years ago? Was it a way to record a hunt, tell a story, pass the time, or educate the young? Perhaps it was a means of conjuring "hunting magic," as French priest and archaeologist Henri Breuil speculated after extensive study of the drawings found in the caves of Lascaux, France, and elsewhere. Though we can only guess, this prehistoric moment marks an important turn in the human story.

When a form of communication—either through words, images, or other means—moves beyond its functional purpose, we have entered the realm of art. The boundaries between art/not art and literature/not literature are subjective, determined by our cultural moment, our training, and our point of view. Yet, there is a critical transition when the sharing of information becomes something more. When does that happen? How do we recognize it?

The poet Lucille Clifton once described the "first poem" as the moment someone "walked off a savannah or out of a cave and looked up at the sky with wonder and said, 'Ah.'" It's no surprise that Clifton's imagined "first poem" is composed of a single word, more sound than meaning. The essence of this first poem reminds us that making art out of the written word requires us to simplify the stimuli of our world and to respond with attention to the wonder of what surrounds us.

We may seem far removed from those prehistoric scribblers summoning "hunting magic," but the storytelling impulse has long been entwined with human survival. Whether that story is told through pictures, spoken word, or written text, we need to tell each other our stories. *Let us slay the bison* is a completely different story than, *He slayed the bison and survived the winter*. And both are completely different from the one that begins, *Guess what? The wildest thing happened today*. Yet, we need to tell, and hear, some variation of these stories.

It is probably no surprise that many of the examples you'll read in this textbook, a book that concentrates on the blurry boundaries between literary genres, would also intentionally push against those boundaries of what is and is not art. Likewise, it should be of no surprise that many (and perhaps all) of the pieces in this textbook locate a sentiment that echoes Clifton's "ah," an exclamation of wonder and surprise.

It can be hard to understand the impact that **orality**, or spoken language, has had on the development of storytelling. As a student of creative writing, it's important to remember that **literacy**, the ability to read and write, accounts for only a small portion of the human experience and as such is a relatively recent skill. Evidence of written language that includes words and not just numbers dates back to just over 5,000 years ago. It's a mere tick of the clock compared to the 30,000–50,000 year span that *Homo sapiens* have been walking the earth.

Some critics have blamed social media and other new technology for waning attention spans and thus the rising popularity of extremely short literature. The invention of "Twitterature," or stories defined by the limits imposed by social media, suggests that attention, both that of the reader and that of the writer, has shrunk to text-box size. It might be tempting to think of short-form writing as a response to the Information Age, a way to compete with the mediated flood for the limited attention span of overtaxed readers. However, we see a distinction between writing that is truncated based on external limits and writing that emphasizes the art of compression driven by internal concerns.

At the same time, we agree with Pía Barros that "literature and life are tied up in a knot that cannot be untangled." Like many readers, we read flash texts during lunch breaks or daily commutes. We write flash texts during our kids' naptimes, while on hold with our medical provider, or in other stolen moments of the day. However, we also posit that the short-form writing you will encounter in this textbook and beyond is part of a long tradition that predates Twitter.

Epigrams, maxims, aphorisms, fables, parables, allegories, and jokes are all examples of short forms that thrived alongside longer forms of storytelling and have roots in the oral tradition. In the early English tradition, you might compare the 3,182-line Old English epic poem *Beowulf* to the short riddles, maxims, and bestiaries from the *Exeter Book*. Some of the riddles are as short as five lines and exemplify the natural compactness of the form. Although these texts served different literary purposes, they coexisted, roughly speaking, side by side. Perhaps just as importantly, within the epic of *Beowulf* there are examples of the smaller compressed forms like hymns, riddles, gnomic verse, and maxims. So, short forms and long forms haven't simply coexisted: they are often part of the same literary milieu.

There has always been an audience for the intense illumination of the fable, just as there has always been an audience for the immersive experience of the epic. **Fables**, those lessons about human error enacted by a cast of animal counterparts, were short because they served as conversation starters for lessons about morality and societal expectations. Epigrams, originally found carved in stone as memorials, were kept brief because of the materials of composition. Every word had to be worth the effort it required to chisel it. Aphorisms and maxims got straight to the point. They used pithy statements to relay an everyday truth or to jolt us into noticing where the paradoxical resides. Sometimes they were funny, sometimes they were profound. Sometimes both.

To shape one's experience of the world requires paring down, recognizing patterns, and managing complexity. Short-form writing offers that opportunity to practice these skills. Today's short-form writing is popular and widely practiced because brevity chisels language into an intense, focused narrative unlike any other mode of storytelling. It drops readers into a moment, a scene, a crisis, or an idea. It offers them an ultra-quick view, and then lets them go.

Long or short, narratives sustain us. We use them to lull children to sleep at night. We use them to frighten ourselves into good behavior. They enliven the dull moments and preserve the moments we want to savor. They explain and entertain. They document a different perspective. This is by no means an exhaustive history of the short form. Rather we hope it helps you glance backward from contemporary short-form writing so that you can recognize how today's short form echoes and amplifies elements of its literary predecessors.

A note on genre

So what is the difference between prose and poetry? **Prose** is defined as any kind of written text that uses the sentence as its main unit of composition. Under the umbrella of prose you can find journalism, memoir, fiction, romance novels, or textbooks; most writing in English is formatted onto a page, either paper or electronic, that determines the appearance of the text. On the other hand, we have poetry, or in more technical terms **verse**, a written text that uses the line as its main unit of composition. You can immediately distinguish poetry from prose based on what it looks like on the page. The poem may be considered traditional verse, meaning that it is composed according to some predefined pattern of rhythm or rhyme scheme, such as the sonnet, or it may be free verse, with rhythmic patterns and sonic devices determined by the author. Yet, we generally can determine we are in the presence of a poem based on the white space after line breaks and between stanzas. Later in this chapter, we will talk in detail about the prose poem, which defies this definition.

When we say **genre**, we mean the type or kind of writing. For example, this book mainly explores the genres of fiction, creative nonfiction, and prose poetry. One of the challenging things about genre is that there are many types of genre. There are the traditional literary genres of fiction, nonfiction, poetry, and drama. As writer Josh Rothman explains in his article "A Better Way to Think about the Genre Debate," there are "period genres (Victorian literature), subject genres (detective fiction), form genres (the short story), style genres (minimalism), market genres ('chick-lit'), mode genres (satire), and so on." Genres are merely labels, like those signs hanging in your favorite bookstore that direct you to the graphic novels or the large print texts or biographies. Genres help locate the reader and the reader will generally have some expectations of what a book within a specific genre might contain. In this book, we argue that the choices a writer makes at the level of language, image, and form are more likely to define a text than its genre.

What joins prose and poetry under the category of short-form writing is the way both challenge and resist the formal expectations of their home genres. Short prose resists the expansiveness of its home genre, and prose poetry resists the formal line breaks that clearly identify its poetic intent. While there may be differences in approach and perspective—the prose poet may prefer one literary technique while the flash fiction writer may be more concerned with another—the result is still a block of text on the page. The impact and potential of the short form transcends the genre distinctions and invites us to explore the ways a text can push against our expectations.

Most works included in this textbook are fewer than 1,000 words, though occasionally we include slightly longer pieces that demonstrate an important technique of the short form. Within these pages you will find stories of varying length. We even found a story with a word count of zero. Guillermo Samperio's "*El fantasma*" (The Ghost) is just a title and the blank page.

Word counts are but one way to limit the short form. Edgar Allen Poe, in an 1842 review of Nathaniel Hawthorne's collection *Twice Told Tales*, defined a short story not by word count but by the reader's investment of time and effort. To be deeply moved, explained Poe, a short story must have a "unity of impression" and "continuity of effort" that can only be achieved when read in a single, uninterrupted session. Short-form writing similarly requires an investment from the reader's imagination that far exceeds the number of words on the page. Prose poetry, flash fiction, and flash nonfiction require concentration on both sides, from the reader's close attention to the writer's distillation of an idea, moment, or story.

While there is very little agreement among editors and writers about what to call extremely compressed literary works, there is one thing we know for sure: short-form literature is as old, as universal, and as vital as any kind of storytelling. Known as palm-of-the-hand stories in Japan and smoke-long stories in China, short-form writing abounds with terms to describe these distilled works of literature (Table 1.1).

This book emphasizes the commonalities in this diverse form, the discoveries writers and readers can make when they practice the techniques of short-form writing, and the way these short works share in a literary tradition that can teach us to make the most of every word.

The short forms we examine in this book are not just miniaturized versions of their home genres. Instead, they have traditions and histories that run parallel to the more established genres and which influence and reinforce each other. In the shadow of their longer and more "serious" counterparts, short forms enjoy a level of freedom and experimentation that would be hard to sustain in longer works. Compact and multifaceted, short-form writing unfolds like a Swiss Army knife. It is a tool for adventurous and resourceful writers.

You'll notice in this textbook we often use "short form" to deliberately resist categorizing texts by genre. We emphasize that the boundaries are blurry: in the short form, some stories act like poems. Some poems act like essays. Some essays act like inventories. In the realm of short prose, if it looks like a chicken and clucks like a chicken, you never know: it might be a person in a chicken suit.

As an instructional stance, we like to encourage a bit of healthy skepticism when it comes to identifying genre categories. We also take the approach that a lot can be learned from studying craft techniques across the genres. With that in mind, below we briefly introduce flash fiction, prose poetry, and short-form creative nonfiction so that you can begin to examine your own ideas and assumptions.

Flash fiction

Every aspect of our modern lives has been shaped in some way by the unprecedented technological advances of the Industrial Revolution, and

Table 1.1 What's in a name? Chart of short-form terms

Anecdotes	Micro-stories
Aphorisms	*Микро разказ* (Bulgarian—"micro narrative")
Apothegms	*Minicontos* (Portuguese—"tiny tales")
Briefs	*Minificción* (Spanish—"miniature fiction")
Brief essays	*Microstorias* (Italian—"micro story")
Casos (Spanish—"cases")	Minisagas (50 words)
Crônica (Portuguese—"chronicle")	Minute stories
Definitions	Monostich (one-line verse)
Denkbilder (German—"thinking pictures")	Nanofiction
Drabble (100 words)	Napkin stories
Dribble (50 words)	Notes
Espresso stories	*Очерка* (Russian—"short nonfiction essay")
Extracts	Ouroboric novels
Fables	Parables
Fantasies	Paragraphs
Feuilletons (French—"serials")	*Pensées* (French—"thoughts")
Ficciones relámpagos (Spanish—"lightning fiction")	Palm-of-the-hand stories (from Japanese)
Figures	Pocket-sized stories
Flash fiction	*Poèmes en prose* (French—prose poems)
Flash nonfiction	Postcard fiction
Fragments	*Prosa d'arte* (French—prose of art)
Gnomes	Prose poems
Greguerías (Spanish—similar to aphorism)	Quick fiction
Hint fiction (25 words)	Reflections
Ideas	Riddles
Idylls	Sentences
Instructions	Shorts
Jottings	Short-short stories
Jokes	Situations
Koans	Six-word memoirs
Kurzprosa (Danish—"short prose")	Sketches
Kürzestgeschichten (German—"shortest stories")	Smoke-long stories (from Chinese)
Lists	Stamp stories (50 words)
Lyrical essays	Sudden fiction (750 words)
Maxims	Tableaus
Microcosmography	Tales
Micro essays	Transmutations
Microcuentos (Spanish—"micro-stories")	Tropisms
Microfiction	Twitterature
Micronouvelles (French—"micro-novels")	Utterances
Microrrelatos (Spanish—"very short fictions")	Vignettes

literature is no exception. During the late 1700s and early 1800s, major developments in the factory system, steam power, machine tools, and other advancements signaled changes in living conditions, population density, and production of goods. The population of cities grew exponentially, resulting in a gradual shift in the Western world from an agrarian lifestyle to a more urban society. Higher wages, shorter working days—compared to the long days in the field—and increased literacy paved the way to a broader and more diverse reading audience than ever before.

The experience of readers in the nineteenth century continued to change with periodicals, which could be produced cheaply and distributed efficiently to a more centralized urban readership. These publications gained prominence over the course of this century and provided a venue for short-form writing. Writers of short stories, brief anecdotes, sketches, and tales could sell their stories to periodicals and make a profitable living. Short-form writing has always existed alongside other forms of literature, but it was this period in history that popularized it and also made it profitable for writers. Increased interest in short pieces solidified formal characteristics that emphasized thematic unity and restraint.

It wasn't until the later part of the twentieth century that a tendency toward extremely short stories came to the attention of editors Robert Shapard and James Thomas. In their reading, they noticed works of fiction totaling no more than a few pages in length that seemed to position themselves between the genres of fiction and poetry. These highly compressed narratives took cues from the short story, but they also contained language charged with the lyric intensity of a poem. In the first of a series of anthologies, Shapard and Thomas coined the term for these stories: flash fiction. They were not the first to attempt to label these extremely brief stories, and they certainly weren't the last. In fact, more than any kind of writing, short-form fiction has inspired the most diverse array of appellations, not just in English but in languages from around the globe.

The word count for these short forms varies just about as much as the names that have been used to describe them. Yet they all point to a kind of writing that thrives on limits. In his introduction to *Flash Fiction: Very Short Stories*, James Thomas points to Ernest Hemingway's "A Very Short Story," published in 1925, as an archetype of the short form. Thomas used this story to set the limit of 750 words for the stories in his anthology. His editorial partner Robert Shapard, in his series of *Sudden Fiction* anthologies, took another route and defined sudden fiction as works of 1,500 words or fewer, essentially anything shorter than a short story.

The appeal of the miniature is nothing new. Perhaps its transmission has been facilitated by technology, but the human instinct for novelty and portability is as old as hunting and gathering cultures. In North American indigenous cultures, scaled down replicas of watertight birch bark canoes were made following the same ancestral techniques as their full-sized counterparts. Initially used as toys for children, they later became souvenirs for tourists who wanted a portable piece of culture to represent their encounter with the "other." These replicas have found their way into exhibits around the world because, in addition to other things, they can fit neatly into a museum display case while suggesting a larger tradition, history, and cultural narrative. Similarly, the Venus of Willendorf, a four-inch carving of a voluptuous female figure found in Austria and estimated to have been crafted in 28,000 BCE, is small enough to fit in a hand or pocket. Perhaps she was meant to be carried as a kind of good luck charm, similar to a rabbit's foot or worry stone. The short form has the qualities of a talisman that can be carried in our pocket.

The short form is frequently playful and portable. It can allude to a larger narrative while exercising a poetic restraint through the meticulous choice of language and form. In this book, we've elected to use the term **flash writing** to describe fiction, poetry, and creative nonfiction that ends where the short story generally begins, at about 1,500 words. We like the term "flash" for its multivalent potential. It suggests the illumination, immediacy, and electric surge of lightning; it makes use of the breezy, informative, democratic voice of the news bulletin; it assumes the collective craziness of the flash mob or the frenetic energy of the flash dance; and it is reminiscent of the explosive, blinding flash bulb of early photography.

Prose poetry

Paris is referred to as the City of Lights, primarily because it is known as the birthplace of the Enlightenment, or the Age of Reason (1685–1815), and secondarily because of its early adoption of gas lighting along the Champs-Élysées, the broad avenue that stretches through the city from the Place de la Concorde to the Arc de Triomphe. But Paris could also rightly be called the City of the Prose Poem for its enlightened role in the development of this distinctive hybrid form. It was this city that inspired the prose poems of Charles Baudelaire, which were published as a slim volume in 1869, two years after the author's early death.

For most of Baudelaire's writing career, French poetry had been dominated by the **alexandrine**, a tightly controlled verse of twelve-syllable iambic lines, a literary descendant of French heroic verse. Baudelaire's *Petits Poèmes en Prose* (Little Poems in Prose) broke from convention in several ways. Not only did it toss metrical verse out the window, but it abandoned the line break as well. Baudelaire's poems appear as little blocks of text on a page and focus on the strangeness and estrangement of urban life.

Baudelaire was not the first person to write poems without line breaks. He was most immediately influenced by the *ballades en prose* (prose ballads) in *Gaspard de la Nuit* by Aloysius Bertrand (1807–41). But it was Baudelaire who launched the prose poem as its own entity, a modern form that blurred boundaries and was energized by the author's intentional break from tradition.

In a letter that opens the book and serves as its preface, Baudelaire defines his literary aspirations: "Which one of us, in his moments of ambition, has not dreamed of the miracle of a poetic prose, musical, without rhythm and without rhyme, supple enough and rugged enough to adapt itself to the lyrical impulses of the soul, the undulations of reverie, the jibes of conscience?" With this letter Baudelaire speaks from beyond the grave to clarify what he called the "haunting ideal" of the small poems collected into manuscript form during his final days. This ideal would inspire writers, both in his country and abroad, who sought a poetic form that could simultaneously contain and free the "lyrical impulses of the soul."

What we call the prose poem in English comes to us from France, but it has gone through many changes to become the form we recognize today. The first recorded usage of the term *poémes en prose* (poetry in prose) can be found in literature of the early eighteenth century, though depending on how broadly you want to define prose poetry, one could find evidence of the concept in the work of Aristotle. Digging through literary history, both in English and other languages, will turn up a wealth of examples that fit the bill: non-lineated verse or poetic prose. American prose poet Russell Edson once quipped that, "Heck, one can call most anything a prose poem. That's what's great about them, anything that's not something else is probably a prose poem." While many critics have focused on attempting to define what prose poetry is—a genre? a subgenre? a mode? a form?—the single most defining element (other than its brevity) is that it artfully and intentionally blurs the boundaries between prose and poetry.

Flash nonfiction

Creative nonfiction of any length is perhaps the hardest term to explain because it is defined by what it is not. We are surrounded by writing not intended to be fictional—news articles, instruction manuals, advertisements, and so on—that have the purpose of being informative or persuasive. Such texts might be well written and interesting, but the primary function of nonfiction is to convey information. When "creative" joins this term, it modifies the informative or persuasive style to include creative approaches associated with fiction or poetry. **Creative nonfiction** tends to be personal, reflective, exploratory, and focused on human experience or memory, but it also has a more public face in the form of literary journalism. Creative nonfiction, like the other creative genres, emphasizes language, image, story, character, setting, and other literary elements to set itself apart from writing that is purely informational.

Creative nonfiction may not have always had that name, but it has always been with us. From the earliest aphorisms, epistles (or letters), diaries, and journals, creative nonfiction has been rooted in the attempt to make sense of and communicate the personal experience. The sixteenth-century French writer Michel de Montaigne is the writer best known for his *essais* (attempts), many of which were written in the short form. Many writers point to Montaigne as the originator of the essay as a distinct literary genre. In the United States, Ben Franklin published *Poor Richard's Almanack* as an annual beginning with the year 1733. For twenty-five years, Franklin published this collection under a pseudonym with original and adapted writing in the form of proverbs, recipes, weather predictions, folk wisdom, and other memorable adages that have entered in the American vernacular, such as "visitors and fish stink after three days." Franklin is also known for his influential autobiography, which was published after his death and considered a foundational text of the literary genre of autobiography.

Personal narrative, memoir, and autobiography are often used interchangeably, and while there are important distinctions between these modes of writing, they all fall under the literary genre of creative nonfiction. Personal narrative tends to be event driven, while memoir focuses on an individual and memories within that individual's life. Autobiography tends to take a more comprehensive approach, organizing the personal story of an individual's life by chronology rather than events or memories.

In 1994, Lee Gutkind founded the literary journal *Creative Nonfiction* with the tag line "true stories well told." A few years later in 1997, Dinty Moore began *Brevity: A Journal of Concise Literary Nonfiction* as an outgrowth of Gutkind's creation. *Brevity* retains the same goal of "true stories well told" but adds to it the limitation of 750 words. Moore describes the reader of flash nonfiction as "a smokejumper, one of those brave firefighters who jump out of planes and land 30 yards from where the forest fire is burning. The writer starts the reader right at that spot, at the edge of the fire, or as close as one can get without touching the actual flame."

Influenced by flash fiction and prose poetry, flash nonfiction wrestles with the double bind of "what actually happened" and the limits of word count. It's a challenge that has produced stunning results, as can be seen in the four anthologies of short nonfiction edited by Judith Kitchen: *In Short* (1996), *In Brief* (1999), *Short Takes* (2005), and *Brief Encounters* (2015). The flash form is well suited to the fragmentary nature of memory itself. To take what life has given you, to see the connections and find the story, and to retell it artfully and with extreme brevity makes this form of flash writing a worthwhile challenge.

What is short-form writing?

We write in short forms every day: grocery lists, tweets, memos, postcards, text messages. These serve a practical purpose as reminders, quick communications, and headlines to help us navigate the flood of information that comes at us from every possible direction. According to recent studies, the average American consumes 100,000 words every day in traditional print media. How can this be? How is it possible to quantify the tsunami of words we encounter during a single day?

If we could quantify it, though, it would mean that the average American reads the equivalent of Emily Brontë's *Wuthering Heights* every day. We are not, of course, reading every one of these 100,000 words. Rather, we are seeing the words everywhere from billboards to flyers posted on telephone poles. Add to that what we receive through visual and digital media from all the screens and other media we encounter in our daily lives. This stream of information swells every year. Out of necessity, we ignore much of what we hear and see.

Literature of any length aims to refocus our attention, to make us see clearly and hear anew the essential human story. American novelist John Gardner once said that there are only two kinds of stories we tell ourselves: someone went on a journey or a stranger came to town. Looking closer at Gardner's two narrative categories, we see that they are in fact two sides of the same coin. The short-form equivalent of these narrative categories might be "there goes so-and-so" or "hey, look, a stranger." The story changes depending on who is telling it and where they stand in relation to others. The short form gives us just the tail end of this journey or the first point of contact where the unknown and the known meet.

Many scholars have written at length on archetypal characters and plots, those universal elements that show up in stories throughout time and across cultures. But to stand out from the 100,000 other words that slide across our field of vision, a story that aims to be literature must do something different from what we see every day even as it appeals to those universal desires. The advice of modernist poet Ezra Pound still holds true: "Make it new!" And it can't just be new to us: it has to be new to our readers. We need to study the old stories like a map so that we can find our own way.

Two worlds collide

Let's take a moment to examine an extremely short story written by the esteemed Latin American writer Augusto Monterroso:

The Dinosaur
When he awoke, the dinosaur was still there.

Take a moment to consider your first response to this piece. Whether it's confusion, skepticism, or admiration, your response is critical to making this story come to life. Perhaps one of the greatest risks a short-form writer takes is being dismissed by the reader, so notice the ways that the author hooks the reader's attention. The central conflict in this micro-story revolves around the collision of worlds—human and prehistoric reptile. What becomes of the protagonist in this story? The author leaves us wondering. As readers, we must piece together the narrative from the fragmentary evidence provided.

"The Dinosaur" was originally published in Monterroso's collection *Complete Works (and Other Stories)*. In an interview about the book, the writer acknowledges criticisms of this extremely short story. While readers generally enjoyed the piece, critics hated it. The most frequent complaint was that something so short could not be a story. "My answer," responded

Monterroso in an interview with the *Massachusetts Review*, "True, it isn't a short story, it is actually a novel." Monterroso's playful response gives insight into the author's resistance to labels. In the same way that the author upends expectations of narrative in his micro, he challenges genre boundaries by acknowledging the critics' skepticism then upping the ante by making an even more outrageous claim.

Small as it is, this story exhibits a two-part plot structure: then and now. It actively resists the expectation that a story must be longer with developed characters, plot, and setting. In its brevity, it manages to be funny, unnerving, compelling, and odd. We could argue endlessly about whether this is truly a story and what the difference is between an incident and a story. Go ahead. And while you're at it, look for the other extremely short pieces in the anthology. We believe that the surest measure of a good piece of short-form writing is that it engages the imagination and the intellect. It keeps us talking and thinking long after the final word.

Dissecting the dinosaur

To understand how "The Dinosaur" has managed to intrigue readers and confound critics since its publication in 1959, let's begin with the title. What if we substituted "dinosaur" for something equally terrifying?

> When he awoke, the _____ was still there.
> Example: alien, ghost, axe-murderer, zombie, Sasquatch, fire-breathing dragon

What becomes apparent when you experiment with substitution in this story is that the subject of the dinosaur allows for several transformations to take place in a single sentence. First, there is the transition from dream state to wakefulness, a transformation of the consciousness of the "he" in the story. Second, "still" indicates that the dinosaur was present in the dream and remains present even when the person wakes up, producing a transformation of the dream dinosaur into a real dinosaur. Third, since at no point in history did dinosaurs and humans co-exist, there is a transformation of time and logical connections. Reality itself is transformed; the old rules no longer apply. You would be hard-pressed to find a substitution that accomplished all these maneuvers, all at once, in so few words.

Monterroso writes in the tradition of **magical realism**, a genre of realistic fiction that incorporates magical elements, but you can see how easily this mode can be changed if you shift the subject:

"When he awoke, the horse bandit was still there." (Western)
"When he awoke, the mother ship was still there." (Sci-fi)
"When he awoke, the bowl of hot porridge was still there." (Fairy tale)
"When he awoke, the chainsaw-wielding clown was still there." (Horror)
"When he awoke, he was still there." (Realism)

Through substitution, we can see that this piece takes the structure of one of the oldest forms of storytelling: worlds collide. Whoever awakes and whoever is *still* there must necessarily be from different domains. This creates the friction from which narrative is born.

While this story does possess conflict, it doesn't have the other traditional literary elements. Consider **Freytag's Pyramid** (Figure 1.1), a representation of narrative structure developed by the German novelist and playwright Gustav Freytag that shows the progression of dramatic events within a story.

Many stories begin with exposition, which leads to an inciting incident that produces a rising action leading to a crisis moment. From that point of no return, the story begins its descent through falling action, the untangling of the plot's knot (dénouement), and finally, resolution. We think it would be a mistake to suggest that flash fiction is nothing but a complete story shrunk down to miniature form, like a wool sweater gone through a hot dryer. In

Figure 1.1 Freytag's Pyramid, also known as a traditional narrative arc. Courtesy of Savannah Adams.

Monterroso's example, there is no lead-up and no resolution. The author offers us only the tiniest glimpse into the story's climax. From this the reader constructs the before and after. The story becomes a story not because it is printed on a page or published in a book, but because of the life it takes on within the reader's mind.

Conclusion: Stealing strategies

You may be a novelist with a natural tendency for Tolstoyan epics. You may be a poet with an ear for iambic pentameter. Your nonfiction might be a sweeping investigation into personal history and memory. If you sat in on either one of our classes where we teach, you'd quickly notice we are both nerdy in our passion for the traditional literary canon, too. However, in this textbook, we make the argument that when it comes to literature, brevity matters more than anything else. Six words can accomplish surprisingly stunning feats. Take for example, the six-word story attributed to Ernest Hemingway: "For sale: baby shoes, never worn."

Using the language of the classified advertisement, where each word literally comes at a cost, this story leaves much to the imagination. The story exists in the assumptions we make based on the meager evidence of the unworn pair of shoes. Who is the seller? Why are they selling the shoes? Why are the shoes unworn? Why shoes? Who might the buyer be? What happened when the seller and buyer met for the exchange? Through questions, we can uncover implied characters and situations. The unworn shoes can be interpreted as an image of unfulfilled potential. The story unfolds off the page.

The allure of extreme brevity is one reason six-word memoirs have become so popular. An entire collection has been published in *Not Quite What I Was Planning: Six Word Memoirs from Writers Famous and Obscure*, edited by Larry Smith and Rachel Fershleiser. The challenge of sketching a life, or capturing a single moment, in just six words is what draws writers and readers to this form. There is also a social quality to the short form that invites response and imitation. Short forms leave space for the ongoing conversation of literature. For example, consider this tweet by writer Amelia Gray (Figure 1.2).

Gray plays off the familiarity of the original six-word story and reconstitutes it. As a result, her thirteen-word story is retweeted and others join in to riff on this literary oddity.

As you examine the pieces in the anthology at the back of this book, we hope you'll begin to notice how much careful crafting has gone into each

Amelia Gray ✓
@grayamelia

For Sale: baby shoes, worn a lot.
Please buy these old-ass baby shoes

4:48 PM - 7 Apr 2015

💬 1   ↻ 54   ♡ 183

Figure 1.2 Tweet by Amelia Gray. Courtesy of Savannah Adams.

brief text and discover some useful strategies to steal as you craft your own writing—whatever form it might take.

Exercises

The following activities will help you practice the concepts from this chapter:

A. Discuss the variations on Hemingway's six-word story in the examples below. Compare the original included in this chapter with these new versions. What is gained? What is lost in translation? Try it yourself and discuss how word choice and level of detail affect the story.
   - Special offer: new shoes, size 0.
   - Sale: unused infant clothes and stuff.
   - Make your own:

   _____

B. Taking inspiration from the party game Two Truths and a Lie, tell or write down a familiar story that *actually happened to you* (nonfiction) and insert an invented detail (fiction). Distill this story into one paragraph. Read it to your classmates. Can you detect the made-up detail in the stories of your peers? How does the added detail in your story affect the way you tell it?

C. Select at least three anthology pieces and read them in a small group. We have deliberately left out the genre identification of these pieces so you can engage in a conversation about classification. Are the pieces prose poetry? Flash fiction? Flash nonfiction? Support your claims using evidence from the text.

Prompts

The following writing prompts will help you practice the concepts from this chapter:

A. Write a short piece in which you integrate the four elements of tension: a person (with a problem), a desire (for something specific), high stakes, and obstacles.

B. Write a short piece that explores one of John Gardner's ideas of the two main narratives in literature, "A stranger comes to town" or "Someone goes on a journey."

C. Take the draft or idea of the story you told for exercise A or B and add seven new, surprising details that use the senses. Feel free to write what you know or invent the details.

D. Craft a six-word memoir in which something changes and where the piece has the feeling or suggestion of a beginning, middle, and end.

One-sentence workshop

The following exercise will help you practice the art of brevity:

Take a sentence from a working draft or from one of the exercises above and see if you can make it six words shorter without changing the sentence's meaning. To demonstrate this technique, we've revised a sentence that appeared in an earlier version of the opening vignette. Notice what changes in the revision and discuss how the revision compares to the original in terms of clarity and concision.

Example sentence: I was an English major with dreams of becoming a writer, so working in food service was my version of a paid internship. (23 words)

Example revision: My restaurant job felt like a paid internship for an English major dreaming of becoming a writer. (17 words)

Part II

The Craft of Short-Form Creative Writing

2

Picture This

Relevant readings

"For My Sister in the River" by Danielle Cadena Deulen
"My Devils" by Brian Doyle
"Time Travel" by Grant Faulkner
"Poland" by Thaisa Frank
"La Jungla" by Nancy Jooyoun Kim
"The Girl Who Likes Dogs" by Calvin Mills
"The Inventory from a Year Lived Sleeping with Bullets" by Brian Turner
"Immigrant Haibun" by Ocean Vuong

Flash interview with Calvin Mills

Calvin Mills is a writer who lives in Port Angeles, Washington. We chose "The Girl Who Likes Dogs" for the anthology because of the way he scrutinizes a moment in time. It produces a complex, hi-definition sensory experience. It's unflinchingly honest, which makes it a little uncomfortable, a little funny, and completely memorable. Here's what he has to say about writing short.

How do you define the kind of short-form writing that you do?

I refer to "The Girl Who Likes Dogs" and my other short-form nonfiction as "creative nonfiction" rather than "nonfiction" or "memoir" for one particular reason. When I began submitting nonfiction to my writing teachers, the pieces raised a few eyebrows. I was told that my work "read like fiction"—referring not to the content, but the style. But I didn't back down. I worked primarily with scene rather than summary, and I pushed tone, voice, and all five senses in my description. Others scoffed at the term when I used it back then but I felt vindicated later when *Creative Nonfiction* became such a notable journal. And, I felt vindicated again as I sat down to write this tonight, when, upon googling the term for the first time in many years, I found definitions that more or less mirror my old sentiments exactly.

How does your approach to writing in short forms differ from the other kinds of writing that you do?

For me, novels and musicals take years. Short stories take weeks. I'd like to say that I sit down and write one flash essay or piece of flash fiction every day, and at the end of the year I have three hundred and sixty terrible pieces and five really good ones. But the truth is, I don't. Instead I think for hours or days about something that happened to me that really hit me hard. I muse on that moment, then that day, then what I was doing that year, and I try to expand on that moment. I reach out for the details: the sound of the car I was driving, the cool air that night, the song that was most likely playing on the radio. And it takes me anywhere from two hours to a week to write the essay—to imbue it with sufficient life. Then the work of resting the manuscript and editing it begins.

What demands does the short form make of its writers or readers?

Intent focus, because every word counts in short-form creative writing. Every word is sacred. It reminds me of that amusing song from *Monty Python's The Meaning of Life*—if it were about words instead of sperm: "Every

[word] is sacred. Every [word] is great. If a [word] is wasted, God gets quite irate."

Free dive

"Images haunt," says poet Robert Hass. Fragments of memories roam our minds like restless spirits: happy or heartbreaking, intensely uncomfortable or pleasurable, real or fantasized, they circle and surface again and again. Write down a list of images that haunt you. What images appear and reappear in your mind? After you collect your own list of haunting images, choose one and try to describe it in as much detail as possible. As Mills explains in his interview above, "muse on that moment ... reach out for the details." Close your eyes and immerse yourself in it: what details do you see, hear, taste, or feel? Do you see faces or hear fragments of conversations? Where are the borders of the memory? Where does it go blurry or dark? Where does it begin and end? When does it come back to you? Take ten minutes and describe as many of the details as you can.

Vignette: If you hand me the right map

I know the specific line of coast, the surge of shore break, the backroads into town. I know which sidewalk cafes get drenched in warm amber light, which alley shortcuts lead back to the office when I've taken too long at lunch. I know the feeling of the emptied-out apartment after a lover fades into thin air, the escalating tension of unrest when the quad swells with protesting students, placards, police in riot gear. My body knows the tired gladness of returning home through the undulating dusty yellow hills at the end of a long road trip. I could show you where I live, work, sleep. Where I linger over coffee and a newspaper. Where I listen to the sounds of idle laughter mixing with the effervescent crash of breakers. Where I am bored and elated, heartbroken and satisfied. Where I lay out picnic lunches. Where I slide my finger under an envelope flap and tear. The white seam splitting open. The yawns and sighs. The mmm hmms and ohs and quietest of oh no's. I want to take you there.

But, the thing is, it's a dreamscape. It's a place I inhabit when I sleep. I dip into and out of the subterranean tunnels of my dreams, and the dreams of others. Sometimes I am here in the place I think of as my dreaming life. Sometimes I am in another, more fragmented and surreal dream that remixes the worries and desires from my day. I've been told I sometimes appear as an apparition in the dreams of others. As a teenager, I rode one perfect wave into and out of my father's co-worker's dream, and I'd never even met him. And once, my childhood friend and I dreamed the same dream, from the same perspective: for the length of one nightmare, we were one person.

The first time I lucidly walked through that empty apartment, ran my hand across the kitchen table and understood it was my dreaming life, it might have been the first time I grasped the theory of a multiverse. I am here and there and every other somewhere: I am walking down some street or beach or hallway in a kaleidoscope of daughter universes. Time projects holograms, heat mirages, sphinx-like apparitions. For an instant, the world lights up, and I'm stepping into cobalt water, inhaling heavy marine air. Or unfurling a red and white checkered cloth. A strand of hair blows across my face, a thumb brushes my lips. And then it's over, and here we are.

—Heather
Word count: 423

Stare: Educate the eye

When we look at something, we experience it with our entire body. We perceive all the nuances of the surrounding environment, including the sensory details of sound, scent, air temperature, and light quality. We analyze and interpret the subtleties of physical texture, vocal tone, body posture, and more—even when we may not be aware of it. This is true when we read, too. The written image is not a flat picture. An **image** is a complex, multidimensional sensory object, and a writer uses it to help a reader imaginatively experience the words on the page.

Consider how images work in the opening scene of Steven Spielberg's cult classic, *Jaws* (1975). A teenage girl strips off her clothes as she runs away from a bonfire on a beach and dives into the moonlit ocean. With only the gentle lapping of waves and the clang of a bell buoy, the girl backstrokes out into the calm, deep water and kicks one leg into the air like an aquatic dancer. The silhouette of the shapely leg with its pointed toe slowly slips down and disappears beneath the surface. The scene is terrifying, but only because of the danger that it suggests: on the surface, everything looks placid, sexy, gorgeous. However, the ominous threat is undeniably present in the angular outline of the leg. It provides a visual reminder of what we expect to see appear at any moment—the shark fin. The corresponding images of the skinny dipper's leg and the shark fin are inextricably linked, and as the leg disappears below the dark surface of the water the viewer can't help but think about what else appears and disappears, what lurks invisibly below the surface. The image reverberates and haunts us as much as the film's theme music.

The thin, fin-like triangle of the girl's extended leg captivates movie viewers because it is such a simple concrete image (a human leg!) that represents so much about the beauty, grace, and fragility of human life. Think about ancient Greek and Roman sculptures that capture abstract ideas about beauty, innocence, and mortality in the form of a half-draped body. Acclaimed neurologist Oliver Sacks says,

> The concrete, equally, may become a vehicle of mystery, beauty and depth, a path into the emotions, the imagination, the spirit—fully as much as any abstract conception (perhaps, indeed more …). The concrete is readily imbued with feeling and meaning—more readily, perhaps, than any abstract conception. It readily moves into the aesthetic, the dramatic, the comic, the symbolic, the whole wide deep world of art and spirit.

Sacks says we may intellectually understand **abstractions**—those concepts we can't touch, like *good* or *bad* or *love* or *hate*—but they don't trigger our imaginations nearly as effectively as the way real things do.

We live in a world of objects. We know that soft shirts make us feel cozy and tight shoes make us feel cramped. We know that certain places (a placid lakeshore) make us relax, while other places (an abandoned house) creep us out. Imagine the scent of your grandmother's perfume, the smudge of red lipstick on a cigarette, the sight of full dinner plates abandoned on a table. These concrete images lead to a different kind of knowing. They lead to comprehension. Images matter, whether we are talking about a marble sculpture of Aphrodite, the opening shot of a horror film, or a close-up in a flash text. A well-placed image can haunt, arouse, or terrify—all depending on how you frame it.

We know that images are powerful. C. S. Lewis says, "It is of the very nature of thought and language to represent what is immaterial in picturable terms." In other words, although humans have the unique capacity for abstract thought, we are still creatures of the world. We anchor our thoughts to the world around us. We're familiar with the adage, "A picture is worth a thousand words." This is unequivocally true in flash work. When an entire piece might have fewer than a thousand words, each image must do double or triple duty in the limited space of a page.

Particularly successful images can telegraph essential information, carry layers of emotional or psychological understanding, and leave a permanent afterimage in the reader's imagination. For instance, consider the parka in Mills's story that is used to carry the dying dog to the vet. A parka is typically associated with warmth and protection from the harsh elements, but this article of clothing takes on added weight by suggesting the impending coldness of the wounded dog as well as the coldness of shock the narrator experiences. Later, the bloodstained parka is balled up and thrown away in a garbage can behind the house. This act takes on ceremonial significance, "a little like grieving," which is about as close as the narrator can get to the feeling as he copes with the accident. The parka in this story is more than an object: it is an image that reveals layers of meaning.

When we see an image in our mind, our brains process the image by linking it to other images that we have seen. We associate it with other experiences that we've had, and we try to connect it to other logical, symbolic, or metaphorical meanings. Without even realizing we are doing so, every time we see an image we follow what Roland Barthes calls a "floating chain" of ideas to make sense of it. This interpretative process happens whether we are watching a film, sitting on the couch reading a book, strolling through an art gallery looking at paintings, or simply talking with a friend. One image, one word, one idea leads to another.

Although the mind seems to ricochet from one image or idea to another when we're thinking, it isn't completely unpredictable. This is good news for writers: strategically placed images can establish a predictable trajectory. For example, in Brian Turner's "The Inventory from a Year Lived Sleeping with Bullets," one section of this prose poem ends with the sentence fragment, "The fresh dark soil over the bodies." The reader's mind fills in the missing action and must leap over the white space that separates one section from another. The imagery invites readers to imagine the shovel scattering soil over the bodies, to hear the scrape of metal against dirt, or see the glint of the shovel. They might glimpse a larger view: graveside mourners, soldiers in fatigues, a searing blue desert sky. In some ways, this kind of strategic thinking is similar to target practice. It requires a discerning eye, some skilled application, and confidence. And it doesn't hurt to have a steady hand.

One way to get more strategic about images is to do a self-study: which images capture your attention? Which ones move you? Where do they take you? Like you did in the free dive at the start of this chapter, practice following the sight line of your thoughts and you can learn a lot about the path of an image traveling through your mind. Granted, no one thinks exactly the same. This, too, is good news for writers. But, there are points of connection, generally speaking. Humans are incredibly adept at reading physical cues like facial expressions, body posture, and external indicators of personality, such as haircuts and clothes.

We have to teach ourselves how to watch, listen, and notice more. American photographer Walker Evans says, "Stare. It is the way to educate your eye, and more. Stare, pry, listen, eavesdrop. Die knowing something. You are not here long." Evans reminds us that artists educate themselves with awareness. This quality of watchfulness applies to daily observations, but also to the unfolding of memories or fantasies in our imaginations.

We have to train ourselves to look for the details. Mills explains in his interview how he does this as part of his writing process: "I reach out for the details: the sound of the car I was driving, the cool air that night, the song that was most likely playing on the radio ..." He looks for the specifics that describe the moment: the sounds, the weather, the physical sensations, and other details from his surroundings. You can do this, too, by making written observations of your surroundings. Take time to notice three things about the room you're in right now. Use your senses to make sense of your world.

Images can be profoundly moving. One example of this is Marina Abramović's 736-hour silent performance of *The Artist Is Present* (2010) at the Museum of Modern Art in New York City. For two and a half months, Abramović sat in a wooden chair and silently met the gaze of every museum visitor who sat down across from her. There were two rules: no talking and no touching. Over the course of the performance, it is reported that 1,545 people sat with Abramović. In the documentary footage of this performance, some of the participants maintained a dead set gaze, some cried, some sneered. But the most moving part of the performance came when Abramović's former romantic and artistic partner Ulay sat down across from her. They hadn't seen each other in twenty-three years.

A viewer doesn't have to know anything about their history together to be moved by the moment they reunite; their expressions say everything. Ulay walks up to the table wearing a black suit jacket, black jeans, black Chuck Taylors, and eyeglasses pushed back in his tousled gray hair. He adjusts his jacket collar, stretches out his legs, and carefully composes himself as he takes the seat across from Abramović. She hasn't caught his entrance: she has been meditating with her eyes on the floor. Her glance travels up from his toes to his face. When she meets his gaze, she smiles (just a hint of a smile).

Ulay shakes his head and blinks. Her eyes water. His eyes water. He exhales and nods (just a hint of a nod). Both of their throats constrict and swallow. Her lips tremble as she reaches her hands across the table. He smiles and takes her hands in his.

The audience doesn't need any words: watching their unguarded expressions for a minute and a half tells us everything about lovers after a lifetime of separation. Each discrete image—when their eyes meet, when they swallow and breathe, when they reach out for each other—tells viewers volumes of information about their personal connection, as well as about the abstract idea we call love. And maybe also the abstract ideas of heartbreak and aging. Real, tangible things like watery eyes and swallowing throats and trembling hands reveal information about real but untouchable things like emotions. Concrete details, like facial expressions and body posture, lead us to an understanding of abstract things, such as love, anger, disappointment, or fear.

We read each other like texts in real life too. Think about the look on your parent's face that says, "You're in *big* trouble" or the glance a friend gives you that sets you off laughing. There's the ever-so-slight deviation in an expression that signals someone is lying. Brian Doyle examines these subtle ways we communicate in "My Devils." The narrator describes the mother's hand gestures as "another language in our family . . . . If she turned her hand one way it meant *Go get my cigarettes*. If she turned it another way it meant *What you just said is so silly that I am not going to bother to disabuse you of your idiocy.*" Doyle's essay clearly connects the external, concrete image of the mother's hand and its slight variations of movement with the unseen and internal characteristics of the mother's personality. In this piece, hands dispel demons, dismiss annoying children, and describe a nuanced understanding of the way this particular family communicates.

As writers, we have to school ourselves in how we read behavior so that we can recreate it on the page. Danielle Cadena Deulen's "For My Sister in the River" portrays a sister in a moment of crisis and demonstrates how one sibling reads another:

> My sister is small and stronger
> than she looks. In a decade she'll arrive late at the door, her lip split,
> eye swollen shut, her baby girl blushed with tears (wound around her
> like a delicate vine.) She'll walk into the kitchen, sit down on linoleum,
> say *I'll never go back*. I'll want to believe I hear her voice filling with
> her voice from the river we swam as girls, where we'd take turns being
> John the Baptist, drenching each other in the muddy tide. Underwater,

I could feel my sister's skinny arms straining to pull me through currents, lift me through the dark surface, press her fingers to my forehead, say *You're forgiven. You're healed.*

This image superimposes two moments of time: one when the sister is a strong, young girl full of a powerful faith, and the other a decade later, when she is a mother finding the strength to escape an abusive partner. Deulen lets the reader see the sister at both her weakest and strongest. She allows the reader to experience the precise moment in the sibling's history that anchors the element of redemption in the present. Just like Doyle's young boy watches his mother's hands to interpret her emotional signals, you can read this scene closely and know everything you need to know about the sisters' relationship.

For most of our language transactions, we move from the real to the abstract, from the image to the idea. We move from micro-expression to a broader understanding. The question then, for writers in the short form, is how might we use the potential power of an image to its full advantage with a handful of words? How do we use a concrete image, as Sacks says, to "become a vehicle of mystery, beauty and depth, a path into the emotions, the imagination, [and] the spirit"? We answer this question by looking at a few theoretical ideas about images and then consider the different ways images function in short-form writing.

Image as epiphany

Poet Ezra Pound's 1913 manifesto, "A Few Don'ts by an Imagiste," declared:

An "Image" is that which presents an intellectual and emotional complex in an instance of time .... It is the presentation of such a "complex" instantaneously which gives that sense of sudden liberation, that sense of freedom from time limits and space limits; that sense of sudden growth, which we experience in the presence of the greatest works of art.

Pound suggests the right image acts like an epiphany that springs open with sudden awareness.

You can see this awareness in Nancy Jooyoun Kim's "La Jungla" in the narrator's description of an English-speaking parrot trapped among the stands of clothes, shoes, and stereo equipment in a predominantly Spanish-speaking neighborhood of southeast Los Angeles. The narrator is at first amused by the "dazzling macaw [that] spent his days in a cage, squawking and screaming, 'Help me! Help me!'" But when the parrot cries out for help in Spanish, the narrator is forced to recognize that the bird means what it says. It is no longer a brightly colored prop set against the backdrop of the dull warehouse. It is a fellow creature calling out in need.

It's important to make a distinction between image and description. Both words in this context are nouns, but an *image* is a thing while a *description* is the act of describing a thing. In other words, an image shows, a description tells. Pound also warns writers about the dangers of description: "Don't be descriptive; remember that the painter can describe a landscape much better than you can, and that he has to know a deal more about it." You'll hear this advice ("Show, don't tell") repeatedly in creative writing classrooms, and this tip is especially pertinent for short-form writers. When you are trying to pack the most into your limited word count, images can serve to both show *and* tell.

The stereoscopic image

Stereoscopes, a common parlor game in the late 1800s, demonstrate one of the most basic tricks of image depth perception. If you've ever slid a round photo disc into a View-Master projector and peered inside to see a three-dimensional image of Saturn or the Grand Canyon, then you've played with a stereoscope too. The early stereoscopes produced the 3D effect in a surprisingly simple way: two nearly identical photographs would be taken at slightly different angles, and then they would be printed side by side. When the viewer looked at them through the stereoscope, the images would seem to converge in the middle, with one image appearing to hover just over the other. The result: an illusion of depth perception.

One famous stereoscopic image depicts John Muir, one of the founding fathers of the environmental movement, standing with President Theodore Roosevelt at Glacier Point, above Yosemite Valley (Figure 2.1). It is a historic moment in environmental conservation: Muir convinced President Roosevelt to make Yosemite a national park by taking him camping in the Yosemite wilderness, and that decision set a precedent for future wilderness legislation. Other than a few written artifacts, that stereoscopic image is all we have to illustrate that monumental moment. Somehow, that three-dimensional parlor trick still feels powerful: if viewed properly, through a stereoscope, it produces the shiver of a hologram—Muir and Roosevelt forever caught with a faint aura of movement surrounding them.

Figure 2.1 Theodore Roosevelt and John Muir on Glacier Point, Yosemite Valley, California. c. 1903. Underwood & Underwood. Photographic print, Library of Congress. Reproduction numberLC-DIG-ppmsca-36413. http://www.loc.gov/ pictures/item/93503130/

Lia Purpura explores how different ways of looking focus our attention in "On Miniatures": "Sometimes we need binoculars, microscopes, View-masters, stereopticons to assist our looking, but mediated or not, miniatures suggest there is more there than meets the eye easily. They suggest there is much to miss if we don't look hard at spaces, crevices, crannies." The opening scene to Calvin Mills's "The Girl Who Likes Dogs" achieves that same stereoscopic three-dimensionality that makes the Roosevelt–Muir image so memorable, and the holographic shiver surrounding it tells us to look hard. Mills begins:

> Picture this: me in a ragged black sweater, her sitting on the edge of my bed, me staring out the window into the dark street feeling bad about what happened half an hour before. She comforts me, tells me it wasn't my fault. I think about the thin black dog, about seeing it in the headlights, about jabbing the brakes, about the gasps in the car that were obvious even through the music as the girl and I and my best friend and his girlfriend went over the dog, and I felt it bang under the thin floor pan of my old Volkswagen Beetle.
>
> Looking out the window, I'm thinking about all of this, and I'm feeling like shit. But look at it from a lonely teenager's perspective.

The narrative captures dimensionality the same way that the stereoscope does: it overlaps the images while skewing the layers slightly, just enough that each layer feels a little off-center. Notice the layers of repetition in these opening sentences: "Picture this ... me staring out the window ... looking out the window, I'm thinking.... But look at it from a lonely teenager's perspective."

They are teenagers in a bedroom. The tension is already palpable. The physical arrangement of the characters emphasizes this tension as the teenage boy stands at his bedroom window with his back turned to the girl sitting on his bed. He feels awful about what just happened, but there is *a girl* sitting on his bed. He doesn't know what to do, so he freezes with his back to her and stalls for time so he can think. The image is a quintessential teenage vortex of dynamic energy: angst, lust, guilt.

Mills lingers on the image and makes us wait with the teenage boy stalling at the window. The narrator directs the reader's gaze, describes his own direction of focus, and then redirects the reader's viewpoint so that the reader sees everything at both points in time: from the teenager's viewpoint the night it happened, as well as from the mature narrator's viewpoint in the future. The layering effect emulates the narrator's conflicted feelings about that night and his response, and it simultaneously makes room for the narrator to look back and reflect on the evening with some empathy and insight.

Moving images can include more dramatic action too. Grant Faulkner's "Time Travel" leaps through time and space with a kind of sci-fi panache: "'My life isn't some cheap reality show,' he said to her when he left. It was 1979, years before reality shows even existed." The title and the first two sentences suggest that the protagonist is a time traveler and that he's just had a fight with a woman and left. The story contains only six more sentences, but it continues to plunge ahead, defying time and space. Read the entirety of "Time Travel" by Grant Faulkner, and pay attention to the touchstone images throughout the narrative:

> "My life isn't some cheap reality show," he said to her when he left. It was 1979, years before reality shows even existed. He was like that, stepping in and out of time periods. When she first met him, he was wearing a top hat. Once he asked her to wear a garter for him on his birthday. She still had the garter. Yesterday, she tried to put it on, but her flesh wouldn't allow it after all these years. She'd had the crazy idea of surprising him, showing up at his offices at NASA, a vision from the past.

In one hundred words, fashion changes, television changes, their bodies age, their relationship ends and starts and ends. If we return to the comparison between the image and the experience of the 3D photograph that we started with, this story moves from image to image with the decisive click of the View-Master lever spinning the photo reel to a new glimpse of the cosmos.

"Time Travel" makes great leaps from one sentence to the next, but the reader doesn't get lost because the narrator stays within the parameters of two paradigms: time travel and relationship cycles. The narrative marries these two concepts and doesn't deviate from them. Consequently, the reader follows the strand of time travel (stepping in and out of time periods, his office at NASA) and the strand of relationship ups and downs (first meeting someone, celebrating birthdays, leaving someone) and doesn't get lost. What might happen if, in the final sentence, the woman had the crazy idea of showing up at his office at a bank or an accounting firm? That kind of detail would deviate from the time travel paradigm. It makes sense that the time traveler works at NASA, of course. Why would a time traveler work as a banker or accountant? How might a banker spend his days managing finances and also happen to become a time traveler? That kind of deviation opens up questions at the end of the narrative instead of closing the loop, the way the NASA detail does.

In other words, making bold moves with the narrative by using a logical pattern of images—in this case, weaving together two distinct patterns—and then not deviating from this pattern gives readers confidence that they know what is going on. It establishes systems of logic in the narrative that are reinforced by the details.

Not just scenery

The reader's imagination sometimes functions like an empty stage: the characters will remain disembodied voices behind the theater's curtain until they step into the footlights. Likewise, the character's plight will remain unclear until you place a chair for your character to slump into, a kitchen table to rest upon, or a dog to whimper beneath it as a grainy dawn filters through a curtained window. Without images, the stage remains empty and the audience waits expectantly in the dark. We need images to define the imaginative space. However, images are not merely props surrounding the characters. Beyond putting images into action, here are a few other ways to handle them in your short-form writing.

Any artistic genre—film or painting or writing—can use what critic George P. Castellitto calls a **suspended image** to focus and hold the audience's attention. While visual mediums like film or television might use silence, up-close shots, delayed timing, or even saturated color to isolate images, texts might use fragments, punctuation, or space on the page to suspend an image.

Brian Turner uses a quick succession of sentence fragments to slow down and look in "The Inventory from a Year Lived Sleeping with Bullets." It begins, "Rifle oil, *check*. Smoke grenades, *check*. Desert boots, *check*. Plates of body armor, *check*." The reader's attention concentrates on each item getting packed into a soldier's rucksack. That hyper-close focus magnifies and isolates each item to relay shock. The list escalates with horror and confusion as it goes: "A dead infant .... A combat load of ammunition .... Sgt. Gould sucking a woman's nipple .... Glow sticks in mouths .... A man in an Energizer bunny suit, on roller-skates." The reader can't quite process the opposing images, and that's the point: neither can the soldier. Turner describes them as "torture fragments" and each item on the list stalls and hovers for a moment, midair in the imagination.

The suspended image momentarily delays the narrative to affect the reader visually, and the result might heighten the reader's physical awareness or emotional experience, and/or escalate narrative tension. This is an amplification technique: the image becomes larger than life as its normal movement through time and space changes. But an image that's treated slightly differently can garner significantly different results. For instance, a **multidimensional image** deliberately packs together layers of literal and symbolic meaning similar to psychologist Carl Jung's idea of an archetypal image, which he describes as "a condensed psychic situation as a whole." Notably, he also calls these "primordial images."

Multidimensional images don't have to include archetypal images, but they do often trigger our instincts at the gut level first. Consider, for instance, the barking dogs in Karen E. Bender's "The Man Who Hated Us and Then Forgot": "There was the time he let his dogs, muscled German Shepherds with sharp teeth, bark at us. They barked so loud we could feel it in our gut. They barked at us whenever we went into our yard, even when our daughter had her second birthday party. He never told them to stop." The image of the snarling dogs conveys two layers of information: physical details about the disruption the family encountered in their own backyard and symbolic information about the neighbor's aggressiveness.

The final image treatment to consider is a **surreal image**, which is often dreamlike or hallucinatory in nature. Surrealism, influenced by Freud's theories of the unconscious, often uses free association, dreamscapes, or symbolism to convey unconscious fears and desires or make us question our perceptions of reality. In 1928, the Belgian surrealist painter, René Magritte painted an image of a smoking pipe on a plain off-white background with one sentence written underneath: "*Ceci n'est pas une pipe.*" This is not a pipe. The painting, titled "The Treachery of Images," explores the confounding nature of things and the representation of things. In other words, we can look at a painting of a pipe, a cat, or a monster, and it is not a pipe, a cat, or a monster—it is only an *image* of a pipe or a cat or a monster. Thus, the treachery: to a certain extent, all art (painting, creative writing) necessarily requires a deception of the senses.

Surrealist images expose this deception as a way to explore the nature of our perceptions, fears, and desires. They rely on **defamiliarization** to make the known feel unknown. Ocean Vuong's "Immigrant Haibun" tells the story of his refugee parents escaping by boat. In the fifth section, it takes a surreal turn: a storm rises on the sea and they realize they are on a miniature ship, encased in a bottle. Outside the bottle, a Christmas party is in full swing. Here's the scene:

> Furious roar. The sea splitting at the bow. He watches it open like a thief staring into his own heart: all bones and splintered wood. Waves rising on both sides. The ship encased in liquid walls. *Look!* He says, *I see it now!* He's jumping up and down. He's kissing the back of my wrist as he clutches the wheel. He laughs but his eyes betray him. He laughs despite knowing he has ruined every beautiful thing just to prove beauty cannot change him. And here's the kicker: there's a cork where the sunset should be. It was always there. There's a ship made from toothpicks and superglue. There's a ship in a wine bottle on the mantel in the middle of a Christmas party—eggnog spilling from red Solo cups. But we keep sailing anyway. We keep standing at the bow. A wedding-cake couple encased in glass.

Vuong magnifies the storm and then uses the ship in a bottle image to suddenly shrink his parents and their crisis at sea to tiny, toy-like proportions. The paradoxical displacement of a ship inside a bottle illustrates their sense of displacement in the world. A person who looks at a ship inside a bottle can't help but wonder, *How did it get in there?* Likewise, Vuong employs the cartoon-like scene to distort the reader's sense of logic, scale, and reality; as a result, the reader experiences the psychic crisis of arriving in an utterly foreign land. They can't help but wonder, *How did we get here?* The surreal image disorients everything and renders unknown the people, the crossing over, the imminent danger, even the Christmas party.

Conclusion: Moving images

Images—of all varieties—lend real-world rationality, energy, and insight to writing. Some of the best images steal techniques from other artistic mediums. This borrowing is a back-and-forth trade across artistic lines: it's one of the ways we keep learning how to reinvent what we are doing. Think about how fiction might use a jazz-like syncopated rhythm to emphasize an action sequence, or a film might incorporate an up-close shot that seems as textured as a sculpture.

In writing, movement might get captured like stop-motion animation, or an angle of perspective might widen into a panoramic shot. Heather Sellers, author of *The Practice of Creative Writing*, says, "Finally, the stock-in-trade of creative writing is creating images—that's what we do. We try to put on paper words that will create a vivid, continuous, sensory dream in our readers' brains." As you read, pay attention to images as they appear in your imagination: how do they move, how do they act, and what kind of dynamic energy do they contain? Notice when they feel clear or blurry, when they move erratically or sluggishly, when they feel hallucinatory or flat. Look for ways to recreate a similar dynamic effect in your own work.

If an image doesn't feel like it's working for whatever reason, if you can't see it clearly, and if it doesn't capture your attention, try changing it up. Perhaps the simplest questions might be, how can I make this image move? What kind of energy is it asking for? Where have I seen that feeling, that shiver of tension, the tone or texture before? A good image works like flint: strike it right and you've got fire, heat, and light. All you have to do is learn to handle it right.

Exercises

The following activities will help you practice the concepts from this chapter:

A. With a partner, create a storyboard of each scene in Ocean Vuong's "Immigrant Haibun." Write down the predominant images in each scene. How do the images echo one another, build on each other, or ping off each other as tangencies? Identify the different kinds of images you find: suspended images, dynamic images, multidimensional images, or surreal images.

B. Collect a set of three to four photographs that focus on a single subject: one object, person, or landscape. Take a minute or so to look at each image. While you do, follow the cue ball of your imagination: what words do you think of when you look at an image, and where do those words take you? Follow the tangential path as one word triggers another, and write them down. Then, if possible, switch your images with a partner, and repeat the exercise with the new set of images. At the end, compare your notes with your partner: Did your lists include similar words? How are they similar or different?

Prompts

The following writing prompts will help you practice the concepts from this chapter:

A. Surrealist poet Larry Levis says, "I refuse to explain." Taking inspiration from Levis, list any images that represent some abstract idea for you—like joy, beauty, bravery, shame, fear, love, or holiness—and record a cluster of images that represent that idea. What do you think is beautiful? What represents joy to you? What fears have you lived? Don't explain: just document and describe.

B. Sift through your memories and identify one that is unreliable. What makes you doubt its accuracy? What do you remember? What details are you sure of? What happened or might have happened or didn't happen? What have you been told that you have no recollection of? Try to capture the mystery of the memory.

C. Calvin Mills says "The Girl Who Likes Dogs" was written as a personal challenge to deliberately go against the tendency writers have to present themselves in a flattering light. Write a flash essay in which you examine a failure or imperfection. You might use it as a way to search for an unexpected truth about your actions or motivations.

D. Pretend you are selling a small, worthless object on eBay or Craigslist. Instead of writing a traditional description of the object for sale, write a narrative that gives the object's backstory. This exercise is inspired by the social experiment conducted by researchers Rob Walker and Joshua Glenn, who proved that a narrative can significantly increase the subjective value of an object. (You can read more about their experiment on significantobjects.com). This exercise asks you to consider the connections between an abstract idea and a concrete object; the ways in which details and precise description contribute to the believability of the narrative and the value of the object; and perhaps reflect on the larger idea of what we value.

One-sentence workshop

The following exercise will help you practice the art of brevity:

Look at the way Ocean Vuong uses oppositional images to create tension: "The sky was September-blue and the pigeons went on pecking at bits of bread scattered from the bombed bakery." In one sentence, we see evidence of destruction and peace. Notice how the sentence controls the way the reader views the scene by panning from peaceful to chaotic: the focus moves from blue skies to pigeons pecking crumbs to scattered bread to bombed out building. Creative writing professor Heather Sellers calls this "sliding." See if you can mimic this technique to direct the reader's gaze as they look around a scene. Write a sentence in which you start by showing one corner of the scene, and swivel the focus so that it eventually lands somewhere completely different. Use this tactic to establish tension by balancing the sentence like a teeter-totter with contrasting images at each end of the sentence.

3

Voice, Character, and Narrator

Relevant readings

"Cookie Monster on the Dole" by Henry Alford

"A Story Possibly Heard in Some Bar at Three in the Morning" by Pía Barros

"Thin Cities 5" by Italo Calvino

"The Cat" by Matthew Clarke and Coco Harrison-Clarke

"My Devils" by Brian Doyle

"Dust" by Sarah Evans

"Dinner Party" by Sherrie Flick

"A Modern Fable" by David Ignatow

"the invisible girl can be anything she wants when she doesn't want to be invisible" by Shivani Mehta

"Consequence" by Ira Sukrungruang

"Immigrant Haibun" by Ocean Vuong

Flash interview with Sarah Evans

Sarah Evans is a nonfiction writer who lives in Salem, Oregon. We chose "Dust" for the anthology because of how skillfully it captures the relationship of parent and child. The imagery of dust floating like fireflies or plankton makes this piece one we kept returning to. Here is what she has to say about writing short.

How does your approach to writing in short forms differ from the other kinds of writing that you do?

Often when I'm writing a short piece, it's with a specific word count in mind—whether that's the 140-character limit of a tweet or the 250- to 750-word limit of most publications that accept flash nonfiction. This differs from my longer works where I just keep writing until I feel like I've said all I need to say. With shorter pieces, I am more specific about my goal before I even start, and I don't veer as far from my central theme or idea as I might in a larger piece. With that in mind, my short-form pieces also tend to have a much narrower topic or focus. Rather than exploring an entire relationship with an ex-boyfriend, as I might do in an essay or memoir chapter, I might instead focus on the first conversation we had when we met, or even on just the moment I first saw him. Even with the narrower topic focus, the piece still has to speak to larger themes that resonate with readers, and therein lies one of the great challenges of the form.

What demands does the short form make of its writers or readers?

For the writer, one of the greatest demands is making every single word defend its place. With such a limited number of words on the page, each one must work hard to move the story along. You have to become your own tough-as-nails line editor. This approach also has made me better at long-form writing. I'm constantly pruning my work and taking out unnecessary phrases. Is there one powerful word that could replace these three so-so words? Often the answer is yes.

Free dive

As writer Sarah Evans explains, the short form requires extreme focus. In the best flash, a first encounter or conversation can suggest the arc of an entire relationship. We'd like you to set a limit of fifty words for your free dive, otherwise known as a stamp story, and see if you can conjure a character with a handful of deliberately chosen words. Put your character in motion with a name, a desire, and some unexpected roadblocks. Go beyond character description and locate your character in a scene, encounter, or conflict that reveals something about that person and gives voice to what he or she wants. Then, be your own "tough-as-nails" editor, as Evans describes. Test every word. What do you need to make a character come alive? How much is enough?

The name "stamp story" originates from a literary experiment conducted by Mud Luscious Press, a publisher who invited one hundred writers to write stories to test the limits of narrative. The stories were printed and distributed on cardstock before being collected into *[C.] An MLP Stamp Stories Anthology* by Andrew Borgstrom and J. A. Tyler.

Vignette: Stephanie's stamp collection

Hunger
For the third time this year, Marvin's name adorned the "Sandwich Maker of the Month" plaque. He was good, very good, but his meticulousness was not

enough. *Clutching his final paycheck, thin as sliced meat, between two doughy hands, Marvin noted his stomach's subterranean rumbling and walked out the door.*

Intimacy
At the clinic, Joe awaited his blood draw, hoping to see Patricia again in her lab coat. Of all the phlebotomists, Patricia's effortless needlework was best, fingertips searching out the most prominent vein. With her breath on his arm, his blood in her vial, the sterile transaction gave him butterflies.

Communication
Jamaal, the multilingual Humane Society volunteer, preferred not to talk. Even if he had, the old, stray, ill-behaved flea bags would not have listened. On early morning walks, they pulled him through tall grass behind the shelter, pissing prolifically, eager to acquaint him with the delicacies of a dead rat.

Anger
Spend your days with your fingers in someone's mouth, as Donna does, and you might feel the world is out to bite you, too. Before bed, the dental hygienist flosses with a vengeance. Floss only the teeth you want to keep! she spits. *Vicious-red blooms fill the sink's white bowl.*

—Stephanie
Word count: each 50 words exactly

Overview

Writers often use familiar characters as a shortcut to humor and social commentary. For instance, *The New Yorker's* Shouts & Murmurs column regularly publishes short features under 1,000 words that are witty, satiric, and, quite often, written in the imagined voices of other people. One week, a reader might eavesdrop on the internal musings of a famous figure; the next, one might glance over the shoulder of an out-of-touch socialite writing a college admissions essay. The writers create sparks by banging together the flint of opposing ideas: public/private, high/low, urban/rural, celebrity/commoner, and so on.

In "Cookie Monster on the Dole," journalist Henry Alford relies on our knowledge of a character from a beloved children's show in order to drive home his point. The speaker's unique voice can be clearly heard by the third sentence: "Me think unemployment not easy for puppet with addiction issues." Cookie Monster's childlike and telegraphic syntax paired with adult concerns produces a delightful incongruity. The image of the distraught yet determined puppet with his eyes forever open prompts laughter and reflection, and perhaps relieves a crumb of the uncertainty that comes from political and social upheaval. The voices of characters, speaking to themselves or to each other, are powerful tools for short-form writers who want to build a fire out of that brief spark.

As a writer in the short form, you cannot afford long passages of back and forth banter that build tension and reveal character. Neither can you delve into a long, drawn-out internalized monologue or character development. Though space is at a premium, you should not overlook the vital tool of dialogue. Both short-form writing and dialogue rely on **subtext** (what is below the surface of the story) and **implication** (what is implied or indirectly stated) to reveal more than what is on the page. This chapter explores how to craft effective and efficient conversations in your writing that give equal attention to what is said and what is not said. We'll also discuss the elusive matter of the author's voice, and what it means to find your own voice in writing.

Hearing voices

In creative writing, "voice" can mean several things. We'll use examples from the anthology to illustrate how voice presents itself in short-form writing.

When we hear the voices of characters talking to each other, we call this **dialogue**. You can see this back and forth clearly in the script "The Cat" by Matthew Clarke and his daughter Coco Harrison-Clarke, where each character has his or her assigned lines to speak. The script comes from the web series *Convos with My 2-year-old*, where actual conversations between father and daughter are reenacted by two grown men. The formatting of a script makes it easy to follow the quick movement of the conversation.

When the main character or narrator speaks, either directly or indirectly to the reader, we call this **narration**. The storytelling voice in Brian Doyle's "My Devils" illustrates narration beautifully. While there are conversations between characters within this story, the first-person speaker ("One time when I was seven years old … ") guides us as the story unfolds. The story itself is about a young boy beginning to understand the complexity of how people communicate with each other through words, gestures, and silences.

When the author's voice is heard through word choice, sentence structure, or other decisions that shape the story, we call this **style**. Every piece *has* style, but some stylistic choices are more noticeable than others. For example, Italo Calvino's opening statement in "Thin Cities 5" introduces a self-assured speaker who compels the reader to suspend disbelief and leap into a floating, implausible world: "If you choose to believe me, good." This stylized, take-it-or-leave-it voice is shaped by the author's choice to have the narrator take an immediately confrontational stance.

Dialogue basics

Dialogue, simply put, is a conversation between two or more people. **Direct dialogue** is typically indicated by placing quotation marks around the character's spoken words, like so: "I would like to demonstrate to you the proper formatting of dialogue." Notice how the final punctuation mark goes inside the quotation marks. Dialogue need not be an individual's speech. For example, Sherrie Flick's "Dinner Party" evokes the ambience of an evening through the communal voices of partygoers represented by direct dialogue enclosed in quotation marks.

Speech can also be suggested. **Indirect dialogue** is presented in summary form, as we see in Pía Barros's "A Story Possibly Heard in Some Bar at Three in the Morning": "He told me that the Emperor, moved by his prose, gifted him ten years of life." Formatted as direct dialogue, this sentence would read: He told me, "The Emperor, moved by my prose, gifted me with ten years of life." The indirectness of the original is not merely an interesting approach to dialogue; it's part of the design of the story within a story. The secondhand story and the indirect dialogue that accompanies it work together to form a unified narrative. Indirect dialogue does not use quotation marks because it is described from the point of view of the narrator, rather than the point of view of the character speaking. This can be an effective approach to use in short-form writing because it introduces the voices of others without taking up the space of conventional dialogue.

You've certainly noticed from both life and literature that dialogue does not always require another person. When one person is speaking aloud in an otherwise empty room, it is called an **external monologue**; think of our friend Cookie Monster, spewing cookie crumbs while lamenting the state of the nation. When that person is thinking but not voicing the ideas aloud, it is called an **internal monologue**. Internalized thought is typically italicized to distinguish it from external speech.

A **dramatic monologue** is an extended monologue that stands alone and conveys character, situation, and setting. These solo speeches, often without quotation marks, can be found in both prose and poetry, in short-form and long-form writing. An example of this can be seen in Ocean Vuong's "Immigrant Haibun," which inhabits the voice of the poet's mother. What makes this externalized self-talk different from an internal monologue is the potential that the speaker could be—and perhaps wants to be—overheard.

For internalized speech, the most common way to show this is through the use of italicized text. That said, short-form writing often plays with the conventions of dialogue to heighten the ambiguity of a scene and to open up the possibility of multiple readings. In the work collected in this anthology, you'll read pieces that dispense entirely with quotation marks (see Pía Barros's "A Story Possibly Heard in Some Bar at Three in the Morning") or that use italics for speech (see Shivani Mehta's "the invisible girl can be anything she wants when she doesn't want to be invisible").

Point of view

Every piece of writing has a voice. In addition to characters, creative works often include other voices that explain the overall situation, background, or action. These voices that hover above and beyond the story have different names based on the genre. But it's important to remember that the voice you are hearing is not the author speaking.

To help us differentiate between the author (an actual person who wakes up each morning, turns on the computer, and starts writing) and the voice in a written work, we often use terms like **narrator** or **character** (for fiction) and **speaker** (for poetry and nonfiction). Sometimes it is clear that these voices are invented characters distinct from the author. Often, it's unclear, and intentionally so. Some writers choose to draw exclusively from autobiographical experience, while others rely completely on imagination, but most fall somewhere in between on the fact-to-fantasy spectrum.

In writing, the voice of the speaker or storyteller is described based on the individual's relationship to the story, or the **point of view**. There are three main points of views: first person, second person, and third person. The following examples from your anthology demonstrate point of view and how it frames the reader's view of the story.

First-person singular

"When I wake on the couch to his hand on my hip, he's already wok-fried the shrimp." —from "Rules of Combat" by Katie Cortese

In first-person narration (underlined above), the emphasis is on the individual, and the reader is invited to identify with this central character. Often, first-person narration is paired with the present tense, as seen above, to create the feeling of being in the moment. When you anchor your reader and your characters in a place and time, it affects what can be seen, what can be known, and what can be shown.

First-person plural

"When we moved into our house, our neighbor, who lived beside us, brought us a pie." —from "The Man Who Hated Us and Then Forgot" by Karen E. Bender

It's unusual to see longer works in first-person plural (underlined above), but the short form is great for experimenting with these lesser-used perspectives. Take, for example, the collective "we" in Bender's piece who become the target of the neighbor's loathing. It would be an entirely different story and conflict if the neighbor had a personal grudge against one individual. But instead his animus toward an entire family becomes not just a character flaw but a symbol of a larger ill.

Second person

"You know how to write poetry, it is all you need to be happy, but you will not be happy ... " —from "Short Lecture on Your Own Happiness" by Mary Ruefle

The second-person point of view (underlined above) is relatively rare in literature. It's a difficult one to sustain, but you can see Ruefle experiment with it above in her lecture. In fact, we, your textbook writers, often use "you" when we're in the instructional mode. Second-person point of view can take on various shapes. It can be the epistolary voice of someone writing a letter to a specific reader. It could be the narrator talking directly to you, the reader. It could be the implied "you" of the imperative voice: [you] do this, now [you] do that.

Third-person singular

"<u>She</u> went trekking in Nepal and became infatuated with <u>her</u> Sherpa—a bright and eager young <u>man</u> who spoke perfect English." —from "Kim and Krishna" by Molly Giles

Third person (underlined above) is a conventional storytelling point of view and it has advantages for the short-form writer. Readers tend to grant the third-person speaker a level of authority and objectivity, especially if presented in the all-knowing, all-seeing **omniscient narrator**. Shivani Mehta's "the invisible girl can be anything she wants when she doesn't want to be invisible" provides a third-person, omniscient point of view. Here, the narrator describes the invisible girl's longing, her mother's grief, her conversations with her invisible friends, and even that she was born translucent. The narrator has access to thoughts, feelings, and experiences that are greater than one person could possibly know.

Giles, in the excerpt above, gives us a **third-person limited** perspective. Though the title is "Kim and Krishna," the narrator follows the movements, thoughts, and decisions of a single character. We only know of Krishna through the eyes of Kim. Even if you're writing a story of only one hundred words, the third person can lend subtlety and a sense of depth and distance by its association with longer works of literature.

The unreliable narrator

The **unreliable narrator** makes an appearance in literature when the narrator's telling of a story doesn't match up with what happened, or when the story itself is based on false information. In short-form writing, dissonance (at times slight) between what the narrator or main character says and what they do not say or do creates an immediate sense of conflict beyond traditional plot-induced complications.

You could have some fun browsing through the anthology to see if there are any characters you find entirely reliable. Can we trust a compulsive monster who is having a midlife crisis? Even Doyle's authentic-sounding narrator speaks to us of the long-gone past through the haze of memory. Charles Baudelaire instructs writers to "Be Drunken," but in reading don't you suspect that he has maybe taken his own advice too much to heart? And Calvino's narrator openly acknowledges the reader's tendency toward disbelief. In fact, the more unreliable the speaker, the more rounded he or she becomes as a character in our imaginations.

We trust the unreliable speaker—or at least the speaker who is willing to admit doubt—because we know deep down that human beings are rarely consistent, completely logical, or selflessly honest. These are ideals, not identities. The short form embraces unreliability because it automatically increases the story's tension and adds dimension to the characters' desires. It makes us participate more fully in trying to solve the mystery of the characters and their situation.

Authentic dialogue

One way to learn authentic dialogue is to study transcripts of 9-1-1 phone calls. While potentially traumatizing, these transcripts recreate situations where something is happening or about to happen. This impending crisis is what Jerome Stern calls "The Bear at the Door" story structure in his book *Making Shapely Fiction*. In these narratives, the person on one side of the door must confront the wildness, the unknown, on the other. It's a situation that demands action, and we read with interest because we want to know what it takes to overcome the threat waiting on the welcome mat.

Moments of crisis reveal who we are at our core. This revelation is what has drawn audiences to tragedies since the earliest days of ancient Greek theatre. When it comes to studying dialogue, urgency produces speech stripped of all the niceties. An emergency places the speaker in an extreme moment that requires direct communication. "What's your emergency?" is typically the first question a 9-1-1 operator asks followed by questions designed to draw out quickly the where, what, when, who, and why of the situation. Writers of all stripes, but especially short-form writers, can learn from these rapid-fire exchanges to propel their narratives forward and to reveal their characters' central concerns.

A less alarming method for studying dialogue is to take a look at comic strips. In a traditional three-panel comic, we can see at a glance the fundamentals of dialogue: character, action, and speech. Notice that actual speech is only one of several elements to consider when we want our characters to communicate with each other. In writing as in life, sometimes we offer nonverbal responses to actions. We shrug, we sigh, we look away instead of answering the question.

In short-form writing, dialogue serves as a multitasking tool to create depth, character, and tension. Rarely do people, in real life or on the page, talk to each other in fully formed thoughts, grammatical sentences, or clearly organized paragraphs. Conversations don't always follow an orderly and logical progression. Instead, we interrupt, evade, answer a different question than what was asked, say more than we wanted, say less than we wanted, or look away instead of speaking. As writers, we want to stay true to the way real people talk, but as short-form writers, we want to eliminate all the fillers—the *ums, ahs, likes,* and other verbal tics—that don't move the conversation forward. The rule of thumb should be this: dialogue on the page should be realistic but without all the boring stuff.

Asking questions

Questions also play a powerful role in the trajectory of a story. If you've interviewed for a job or spent any time with a curious kid, you know that the person who asks the questions holds the power.

Return to the script of "The Cat" and look at how questions are posed by the characters. Coco, the four-year-old, opens the scene with a question that has the feeling of a demand. To tiptoe around saying no, the father asks more questions. As the scene plays out, the questions turn from the practical to the philosophical, concerning language and existence, before looping back to the original question. Anyone who has had a conversation with a child will recognize this pattern, but the humor in this scene comes from what is not said. On the surface, this exchange is about getting a cat. But the subtext, the part of the story we cannot read except between the lines ("Coco is disappointed. This disturbs Matt.") suggests that more is going on. The questions are the crowbar that pries off the lid of Pandora's box and releases the existential angst of the father who must confront his mortality and the reality that his child, if he is lucky, will outlive him.

Through question-asking, we negotiate power and information. When we ask a question, we almost always have some other reason for asking. Sometimes the question we ask contains the answer.

Dialogue format

Dialogue tags are phrases added to indicate who is speaking. There are three common places these tags can be found (underlined):

- Beginning: <u>He said</u>, "Tell you what, I'll let you know when I'm ready to give a damn."

- End: "I knew you never really loved me," <u>she said</u>.
- Middle: "Would you two just stop fighting," <u>they said</u>, "and help us?"

The placement of dialogue tags can enhance the speech. A frontal tag lets us know right away who is speaking. A hind tag delays the recognition of the speaker in order to allow for greater uncertainty and ambiguity. A centrally located tag provides a pause that can indicate hesitation or otherwise alter the pacing of the character's speech. The placement of these tags, if they're used at all, can help create rhythm and structure in the short form.

A rule of thumb is to use dialogue tags minimally and only when absolutely necessary to help the reader follow the conversation. The reason for this oft-repeated advice is that dialogue tags interrupt the scene to remind us that we are listening to a created conversation. Of course, we know this. But if we can forget the author's presence and enter the "dream" of the story, as John Gardner calls it, we can be transformed, from a reader with a book to a fly on the wall of an imaginary, yet fully believable world.

Is "said" dead?

Many of us have been taught that "said" is overused as a dialogue tag in creative writing and have been encouraged to find alternatives that are more vibrant and descriptive. By consulting a thesaurus, you could easily come up with hundreds of substitutes, as you can see in Figure 3.1. These verbs act as stage directions that tell your audience how to read the text, which can sometimes be helpful.

Often the advice to use alternatives to "said" is designed to prevent the overuse of adverbs, such as "he said vociferously." While we generally have

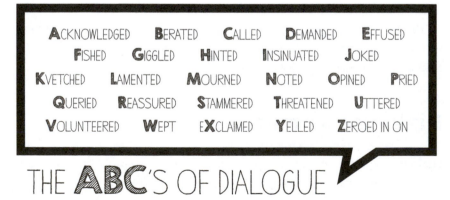

ACKNOWLEDGED   BERATED   CALLED   DEMANDED   EFFUSED
FISHED   GIGGLED   HINTED   INSINUATED   JOKED
KVETCHED   LAMENTED   MOURNED   NOTED   OPINED   PRIED
QUERIED   REASSURED   STAMMERED   THREATENED   UTTERED
VOLUNTEERED   WEPT   EXCLAIMED   YELLED   ZEROED IN ON

THE **ABC**'S OF DIALOGUE

Figure 3.1 The ABCs of dialogue tags. Courtesy of Savannah Adams.

nothing against adverbs, an overabundance of them usually points to an imbalance in the rest of the text. Adverbs are second-string modifiers that swoop in only when the nouns and verbs aren't pulling their weight. Adverbs that modify a dialogue tag should be particularly suspect because they run the risk of distracting attention from the speech itself. The minute a reader becomes more engaged in which new verb or adverb you'll pick to describe what a character has said, you've lost them.

When you were a kid, did you ever repeat a word until it lost all meaning? The use of "said" in dialogue tags has the same effect. Because "said" is expected, standard, and plain, its usage becomes relatively transparent. We don't notice it because it doesn't demand our attention. As a result, we are drawn into hearing the character's voices ourselves and creating the tone, urgency, and volume in our minds. Plain dialogue tags require readers' imaginations to become more actively engaged in the scene, and we must listen closer to what is being said and not said by the characters.

Conventional versus unconventional format

The most common formatting for dialogue is to indent your paragraphs each time a new character speaks. Tags and narration related to that speaker remain in the same paragraph. The result is a streamlined yet space-consuming exchange that can be problematic for writers in the short form. This is one reason you'll see short-form writers circumvent dialogue conventions and construct alternatives that allow them to compress dialogue into a tighter space.

For example, consider "A Modern Fable" by David Ignatow. In the version below, the dialogue is formatted conventionally:

Once upon a time a man stole a wolf from among its pack and said to the wolf, "Stop, you're snapping at my fingers."

And the wolf replied, "I'm hungry. What have you got to eat?"

And the man replied, "Chopped liver and sour cream."

The wolf said, "I'll take sour cream. I remember having it once before at Aunt Millie's. May I bare my teeth in pleasure?"

And the man replied, "Of course, if you'll come along quietly."

And the wolf asked, "What do you think I am? Just because I like sour cream you expect me to change character?"

Compare this to the actual version in your anthology. What effect does this format choice have on the pacing of the conversation?

Multidimensional dialogue

In her book *Reading Like a Writer*, Francine Prose states, "One mark of bad written dialogue is that it is only doing one thing, at most, at once." This cautionary advice becomes more potent when applied to short-form writing. In a story of a few hundred words, each word must not only count but also compound. This can be applied not only to dialogue but also to any formal element within short imaginative writing. Every choice must do more than communicate; it should advance the narrative, deepen the reader's understanding of the character, complicate the action, suggest a time before or after, heighten the emotional situation, resonate with something that happened earlier in the story, foreshadow something that is to come, or insinuate something that has not been fully revealed.

One of the first lessons we learn in writing for an academic audience is that we cannot write like we talk. That lesson holds true in creative writing as well: we cannot write like we talk even when we are trying to capture the particulars of authentic conversation. One exercise Stephanie gives her creative writing students is to visit the campus coffee shop and eavesdrop on fellow students. Listening is one of the most essential skills of any writer, and students who actively listen to other people talking are surprised to discover this very important thing: *we don't say that much*. Often, we talk at or past each other, repeat gossip, misunderstand, brag, or offend.

Unless we are a participant in a conversation, or unless the topic is particularly salacious, most conversations are boring. A conversation is supposed to be an ephemeral pleasure, a way to pass time and build relationships, a meandering thread of ideas that we weave for our own entertainment. A written conversation, on the other hand, takes a more permanent shape on the page and as such can be revised and manipulated to seem authentic but to be more than a direct reflection of reality.

One trap that writers fall into is the attempt to replicate real speech word for word. We tend to be wordier in conversation because, as the saying goes, "talk is cheap." In short-form writing, we can't afford to spend our precious word count having our characters talk about the weather. That is unless the characters are talking about the weather as a conscious evasion of the real topic. In that case, the dramatic tension arises from the insignificance of what is said and the significance of what is withheld. That's what we mean by subtext.

You can hint at what is unsaid through a variety of techniques, but the best way to understand subtext is to look at it in its natural habitat. In intentionally crafted dialogue, the unsaid isn't absent. The unsaid is displaced into action, scene, or image. Subtext is shown in the way the character holds her body rigid while her words speak of love. Subtext is the stifled yawn, or the dirty window that reflects the character's face, or the vase on the mantle that holds the ashes of the main character's husband as she invites her date in for a nightcap.

Sometimes, in an attempt to shape dialogue for our own purposes, we can go too far in the other direction. Dialogue in complete, grammatical sentences too often sounds stilted and unnatural. Dramatic monologues in which a character rants or philosophizes are often seen as the author using the character as a megaphone for his or her own ideas. In this case, dialogue is serving the sole purpose of fulfilling the author's agenda, and as a result, it is not fulfilling its multidimensional function.

Conveniently, the best practices for dialogue also support the goal of compression in short-form writing. You can avoid needless scene-setting and lead up if you locate the dialogue in a place that gives us an immediate sense of what's at stake. For example, the opening statement in Grant Faulkner's "Time Travel" sets up the conflict that follows the characters through time and space: "My life isn't some cheap reality show." The statement locates us in a particular time and hints at the nature of the extended drama between these characters.

Another compressed way to show dialogue is indirectly, through summary dialogue. Rather than a back and forth exchange, **summary dialogue** expresses the gist of a conversation (sans quotation marks) from the narrator's or third-person perspective. For example, Katelyn Hemmeke's "What You Are" intensifies the narrator's conflict about her identity by placing it against the backdrop of her family's conversation around the Thanksgiving table: "Isn't it so scary that Michigan has one of the largest Muslim populations in America, they said. Isn't it such a good idea to build a wall to keep ourselves safe. Isn't it fortunate that we live in a town like ours, with good values and at least one church in every neighborhood and not so many of *those immigrants*." We don't need quotation marks to believe that these words were said. In fact, by providing these statements in the form of summary dialogue, the author creates the effect that these words have been said and heard more than once, and perhaps not just in this household.

The psychological gesture

In a theatrical performance, an audience reads posture and gesture looking for authenticity. To explain how this authenticity is conveyed to the audience, legendary acting teacher Michael Chekhov developed the concept of the **psychological gesture**, a physical action that reveals important clues about the internal nature of a character. The psychological gesture is the doorway into the character's private thoughts and feelings. Chekhov's theory of movement, in simplified form, can help the short-form writer find ways to express a character's inner world through small, deliberate glances or gestures.

More than just a daily gesture or physical tic, like scratching your head or jingling coins in your pocket, the psychological gesture is rooted in what Chekhov considered the archetypal movements that communicate a character's most essential state of being. He identified ten archetypal movements that an actor could use to externalize the inner life of a character: pushing, pulling, smashing, lifting, gathering, throwing, tearing, dragging, penetrating, and reaching. Consider the psychological gesture of Steve Coughlin's "Boy at Night" where the young boy repetitively throws a football against a chain-link fence. This action says more than anything the boy could say. As you develop characters in your writing, consider using this list to reveal movements that fit the scope of your piece.

Perhaps your character lifts a glass of water and sets it down without drinking. Or he smashes a tiny spider crawling across his desk. Or a woman tears at a ragged thumbnail. An accountant throws his coat into the back seat of his car. Someone peels the wrapping paper from a gift so carefully that it does not rip. A child yanks at a tag on the back of her shirt. An old man jabs the toe of his boot into a gopher hole in his yard. Psychological gestures and other deftly handled actions can tell us everything we need to know about a character. This technique is also a useful tool for compression. This technique can be adapted to give depth to the short form.

To illustrate this idea, look at how Brian Doyle's "My Devils" opens with gestures that are both physical and psychological. In the beginning of the story, the seven-year-old's aunt lays hands on the boy in a gesture of religious healing. The aunt's actions give insight into the religiosity of the boy's family and also heighten awareness of the ways that hands communicate throughout the story. Later the boy explains, "Hand gestures were another language in our family, and our mother was the most eloquent speaker of that tongue." The story opens and closes with the movement of hands, and these gestures frame a story of a young boy trying to sort through all the ways we communicate without words to those we love.

The show/tell ratio

Walk into any creative writing classroom and you'll likely hear this phrase: "show, don't tell." What teachers and well-intentioned peers mean by this is that writing should actively give us the scene and put us in the middle of the experience rather than talk *about* what's happening. In our own classrooms, we advocate for a balance between both showing and telling. Good writing often puts its readers in the middle of the action and then takes a few steps back to reflect on the scene. You can test your writing's show-to-tell ratio by focusing on your verbs. If your verbs are specific and lively, in other words if they are active, then you're on the right track.

See, for example, how Semezdin Mehmedinović activates the first three sentences in "Surplus History": "A shell <u>hit</u> one of the facades on Marshal Tito Street. The plaster <u>poured</u> down and, with it, a sheet metal sign. The sign <u>read</u>: Dr. Ante Pavelić 11." The active verbs (underlined) create a tense scene that launches us into the story. Alongside the active verbs, the specific details such as the name of a street and the physical materials (shell, plaster, metal) make the scene feel real even before the speaker can explain what's happening. Imagine if the story had begun with the fourth sentence: "Until then I had no idea, but now I knew: the central street of Sarajevo had a different name fifty years ago, and that name was hidden for years behind the plaster, like a geological diagram of different ages." We can absorb the narrator's telling us what he has discovered only because we have been shown it first.

Recognizing clichés and stereotypes

All writers need to be wary of shortcuts that reduce or simplify characters rather than add nuance and complexity. Two of the most common shortcuts for writers are clichés and stereotypes. A **cliché** is a familiar phrase, expression, or theme that has been so overused that it requires little to no thought on the part of the reader. That doesn't mean clichés are off-limits, though. For example, Joanne Avallon in "All This" uses the phrase "seeing red," a clichéd expression for anger. In her one-sentence story, she brings this familiar phrase to life within the scene as she describes how the narrator "understand[s] for the first time—as [her] hand descends—the phrase 'seeing red.'" In this case, the cliché is made unique by its relationship to the narrator's awakening to an anger that is intergenerational and that has, like the expression itself, been passed down without thinking.

Stereotypes are like clichés in that they are repeated without much thought, but they tend to be generalizations of people who share similar characteristics. A **stereotype** is an assumption based on a person's belonging (or lack of belonging) to a particular group. The assumption may be based on ethnicity, race, gender, nationality, sexual orientation, occupation, physical appearance or ability, religious affiliation, political affiliation, or pretty much any group you can imagine. If you hear someone say, "All ____ are _____," you are in the vicinity of a stereotype.

In literature and pop culture, stereotypes are frequently employed for comedic effect. See the way Sherrie Flick invents new stereotypes in "Dinner Party" to describe the attendees not as individuals but as background noise:

> The smart people at the dinner table murmured, "Hmm. Mmm? Hmm."
> While the middling people added, "Blah. Blah. Blah. Blah."
> The people not in the know asked questions.

Flick uses stereotypes purposefully to accomplish several things. These stereotypes add humor to the scene because we recognize these groups by their conversational patterns. We have all been at social events like this where like-minded people gravitate toward each other. Flick's example is, more precisely, a generalization. She avoids the traps of stereotype because she purposefully applies her generalizations to everyone at the party to give a blurry, impressionistic glimpse of the crowd in action.

Both *stereotype* and *cliché* originated as printer's terms for the reproduction of text using printing blocks. The stereotype was a solid plate of metal used for printing that saved printers time and money. Cliché is a French word originally describing the sound of the individual letters set into the print tray. Say the word aloud, and you'll hear the click and slide of those letters falling into place. These words, once used interchangeably to describe a mechanical process, are now mostly used metaphorically and have a generally negative connotation. Stereotypes are often the result of snap judgments based on biases that may or may not be openly acknowledged. For this reason, they can produce offense (at least) and reproduce ignorance (at worst).

One technique that can quickly descend into cliché is the use of **dialect**, which refers to speech that differs from standard usage and is usually specific to a region or group of people. As a literary device, dialect can provide quick characterization and help distinguish speakers from different areas, classes, socioeconomic groups, ages, and education. But we recommend that you use this device sparingly. Unless you have closely observed the patterns and tendencies of a particular dialect, it will be hard to convey it authentically. Especially in short-form writing, you don't need to write completely in dialect to suggest the flavor of a region. Channel the idiosyncrasies of individuals rather than the general tendencies of a group. For example, it could simply be a matter of saying "lightning bugs" rather than "fireflies" or "cola" rather than "pop." This does not mean that you can only write about places you've been and people you've known. The best writers find a way to balance between writing what they know and writing what they want to know.

Clichés are less likely to offend, unless you bring a story full of them to a writer's workshop. In fact, it's a cliché of writing workshops that someone will take great joy in pointing out the clichés in other people's work. Don't be that person. Instead, recognize that clichés are an inevitable part of human existence. David Shields's "Life Story" is a prime example, composed entirely of bumper sticker clichés. The story becomes more than a sum of its parts, however, through sheer force of will and the accumulation and placement of clichés to create a unique narrative made from the most mundane materials. The lesson to be learned from this piece is to use clichés consciously rather than letting them use you.

While recognizing clichés and stereotypes in your own writing and the writing of others can be helpful, it is more useful to consider ways these generalizations can show us something specific and unique. One way to do this is to substitute archetypes for stereotypes. What's the difference, you ask? An **archetype** is a universal framework upon which an original story or character is built. Archetypal characters are shaped by standout qualities that differentiate them from others. We like to think of them as pairs of characters that represent two sides of the same coin: the ruler and the rebel; the king and the jester; the sage and the imbecile; the villain and the hero; the teacher and the student. What keeps an archetype from becoming a stereotype is that it keeps going and reveals something new about this recognizable character. A stereotype, on the other hand, ends the conversation. It implies a judgment that does not allow for individualization.

Conclusion: What are your characters made of?

Ghost hunters find ghosts by heat, scent, sound, light, movement: your characters should at least have as much substance as a specter. Take the time to flesh out your characters by letting them talk to each other. Listening to how people talk and questioning the automatic ideas and phrases that pop into our heads are two ways to write authentically and purposefully. Short-form writers have to take shortcuts, but in doing so they need to beware of language that comes too quick and too easy. Forgive yourself and others for using clichés. It happens. Don't give up. Let us see what you're made of, and what your stories and characters are made of, by pushing past the familiar into something new.

Exercises

A. Visit a public space like a coffee shop or airport and eavesdrop to observe conversation in its natural habitat. What do you notice about the ways people converse, what they say and do not say, and how their bodies emphasize or contradict what they are saying? Notice the hesitations, pauses, roundabouts, and tangents. Listen to the way people laugh, talk, and interact. Capture the patterns and idiosyncrasies of a conversation as if you are a field biologist taking notes on an elusive creature. Learn about the ecology of conversations in the wild so that you can replicate them in your writing. Then transcribe these conversations (as best you can without looking like a creep) into your journal.

B. To consider the ways that conversation reveals character, think of the phrases that someone you know says all the time. For example, Heather's grandfather, if someone's pants were too tight, would say, "Those pants fit a little too soon." And if they were too loose, he'd say, "There's ballroom for dancing." Record these verbal quirks in your journal or share them in conversation with your classmates to explore how habits of speech can deepen characterization.

C. Watch a favorite scene from a film with the sound turned off. Use this as an opportunity to observe gesture, body language, and subtext.

What can be communicated between characters without saying a word?

Prompts

A. Write a single scene between two characters in an unexpected setting. The characters must be performing an action that is related to the setting while talking about a completely different topic. For example, a mother and son might be talking about the son's decision to drop out of school while they strap themselves into a rollercoaster car. The goal of this prompt is to consider the ways that actions and words work together or resist each other to tell a larger story.

B. Write a micro-play that reveals tension between two or more characters through dialogue, gestures, glances, and action. Let their sidelong looks, squints, or grimaces reveal everything essential about them in that moment. You may only have room for each character to say one line of dialogue, so use it carefully—as if it is your one-shot flare gun when you are stranded on a desert island. The lines of dialogue should reveal some essential tension between the characters, whether directly or through subtext. Cut straight to THE moment (the moment of change, of crisis, of realization, of completion) and describe what happens.

C. Write a completely earnest, over-the-top complaint letter that ultimately creates an intimate portrait of the speaker's character and situation through complaints alone.

One-sentence workshop

The following exercise will help you practice the art of brevity:

Read this sentence from Sarah Evans's "Dust" and notice how it moves from conversation to observation:

My toddler son asks, "What is it?" and I answer, "Dust," and I watch as he watches each speck twirl, like fireflies skimming the night air, like plankton riding the currents in the deep.

This single sentence captures the relationship between parent and child, question and answer, reality and imagination. Using imagery, metaphor, and the interaction between characters, the author navigates different kinds of darkness and gives weight to this miniscule scene. With Evans's sentence as your model, bring together question and answer into a single sentence, and let those few words of dialogue speak volumes about what is most important to your characters at that moment.

4

Moving through Time and Space

Relevant readings

"All This" by Joanne Avallon

"A Story Possibly Heard in Some Bar at Three in the Morning" by Pía Barros

"The Man Who Hated Us and Then Forgot" by Karen E. Bender

"Thin Cities 5" by Italo Calvino

"Boy at Night" by Steve Coughlin
"Time Travel" by Grant Faulkner
"A Thousand Perfect Strangers" by Kathy Fish
"Natalia" by Ilya Kaminsky
"On Miniatures" by Lia Purpura
"Dinosaur" by Bruce Holland Rogers

Flash interview with Karen E. Bender

Novelist and short-story writer Karen E. Bender has taught in MFA programs around the country, including Hollins University, Warren Wilson College, Chatham University, and the Iowa Writers' Workshop. We chose her piece, "The Man Who Hated Us and Then Forgot," because of the way it shows the progression and regression of time. Here is what she has to say about writing short.

How do you define the kind of short-form writing that you do?
The short short fiction and nonfiction that I write is defined by its focus, and the intent—in a short short, I want to capture one small moment or interaction, the way that we experience moments in our lives; but I want to make the moment as strange and resonant as it is in life, which is to say, more expansive than the one moment. A successful short-form piece should feel complete in itself but hint at a world that expands far beyond it.

How does your approach to writing in short forms differ from the other kinds of writing that you do?
Longer short stories and short shorts exist in time in different ways. Both are slightly artificial ways of experiencing time. I view longer short stories as time funneled through a narrative one is relating to a reader—a longer story is what we tell people, shaping the experiences and chaos of life into a narrative arc. A short short, to me, is more akin to how we actually experience life—in unique, resonant moments, in very focused explorations of image or time.

What demands does the short form make of its writers or readers?
The short form may ask the reader to imagine the story outside of the actual story more than traditional short stories; the plot of a short story tends to lie mostly outside of the boundaries of the short short. The short short form also demands that each line be essential and deepen the story in some way, so attention to language and detail is important.

Free dive

Choose a specific place you know where time seems to slow or stop completely, and write about what happens there. For example, in Lia Purpura's "On Miniatures," the author discusses an experiment showing that a person's perception of time is affected by how they perceive the space around them. As you imagine the specific place you want to write about, try to capture the multiple layers of history, memories, and projections into the future. Collect the truths, untruths, and almost truths, the yearnings and regrets. Document how the transitory and changeable nature of life might be perceived in this space. When a photographer sets up a camera to record a time-lapse video or photograph, something peculiar happens to the way the viewer experiences the speed of life: everything in the image that is living rushes, changes, blurs, or disappears altogether. Your time-lapse flash piece might do something similar. See if you can record the deep time of the place you are writing about.

Vignette: Tonight, at the Santee Drive-in Theatre

Here we are, rolling down the windows of a Volkswagen Squareback to a set of car speakers. A hazy, late-July sunset casts a thin silhouette of my parents. My best friend is here, always here. Everyone sits where they can: on aluminum chairs and ice chests, in the open trunk, on the roof. We pass around a bucket of popcorn and listen to the hush as floodlights cut and speakers squawk to life. We must be wearing stripes: brown, teal, burnt orange. We watch Rocky, Grease, Footloose. *Here, again: we choose our spot under the bird-laced electric blue, hitch our Keds on the Chevy tailgate, drink Dr. Pepper through licorice straws. We watch* Edward Scissorhands, Reality Bites. *We'd watch anything. And here: in Chuck Taylors and flannel shirts, at the edge of asphalt and alfalfa, tossing sleeping bags into the bed of the truck. The pillows keep the dizzying scent of teenage boys with thick, wavy tresses that twine my fingertips. We forget to watch the double feature. My best friend eats a hot pretzel with mustard. And then she's gone and I'm reversing into place, unhooking the hatchback and unzipping a sleeping bag to a man who unwinds everything I know. We watch* The Matrix, Mulholland Drive. *Uncertain of the narrative we half-sleep, half-dream: a shaggy-headed palm tree, a meteor shower. Then, we're here: handing wrinkled dollar bills to the guy wearing a retro* Goonies *t-shirt. My sister-in-law and I take our place side by side on fold-out beach chairs in uncanny flamingo pink light. We've snuck out, barely remembering how it's done. At home: pajamas, teeth brushing, story time with grandma. Here:* Atomic Blonde, *the crackle of radio air, low murmurs, tires rolling past. A hush ripples across the still hot blacktop, and the feature begins.*

—Heather
Word count: 298

The narrative dilemma

Even the briefest narrative must confront time. Once upon a time. One time. One day. The strangest thing happened. A man walked into a bar. A girl moved next door. And then. And then what? Well, it all depends on how much time you have to hear the story. If you're on a Greyhound bus riding from Spokane, Washington, to Cheyenne, Wyoming, and listening to your seatmate tell a story—well, that could be a long one. But if you're reading a flash text, what happens next will undoubtedly happen quick. Get ready. Time is short, and the drop is coming.

You've probably noticed by now that strange things tend to happen when you write in the short form. Squeezing the text into a small space produces two results. First, when space is limited, it determines how much of the story can be told. Second, when you squeeze anything into a small space, distortion occurs. Depending on how much pressure you apply to your narrative, and how much air you suck out of the spaces between moments, you'll affect how the reader perceives time, space, and even the relative proportions of objects. This chapter explores how these tendencies affect the reader's experience within a creative work. We'll talk about how you might conceptualize the elements of a micro story and imagine the ultra-close proximity of the horizon. We'll also touch on some of the ways you might use the natural distortion that occurs to your advantage.

Self-contained worlds

A short-form text is compact but not incomplete. As Lia Purpura mentions in "On Miniatures," "The miniature, a working, functioning complete world unto itself, is not merely a 'small' or 'brief' thing, or a 'shortened' form of something larger. Miniatures transcend their size, but like small-but-vicious dogs; dense chunks of fudge, espresso, a drop of mercury, parasites." And if we may add another metaphor to the list, short-form narratives are microcosms—tiny, independently spinning universes.

Time moves fast in the short form. It can also behave a bit wonky. Art history professor Richard Shiff writes, "We *feel* space and time, body and mind, all as sensation." Although Shiff is talking about the way we experience space and time in a work of art, the same holds true with the way we experience these elements in writing. As Karen E. Bender said in her flash interview, short short stories resemble the way we experience time as "unique, resonant moments." Bender's suggestion reminds us that time is fluid and changeable. And, it's not always linear.

Pause for a minute and think about how differently time can feel in these situations:

- If you are waiting in line
- If you have just inhaled laughing gas for a dental procedure
- If you are experiencing an eclipse
- If you are running a marathon or participating in some other endurance sport
- If you are in the middle of breaking up with someone
- If you are witnessing a bar fight

Time misbehaves. It feels hallucinatory. Time can speed by, move in slow motion, stutter step, act glitchy, drift. You should think of narrative time as malleable and adaptable to the needs of the text. You don't have to follow standard time.

What is standard time anyways? It is common practice in the United States and beyond to follow Daylight Savings Time and turn the clock backward or forward to "save" daylight, but some countries such as India, Peru, Russia, and South Korea do not observe this practice. Neither do the states of Arizona or Hawaii. Likewise, when you enter the Fremont neighborhood of Seattle, Washington—a place known as "The People's Republic of Fremont" where nude bicycle parades happen on a regular basis—a sign encourages visitors to turn their watches back five minutes. Briefly imagine what might happen if you were gifted an extra five minutes anytime you entered your own neighborhood. You might strike up a conversation with a stranger. You might solve some problem that's been dogging you. You might spontaneously join that bike parade streaking past. Fremont's approach to time is pleasurably radical—and it might not be so far-fetched.

Time is not fixed according to Einstein's theory of relativity. Scientists have demonstrated the concept of **time dilation**, or the way time can slacken, by sending atomic clocks into space and comparing them with clocks back on earth; although the clocks start out synchronized, the clocks will eventually begin to show slight discrepancies. All this is to say that non-rigid approaches to time tend to make interesting things happen in life, as well as in writing. And when it comes to short-form writing, it's imperative that you think about how you represent time. Otherwise, you reach the end of the page, and nothing has happened.

The flexibility of time: A few illustrations

In its simplest form, a narrative says one thing happens and then another. Linear time strings together a series of events. Think of linear time as having the characteristics of a silk ribbon. The ribbon is supple; it might be stretched out flat, bent, twisted, looped, or tied. If we imagine the simplest version of linear time, it might be illustrated as three knots, evenly spaced apart from one another on the ribbon (Figure 4.1). Each knot marks a moment in time we might think of as yesterday, today, and tomorrow.

To illustrate the traditional narrative arc (or plotline) of a story, the ribbon of time stretches out, but quickly arcs upward (Figure 4.2). A series of scenes escalate the tension until it peaks at the climax. Then, a short series of scenes release the tension and wrap up the traditional plotline, also known as **Freytag's Pyramid**.

You probably recognize this common narrative structure. Think of your average drama. A hero is introduced. Hero gets into a series of surprising

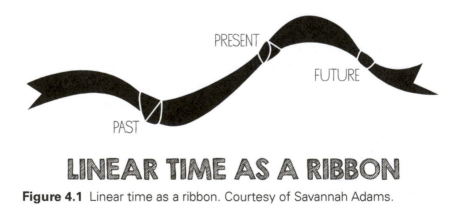

Figure 4.1 Linear time as a ribbon. Courtesy of Savannah Adams.

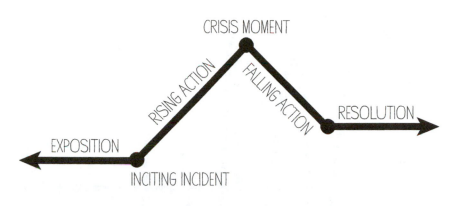

FREYTAG'S PYRAMID

Figure 4.2 Traditional narrative arc. Courtesy of Savannah Adams.

confrontations and learns, bit by bit, about the enemy. The plot heats up. Hero faces off with the enemy. Hero survives. (You know the formula.)

The problem is, short-form writing doesn't have the room to build suspense through a long sequence of dramatic scenes. It doesn't have time to slowly and surely drive the plot toward a climax. And it certainly doesn't have time to resolve every mystery. How might you imagine a narrative structure that works in a flash? What happens to the narrative when a text gets compressed?

If you'll forgive a quick and dirty simplification of some theoretical astrophysics, it can help explain how time and space might work in an ultra-short narrative. The **wormhole theory**, which is based on Einstein's general theory of relativity, provides an interesting way to think about narrative trajectory in short-form writing. If we continue to build on the image of linear time as a silk ribbon, the wormhole theory says that we might fold the ribbon back and forth against itself to create a series of waves. Then, imagine a needle and thread piercing through the folds of ribbon. The wormhole theory predicts the needle that pierces through the ribbon would create a passage way that defies normal modes of space and time and allows you to travel directly from one place in time to another. Theoretically, this offers one compelling possibility for how you might move across vast swaths of time and space. It's a theory that has influenced a lot of science fiction in recent years, but it also offers writers a way to conceptualize the sorts of time leaps that you might take when structuring a short-form narrative. To be clear, this theory, when applied to narrative structure, isn't about writing time travel stories that include space ships and encounters with alien species. It's

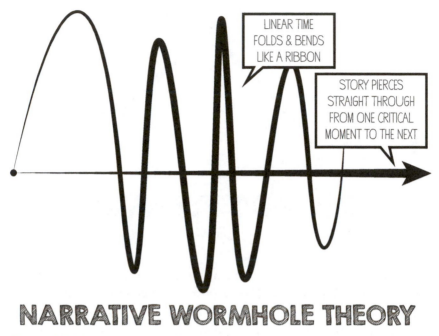

NARRATIVE WORMHOLE THEORY

Figure 4.3 Narrative wormhole theory. Courtesy of Savannah Adams.

about establishing a time-defying trajectory that allows short-form writing to quickly span a long period of time or travel great distances, all in the space of a sentence or paragraph (Figure 4.3).

The wormhole theory can help us conceptualize what a narrative structure might look like in short-form work. Imagine a narrative trajectory that pierces through time and moves from one scene to another without any in-between: the narrative arrows straight from one critical moment to another. Instead of having the tension slowly and steadily rise toward a climax, as it does in a more traditional narrative arc, a compressed narrative might jackknife at an acute angle. Scenes might collide. Different moments in time might align.

The wormhole route allows the writer to tunnel under a narrative to pop up in a new place, or collapse time and juxtapose two scenes side by side. Bruce Holland Rogers's "Dinosaur" works in this fashion. Look at the way the story begins:

> When he was very young, he waved his arms, snapped his massive jaws, and tromped around the house so that the dishes trembled in the china cabinet. "Oh, for goodness' sake," his mother said. "You are *not* a dinosaur! You are a human being!"

After that opening, the man's life gets summarized in a modest paragraph. He grows up. He becomes a tax accountant. He retires. Then, at the end of his life, time seems to collapse, and the man returns to exactly where he started:

> Then one day, when he was out for a walk by the lake, he forgot what his mother had told him. He forgot that he was not a dinosaur. He stood blinking his dinosaur eyes in the bright sunlight, feeling its familiar warmth on his dinosaur skin, watching dragonflies flitting among the horsetails at the water's edge.

The man undergoes a kind of instantaneous de-civilization and returns to a wilder and more natural state. We can sense the weight of the life lessons that tamed the man. But the two scenes that glint with warmth and sunlit clarity are the scenes at each end of the narrative tunnel, when the boy feels powerfully ferocious as a dinosaur and, then, when he stands at the water's edge and embodies that natural wildness once more.

Alternatively, Joanne Avallon's "All This" boomerangs the reader from the present moment into the past, and back. The second person perspective amplifies the sense of disorientation as it leaps from a moment when "you" draw back to slap "your" daughter, all the way back to when "you" were five years old and being punished, and then forward again to the initial moment when "your" cocked arm releases and slaps. The entire time-traveling narrative takes place inside the confines of a single sentence that is 244 words long. It propels the reader headlong toward the moment of impact: the look of shock and understanding on the daughter's face.

Ultra-long sentences like this one are common in short-form writing. We call it a **telescoping sentence** that, like an astronomer's telescope, closes distance and brings far away objects into intimate focus. A telescoping sentence can stretch through a spectrum of experience and thought, and it often does so with a messy mixture of the profound, the mundane, the specific, and the abstract. Translator Michael Helm says that these long sentences "create a synthesis of effect … that seems something like the condition of a lived moment. Certain moments never end." The telescoping sentence is one maneuver you might try to vault the reader forward.

The space-time continuum

So far, we've addressed how a writer might move through the narrative in a variety of ways. Next, we're going to explore how you can change the reader's perception of the dimensions of time and space in a narrative. Time and space are closely connected: in science, they refer to this as the space-time continuum, as if they are woven into the same fabric.

We've been using the metaphor of space/time travel to conceptualize narrative theory with a grand view of the universe. But for the purposes of a story, when we refer to space we are simply talking about the setting in which a scene takes place. It might take place in a desert or a cramped and dusty used bookstore, for instance. The physical details of the setting are important: Is the noonday sun beating down on the protagonist in the arid landscape where all is silent except for the stir of a rattlesnake? Or do cluttered shelves and sounds of street traffic convey a sense of confinement and disarray in the bookstore scene? The setting anchors the characters and their actions. When you demarcate the space of a narrative, you set the boundaries of the narrative's imagined world.

As a writer, you can represent the scene's dimensions in a conventional way. Or you can choose to distort the setting in one of two ways: spatial dilation or spatial constriction. Dilation adds a quality of openness. In Kathy Fish's "A Thousand Perfect Strangers" we glimpse all the possible domestic pleasures of the couple in one sweeping glance: "Now puppies, now children, now rainbow trout, mountain streams, their own warm bed, her hands, her mouth, her body, his desk, his tiny stories, her sky, their bodies, her voice, his smiles, her smiles, their faces, holidays, family, road trips, a thing called game night, walks at dusk, his books, their love." This sentence telescopes into the future and lets the android see what his life could be like if he were to run away with Research Assistant Gem. You'll notice the closeness of this list feels warmly intimate but not claustrophobic. The repetition of "now," "now," "now" allows the experiences to open incrementally; it dilates to expand and let in one more thing, and then another. There are also important distinctions made between the objects: *his* desk, *her* hands, *their* bodies. The pronouns subtly emphasize the individuality and space between each part of their shared future. It's a nuanced, but effective maneuver at the sentence level that makes the future seem wide open.

On the other hand, a setting that constricts creates a feeling of confinement. Objects in a scene can seem to stack on top of each other and feel uncomfortably close. In Steve Coughlin's "Boy at Night," a boy is trapped between the demands of this dead brother's ghost and his mother's grief. Consider this passage from the text:

Let me in, his brother calls from the street in front of the boy's white house. His brother knocks his cold fist against the boy's front door.

Three years after his brother died the boy's mother moved him into his brother's room. There's a record player covered in dust that the boy has never played. His brother's hockey stick still leans against the wall.

He will not open the closet filled with his brother's clothes.

The boy wants to be strong enough to scare his dead brother away. He wants breathing room, but he can't have it. The ghost bangs on the door. The boy wants to knock the fence down, he wants to push his older brother away. He tries and tries but can't. When the fence does, finally, come down, he seems to run and hide forever:

> He keeps throwing the football against the fence because he wants to knock the fence over and run behind the neighbor's brown house. After he knocks the fence down the boy's mother will call his name, but the boy will not come home.

The verb tense shifts at the end from present to future to indicate the boy's hoped-for outcome: the fence comes down and he leaves for good. Or perhaps the fence never comes down. Either way, the confinement of the unyielding perimeter is palpable. So is the ghost's presence and the boy's yearnings. Everyone is trapped within the constricted space, including the reader.

Dilation and constriction work in opposite ways to construct the dimensions of the scene as well as alter how the reader perceives the span of time over which a narrative might take place. A narrative can move through the past, present, and future in several ways by concentrating on one point in time or spreading out over multiple points in time. Although we as readers can tease out these different elements of time and space, we experience them as closely linked. We often experience them as integrated, like the space-time continuum, where the three dimensions of physical space and the fourth dimension of time combine. Consequently, writers must juggle the elements of space and time in their narratives to create for their readers the illusion of a world that is a vivid, unified, and continuous whole.

As with spatial dilation and constriction, there are two basic ways of altering how the reader perceives time to make it behave differently, either by slowing time down or speeding time up. Compare the speed at which the two following narratives move. The first is from Molly Giles's "Dumped: Seven Cautionary Tales":

Sean and Susan

She said the new baby might not be his. He backed the car over her cat. She gained sixty pounds. He cried out his ex-wife's name when he came. She sold his Ted Williams baseball bat for five dollars at a garage sale. He went to Bangkok for two weeks without her. She corrected his boss' grammar at a company dinner. He kissed her sister on the lips. She kissed his father on the lips. He drove off and left her at a truck stop. She found some pot in his sock drawer and threw it out. They're still together.

The second is from "8 Meetings Nobody Scheduled" by Alex Carr Johnson:

> **The Centipede.** As it munched on mites and midges in a sweet recess of rotten log, the centipede could never have known what cataclysm was to visit it next. Even if the creature possessed the cognitive capacity to guess, and even if it had a thousand guesses, it could not have prepared itself. Nor could I have known before I ripped apart the white mycelia and the tender flakes of wood pulp that I was a monster, a giant, a disaster.

In Giles's story, years careen past. The lovers accumulate one screwup after another. The reader assumes that years pass, but the list of break-up worthy failures seems to constrict into a single epic mashup. Johnson's piece, on the other hand, slows down and focuses in on the long moments before the centipede faces calamity. Notice how the syntax draws out the drama of what hasn't happened yet:

> As it munched on mites and midges in a sweet recess of rotten log, the centipede could never have known what cataclysm was to visit it next.

This sentence is filled with **alliteration**, the intentional repetition of intial sounds to produce a sonic pattern. The alliteration (munched, mites, midges; recess, rotten; never, known; could, cataclysm) makes the reader slow down and listen to the music. And the phrases like "as it," "in a," and "was to" draw out the moment as they draw out the sentence. You have to unwind the sentence to understand the nature of the cataclysm. Likewise, the speaker's self-awareness grows bigger and bigger: he's "a monster, a giant, a disaster." All these tactics affect the reader's perception of narrative time by making the moment slowly open. This is time dilation in action.

Writers can use spatial and temporal dilation and constriction to dramatize different elements of the narrative. These strategies are useful tools for emphasizing the dimensionality of scenes or moderating the action. However you choose to represent time and space, it will affect your reader's perception of how the narrative feels and moves (Table 4.1).

Table 4.1 Strategies for representing time and space

Strategy	Effect	Example
Time dilation	Evokes the feeling of slackening, loosening, or slowing down.	"I stood up, I sat down, I stood up again; the clock slowed down, the post came late, the afternoon turned cool; the cat licked his coat, tore the chair to shreds, slept in a drawer that didn't close ..." (From "One Long Sentence" by Sven Birkerts)
Time constriction	Evokes the feeling of quickening, intensification, or speeding up.	"She said the new baby might not be his. He backed the car over her cat. She gained sixty pounds." (From "Dumped: Seven Cautionary Tales" by Molly Giles)
Spatial dilation	Evokes the feeling of vastness, emptiness. Distant things seem close, and close things seem distant.	"Below, there is nothing for hundreds and hundreds of feet: a few clouds glide past; farther down, you can glimpse the chasm's bed." (From "Thin Cities 5" by Italo Calvino)
Spatial constriction	Evokes the feeling of closeness, confinement, and even perhaps claustrophobia.	"It's not as morbid as it sounds, a target pinned above a crib: the place was small, the walls already plastered full with paintings, sketches, pretty leaves, hand-illuminated psychedelic broadsides of poems by my friends. I masking-taped my paper massacre to the only empty space, a door I'd closed to form a wall." (From "Grip" by Joy Castro)

Endless possibilities

Short-form narratives rely on suggestion to hint at the unspoken parts of the story. Readers decode the equivalent of a nod, a bit lip, a sideways glance, or other micro-expressions to comprehend the full story. But another related strategy to expand the narrative in the reader's imagination has to do with the power of "maybe" and the suggestion of multiple possibilities. The strategy offers wide-open futures, and you can see this in the way Ilya Kaminsky's "Natalia" rides on the energy of fantasy and all the possibilities two lovers desire for a lifetime together. The speaker imagines how his ambitions dwell on her shoulder, his wishes linger behind her knee as if her body holds all the things he might want. Nothing is singular: he doesn't promise a vacation, he promises adventures—horseback rides, trips to Mexico, Angola, Australia. He doesn't bring her a box of sweets, he promises scandalous days in their own private sweet shop. The repetition of the phrase "we will" projects the promises, the wishes, and the fantasies into the future. Anything and everything can happen. It's a small shift in language, but instead of describing the scene as singular and determined, he describes it as full of both promise, and promises.

Instead of describing the possibilities of the future, a writer might describe alternatives for the present moment. In a parallel universe, everything seems familiar, but the reality is different. The otherness is often surreal. Writers might integrate elements of magical realism or dream logic, or they might adapt forms like the fable to create texts where animals act like humans or people transform into creatures. In "A Modern Fable" by David Ignatow, for instance, a man and a wolf have a conversation about manners. In Shivani Mehta's "the invisible girl can be anything she wants when she doesn't want to be invisible," an invisible girl plays with the wind, a girl she calls Effie. These narratives often deny the reader stable footing. The narrative might hinge on a series of "and/or" options or lurch the narrative sideways instead of forward. In Bryan Fry's "Hill Street Blues," the speaker tries and fails to pinpoint his first memory: every time he thinks he has it, he decides he is wrong. The reader's sense of reality gets undermined. We have to look, and look again (Table 4.2).

The last narrative strategy that we'll look at is the **Möbius strip**, which creates an endless loop (Figure 4.4). Imagine our silk ribbon one more time. To make a Möbius strip, twist the ribbon 180 degrees, and glue the ends together to create one endless surface. If you imagine this loop effect in a narrative, it keeps the reader confined within a tight sequence. It creates a never-ending story. Look at Pía Barros's "A Story Possibly Heard in Some Bar at Three in the Morning," which begins, "he told me" and ends, "sometimes she goes to the bars, and before she takes off her clothes, she tells stories like this one." The title, the first line, and the closing line create a circuit of

Table 4.2 Strategies for pushing the realm of possibilities

Strategy	Effect	Example
Möbius strip	Evokes the feeling of a never-ending narrative, a fairytale sense of "the ever-after," or a continuous loop.	"Sometimes she goes to the bars, and before she takes off her clothes, she tells stories like this one." (From "A Story Possibly Heard in Some Bar at Three in the Morning" by Pía Barros)
Parallel universes	Evokes the feeling of multiple possibilities or futures. Or, it calls into question the truth of what happened in the past, and then undermines the accuracy of memories.	"No. This is not my first memory. I'm in the back seat of my parents' car. My father is driving my mother to work. We live in Seattle. It must be raining. Yes, I can see it now. It is raining. Small beads of water stick to the glass of the windows.... No. We are driving. I am sitting in the back seat. My mother is smoking. When she notices I am watching her, she blows out small rings that rise toward the windshield. We live in Seattle. It is definitely raining." (From "Hill Street Blues" by Bryan Fry)

Figure 4.4 Möbius strip. Courtesy of Savannah Adams.

storytelling that says this story is heard and will be heard forever because the girl lives on. The story tattooed on her body gets reinvented with each contortion; so too does the story she tells when she strips. A striptease relies on the *tease*: the dancer never completely undresses. Likewise, the story teases the reader by almost—but never quite—finishing.

Conclusion: Sneak in, slip out

Writers construct the reader's experience. There are many ways to move through a narrative and all of them are, to one degree or another, artificial. The story, whether based on truth or not, is an invention. You get to decide how you want to build it. Hopefully this gives you a great sense of freedom. Although the strategies in this chapter might create vastly different effects, they all have one thing in common: they are strategies you might employ as you tackle the challenge of smooshing a narrative down into a confined space.

For the record, you don't have to be a cosmologist to think about developing your own theories of time and space as you try to build your narrative. Your goal is pretty straightforward: How might you represent time so that it best serves your text? How do you want your reader to feel? Rushed, lost, disoriented, dazzled, hyperalert? Identify that sensation and look for ways to make the movement of the text (at the sentence level and at the narrative level) reinforce that sensation. Think about how it should feel to exist in the tiny universe of your narrative, and tinker with the language, the images, the grammar, the syntax, and the rhythm until you capture those sensations.

Exercises

The following activities will help you practice the concepts from this chapter:

A. When was the last time you sent a postcard to someone? Write one now. Imagine you are looking at your surroundings for the first time: take note of what is most surprising. Then address the postcard to yourself and describe what you see and feel in that moment. What is the weather like? Include the names of friends, places, vegetation, wildlife, and geographic features. What looms largest in your mind at this moment? Use the size of the postcard to help you distill your communication. Then mail it to yourself. How has your perspective on that moment changed in the time it takes the postcard to make its way back to you?

B. Find a rooftop near you that affords you a view of your surroundings. For example, Stephanie takes her class to the top of the Oregon State Capitol building. It could be the top level of a parking structure or the rooftop of a campus dormitory. The goal of this exercise is to elevate yourself and gain perspective on your surroundings. How do you see differently what is around you? Try this exercise at night to get a different perspective on distance and scale.

C. A Möbius strip is simply a strip of paper with a half twist in it. When the ends are taped together, you have an infinite loop. There is no beginning, no end, no inside, no outside. This exercise involves making a Möbius strip, so you'll need a pair of scissors, at least one blank sheet of paper, and some tape. Cut a strip of paper of any length or tape multiple strips together to create a longer strip. Label the front of the strip "side A." Flip the strip over, and label it "side B." Half of your Möbius strip story will be written on side A, and the other half with be written on side B. If you hold up side A, the text on side B should be upside down. When you have written your story, bring the two ends of your strip together to form a loop. Take one end of the strip and flip it over before taping it to make your never-ending story.

Prompts

The following writing prompts will help you practice the concepts from this chapter:

A. Identify a record of some moment in time that exists (or existed) even if you can't retrieve it. For instance, in a dusty box in an attic or garage somewhere there is a photograph, a birth certificate, a cassette tape, a super-8 film reel, or a diary. What does it say? The goal is to examine the complexity of the recorded moment. Excavate it like an artifact. What do you know about what happened after that moment was captured? How does it change what you see in the image? Concentrate on the details and immerse your reader in them by using the senses. What truths might be glimpsed in the artifact you are studying?

B. Begin a story with one of the following time–order transitions to suggest that something has just happened: after, before, later, during, meanwhile, next.

One-sentence workshop

The following exercise will help you practice the telescoping sentence:

Watch how this shortened version of the final sentence in Bruce Holland Rogers's "Dinosaur" telescopes outward. Use the guiding questions in Figure 4.5 to experiment with the telescopic technique on a short sentence from one of your drafts. If it helps you get started, experiment with the same core sentence, "He stood there."

Figure 4.5 One-sentence workshop. Courtesy of Savannah Adams.

5

The Microcosmic Sentence

Relevant readings

"All This" by Joanne Avallon
"Be Drunken" by Charles Baudelaire
"One Long Sentence" by Sven Birkerts
"Self-Portrait as a Chimera" by Natalie Diaz
"Dust" by Sarah Evans

"Memoir" by Amy Hempel
"The Letter from Home" by Jamaica Kincaid
"In Praise of Latin Night at the Queer Club" by Justin Torres

Flash interview with Justin Torres

Justin Torres is a writer and professor who lives in Los Angeles. We chose "In Praise of Latin Night at the Queer Club" because of the way it counters violence and hatred with lyrical, rhythmic language that celebrates survival. Here's what he has to say about writing short.

How do you define the kind of short-form writing that you do?
I'm sure I've never defined the kind of short form writing I do. This piece was an op-ed in response to a mass shooting targeting queer Latinos. I've written other short essays in response to the election of Trump, or on literature. I've written short fiction pieces—some more poetic, impressionistic, some more narrative.

How does your approach to writing in short forms differ from the other kinds of writing that you do?
My approach doesn't differ: get the words right, cast a spell.

What demands does the short form make of its writers or readers?
The short form isn't "demanding" of readers. In fact, the precise pleasure of the form is the ease with which the end is reached. The short form is inviting; read once quickly, read again more slowly, read again and again.

Free dive

For this ten-minute free dive, begin with a short, simple sentence that contains the kernel of an idea, a bright flash of image, or some ear-catching turn of phrase. Then slowly build it out, adding rooms to contain more information. Add the word "before" or "after" to the beginning of your sentence and build upon the main idea. What happens before? What happens later? What is happening at the same time somewhere else? Pack your sentence as if you were going on a long trip. Pull out all the stops: parenthetical statements, colons, semicolons, long dashes. Do your best to maintain the grammatical soundness of your structure. Keep rewriting and stretching the sentence out as far as you can take it. Notice where and when the sentence begins to feel unwieldy. As the simple sentence evolves into something else, what happens to the original idea or image? Does the progression suggest a story? Does an image intensify or does repetition become haunting? Read the sentence out loud, and notice its physical effect on breath, pacing, and rhythm. In what situations can you see using a sentence of this length?

Vignette: Beginning and ending with a dot

During a month-long writing residency in an art gallery, I sat in my studio and tried to write as the artist Jon Colburn set up his retrospective entitled "Show of Shows" just outside my door. His artwork features paintings of galleries, drive-in theatres, and movie screens, from which he takes the title of his exhibit. I was impressed by how meticulous he was, returning day after day to make sure the paintings were hung perfectly, taking pictures, mumbling to himself, studying each brushstroke and still finding changes he wanted to make at the last minute.

Many of his works of art show paintings hanging in a gallery, and there was one in particular that I could see through the doorway of my studio. Standing in a gallery looking at a painting of a gallery of paintings made me feel like I was in a hall of mirrors. I enjoyed how Jon's art invited viewers to become a part of the never-ending experience of art. The artist's fussing with his paintings before the opening of the exhibit reminded me of the way writers continuously tinker and Paul Valéry's statement that "a poem is never finished, only abandoned." In the world of art, there's a similar saying: "A painting is never done until it gets a red dot," which means that it's been sold.

Our beginnings and endings are like two mirrors facing each other, and this is what I wanted to explore. I decided to write something in honor of Jon's reception and frame it in a single sentence to replicate both the constraints and freedom of creating art. Here it is.

The Red Dot

Before the exhibit's breathless opening, before the wine's measured pour into plastic cups, before the loud praise and fervently tilted heads, the artist shuffles among unambiguous white walls on which hang his life's work, adjusting lights, straightening placards, deciding at the last moment to change the one called "Heliotrope" back to "Drawn to Flame," each canvas a doorway leading to another room and another, as he reaches out to scrape away a clump of paint, imagining the bright cups held aloft like torches before his paintings, this show of shows of shows of shows where the work is never done, no, not until the long sentence of art and its making is punctuated at last with a small red dot.

–Stephanie
Word count: 394

What is a sentence?

A man robs a bank and is caught red-handed. The authorities arrest him and hold him until his court date. If convicted by a jury, he will receive a sentence from a judge, usually expressed in months, years, or lifetimes, depending on the severity of the offense. While this is the typical order of events in the American justice system, far too many new writers apply this legal definition of a sentence to their writing. Without much cross-examination, they have accepted that a sentence is synonymous with judgement; it is a structure that restricts and punishes wrongdoers.

But the structure of a sentence need not be confining! In this chapter, we will explore how sentences work in short-form writing, how they organize the reader's understanding, and how they can expand and contract to elicit surprise. To get the most out of our sentences, we have to be willing to linger over them. New writers often rush in and out of a sentence like they're robbing a bank. For these writers, every word forward brings the threat of the red pen, so either the writer barrels ahead without looking back or proceeds with trepidation, falling short. We want you, instead of making for a quick getaway, to slow down. Notice what sentences are doing. Notice how they move. What are they saying and what are they withholding? What purposes do they serve, in your own writing and in the writing of others? As Sammy Davis, Jr. sang in the television theme song for a 1970s detective series: "Don't do the crime if you can't do the time." In other words, if you want to write, you must be willing to take your time with the sentence.

The sentence is both grammatical structure and rhetorical design. It is form and content embodied. As a grammatical structure, the sentence is either correct or incorrect. It can be simple, compound, complex, or compound-complex. You can, if you know your grammatical terms and parts of speech, label each word in a sentence. Rules and conventions guide sentence construction. But as a rhetorical design, the sentence aims to *do something*. It asks a question, makes a statement, and links ideas to reveal their relationship. It persuades or proves or contradicts itself all in the interest of propelling the reader forward from one sentence to the next. Grammar tells us how a sentence is built, but **rhetoric** (the art of effective writing) reveals how the sentence moves and how it moves those who read it or hear it.

In the simplest terms, a **sentence** must have a subject and a predicate, which includes a verb and any other words in the sentence. See? There's nothing to be afraid of! A sentence organizes words into sequences of events, cause and effect, or expressions of desire. Not surprisingly these are the elements needed to craft an interesting narrative. The verb tense of a sentence tells the reader if the action is happening now, happened before, or will happen later. A sentence can be a story, a memory, or a wish. That's what sentences really are: a way to "do" time, to show the passage of time through action or thought.

The English language is full of inconsistencies, and here's one of them: grammatically correct sentences do not inevitably lead to well-written prose, but well-written prose more often than not is composed of grammatically correct sentences. Even so, you can find plenty of perfectly correct, efficient, but lackluster sentences in manuals, memos, and other functional documents. The question is not how to write a correct sentence but how to write an eloquent one.

The job of an eloquent sentence in short-form writing involves multitasking. It cannot simply be a conveyor belt of information. An eloquent sentence consists of meaning and music created through a combination of word choice, syntax, and the point of view it takes toward its subject matter. And it's safe to say that this is true for any kind of writing with literary aspirations.

As we talk about sentence-making here, we won't overload you too much with grammatical terminology. We believe it's less important for writers to name the parts of speech or identify mechanical errors by their proper names and more important to listen to the sounds, patterns, rhythms, and pacing of sentences.

If you want to brush up on grammatical terms, the following books offer clear and entertaining explanations as well as level-headed corrections of the myths and misguided instructions that plague students of English: Patricia T. O'Conner's *Woe Is I: The Grammarphobe's Guide to Better English in Plain English*; Lynne Truss's *Eats, Shoots & Leaves: The Zero Tolerance Approach to Punctuation*; and Constance Hale's *Sin and Syntax: How to Craft Wickedly*

Effective Prose. We also enjoy podcasts by Grammar Girl and the website for Purdue's Online Writing Lab (OWL), a comprehensive resource on grammar, mechanics, and much more.

All about relationships

If we take our elementary school teachers at their word, a sentence is a complete thought beginning with a capital letter and ending with a punctuation mark. But this definition throws too wide a net. A sentence is a microcosm, enacting in miniature the various functions of the English language: questioning, commanding, declaring, and exclaiming. A sentence is, as Stanley Fish writes in his book *How to Write a Sentence and How to Read One*, "a structure of logical relationships." Simple or complex, complete or fragmentary, active or passive: whatever their length or form, sentences place us in time and space, offer us sequence and logic, show relationships, or otherwise actively and intentionally defy these expectations in order to produce surprise. Recognizing the eloquence of sentences is the first step in being able to reproduce those graceful moves in your own writing.

An example of a writer who wants you to pay attention to the sentence as a narrative unit is Sven Birkerts. His "One Long Sentence" is a single sentence totaling 1,314 words. It's one of the longest in our anthology, chosen for its use of sentence structure as a metaphor to tell a story about a journey. The story embraces all the elements that a good sentence should consider: pace, space, time, memory, relationship, and comparison. Birkerts builds his story-sentence consciously, even self-consciously. The sentence structure doesn't just hold information, it enacts the story as it mirrors the experience of air travel. Birkerts displays his authorial intentions as clearly as if he's going through airport security, unloading his pockets, taking off his shoes. He explains that "what I'm talking about is travel, going to the airport so as to get from one city to another, the directionality of that process almost grammatical, starting with what I'll call the beginning of the sentence, my arriving through the big automatic doors as through the wide mouth of a funnel." This long sentence carries us incrementally through each tedious checkpoint in the traveler's day, and it is exhausting. The sentence, like airplane travel, is something we must endure to get where we want to go.

Another writer who uses the sentence to its fullest potential is Joanne Avallon in "All This." Her one-sentence story collapses the distant past and not-too-distant past into a single moment to illustrate the way memory moves. Rather than taking us on a journey as Birkerts does, Avallon drills down and exposes the layers of history that are part of the character's present experience. The story begins with the main clause ("your arm and hand cock back instinctively") followed by two subordinating clauses that give us insight into the character's past ("although they have never moved like this before") and an explanation of what has incited the action ("because your firstborn has taken a piece of your thigh between her two-year-old, sharp and white incisors"). The character's instinctive reaction to physical pain shows us the legacy of violence that coexists even within loving relationships, and Avallon accomplishes "all this" by linking present actions with distant memory grammatically in a single, complex sentence.

In both examples, the sentence is the engine that propels the story forward. As John Gardner explains in *The Art of Fiction*, "the writer's most basic unit of expression is the sentence, the primary vehicle of all rhetorical devices." A sentence tells us if we are dealing with reality or potentiality. A sentence gives us the point of view, the mood, the tense. A sentence allows the reader to temporarily embrace an idea. In short-form writing, a single sentence can be even more powerful because there are, ultimately, so few of them.

What is structure?

There are eight **parts of speech** (nouns, pronouns, adjectives, verbs, adverbs, conjunctions, prepositions, and interjections) and four fundamental designs for sentences: simple, compound, complex, and compound-complex. These basic designs can be used as blueprints for different sentence styles. Think of these sentences as houses, each with the ability to be expanded and modified to suit the needs of its inhabitants. These structures in isolation do not accomplish much on their own. But arranged together, in various combinations and patterns, they can produce a wide range of effects, little neighborhoods of style and substance. For short-form writers who need to make good use of every nook and cranny they can find in a sentence, it can be helpful to review these basic structures.

A blueprint for thought

A **simple sentence** contains the essential elements that make it a sentence, an independent clause formed by a single subject and a single verb. Together, this structure provides a modest dwelling for a complete thought. Here are some examples from your anthology, with the subject <u>underlined</u> and the verb in *italics*:

"<u>We</u> *are* bereft." —from "A Thousand Perfect Strangers" by Kathy Fish

"My first <u>memory</u> *fails* me." —from "Hill Street Blues" by Bryan Fry

"The <u>cannibals</u> *dance* around the explorers." —from "Cannibals and Explorers" by Ana María Shua

"*Can* <u>we</u> *get* a cat."—from "The Cat" by Matthew Clarke and Coco Harrison-Clarke

All three examples are first sentences. Notice the way they focus the sentence on feeling, memory, action, or desire, respectively. The final example from "The Cat" is a question expressed as a statement, which will make sense to anyone familiar with demanding toddlers.

Simple sentences need not be simplistic. They can accomplish a lot in a few words. They can be dramatic, blunt, tense, definitive. Shua's sentence, for example, immediately thrusts us into the center of the conflict. The others leave room for questions, for subtext and implication: Who are "we"? Why are we bereft? What has led to the failure of memory?

Molly Giles offers a paradoxically simple sentence in her opening from "Bob and Betty," part of the "Dumped" series: "It was a good divorce." In addition to being a strange statement, the sentence itself is a bit odd. Sentences that begin with variations of "it is" and "there is" are called **expletives**. In Giles's sentence, you might be tempted to assume "it" is the subject of the sentence because "it" is in the place you'd normally look for a subject. But "it" is actually a dummy subject, a placeholder for the actual subject, "divorce." We could reorder the sentence so that it reads, "The divorce was good," putting the subject up front as expected. But we also lose something in the rearrangement, that subtle hint of strangeness that foreshadows what's to come.

Teachers will advise you to avoid expletives (grammatically speaking and otherwise). They take up space without adding content. But in Giles's sentence, the strange syntax sets the tone for her short, one hundred-word story. The displacement of the subject and the strange pairing of "good" with "divorce" anticipates the extreme displacement that comes at the end of the story.

A **compound sentence** has at least two independent clauses with a comma and a word that connects them (coordinating conjunction). You can use the acronym FANBOYS to remember the most common coordinating conjunctions: for, and, nor, but, or, yet, so. Because each part of a compound sentence is an independent clause and could stand alone as a sentence, each side is considered equally important. The structure is like a duplex, two independent units that share a wall, as seen in these examples from your anthology with the coordinating conjunction <u>underlined</u>:

> "It kills mold, <u>but</u> removal of the stain associated with mold and mildew can sometimes be tough." –from "An All-Purpose Product" by Patricia Smith
>
> "Progress doesn't exist in that sense, <u>and</u> we live in a space infected by a surplus of history." –from "Surplus History" by Semezdin Mehmedinović
>
> "There is blood on its face, <u>and</u> its eyes move a little in their sockets." –from "The Girl Who Likes Dogs" by Calvin Mills

Perhaps you noticed as you read the examples above that the structure of a compound sentence is a little more formal. It feels a little more deliberately objective and maybe even distant. While simple sentences abound in the work included in the anthology, true compound sentences are a little harder to find. They are more likely to play a supporting role than take the lead. Too many compound sentences in a row will steal the energy from your writing because the "and … and … and …" structure extends but doesn't develop or deepen the relationship between ideas. When you do encounter compound sentences in a literary work, be aware that the structure is a distinct choice, a refusal to isolate or subordinate ideas.

The final example by Mills also gives us another look at the expletive in action. "There is blood on its face" has a different feel from "Blood is on its face" or even "Its face is covered in blood." The dummy subject holds us at arm's length, creating distance between the reader and the subject, just as Mills's speaker distances himself from the dying dog.

A **complex sentence** is created by linking an independent clause to one or more dependent clauses using a subordinating conjunction. These clauses "depend" on the main parts of the sentence for their meaning. A compound-complex sentence, as the name suggests, is a sentence with two or more independent clauses and one or more dependent clauses. You will see these two sentence structures more often than the other sentence types simply because they offer the greatest opportunity for variation. There are many more subordinating conjunctions than there are coordinating conjunctions, which exponentially increases the number of connections that can be made between ideas. No handy-dandy acronyms exist to help you memorize them, so don't even try. But you should familiarize yourself with these words so that you can recognize them

Table 5.1 Function of subordinating conjunctions

Function	Subordinating conjunction
Causality	because, whereas
Comparison	as if, just as, even if
Contrast	although, even, rather than, though, whereas
Degree	as long as, as much as
Possibility	if, supposing, unless, whether
Simultaneity	as, while
Time	after, as soon as, before, now, once, since, when, until

as you write and read (Table 5.1). In the short form, subordinating conjunctions can quickly introduce tension, sequence, order, or causality, which can be a good way to get the action started. You can think of these words as hot spots, positioning words that give added dimension to a story.

Complex and compound-complex sentences are like more spacious dwellings that include a main floor (independent clause) as well as additional levels in the form of one or more dependent clauses. Most of the action takes place on the main level of this home, but the basement and second floor provide additional living space. Here are some examples from your anthology with the subordinating word underlined and the entire dependent clause in *italics*:

"*When he awoke*, the dinosaur was still there."—from "The Dinosaur" by Augusto Monterroso

"*If you're lucky*, they'll play some Latin cheese, that Aventura song from 15 years ago."—from "In Praise of Latin Night at the Queer Club" by Justin Torres

"I am writing to you to object to the word cremains, *which was used by your representative when he met with my mother and me two days after my father's death.*" —from "Letter to a Funeral Parlor" by Lydia Davis

As you can see, the dependent clause can come at the beginning or the end of a sentence. In Monterroso's single-sentence story, the story hinges on the collision of worlds and clauses (man and dinosaur, then and now, sleep and awake), and the structure makes this impact felt as the human becomes subordinated literally and grammatically to the dinosaur. In the sentences by

Torres and Davis, the authors tuck their most compelling ideas or motivations into their dependent clauses, as if these parts were whispered under their breath. "Dependent" and "subordinating" can be misleading terms if you assume that one part of a sentence is less important than another. Instead, consider the dependent clause and independent clause as two notes struck at the same time to create a harmony that gives depth and context to a song.

While it's important to know how different kinds of sentences affect a reader, it's also important to notice how these sentences work together to create voice, rhythm, pace, and tone. Style in writing is communicated through choices, not habits. If you find yourself relying on a certain type of sentence simply because it's easier, challenge yourself to write in a different way. When reviewing drafts, spend time looking at your sentences to see if you can see any habits of mind that may lessen the effect of your writing. One trick that can help you identify habits of sentence construction is to type your story, one sentence per line, into a spreadsheet program. Using the sort function to alphabetize your sentences, you can see if your sentences start in similar ways. At a glance, you will also be able to see how the length of your sentences compare to each other. Variety and intentional repetition is key to dynamic prose.

What is syntax?

The order of words in a sentence is called **syntax**. In English, the pattern of words in a sentence most often falls into a sequence of subject, verb, and object, as in the following example:

> The child ate the cookie.
> |----S----|----V----|----O----|

English is mainly considered a syntactic language. This means that our understanding of an idea arises from the placement of words in relation to each other. Consider how the placement of the word "only" affects the meaning of the original sentence:

> Only the child ate the cookie.
> The only child ate the cookie.
> The child only ate the cookie.
> The child ate only the cookie.
> The child ate the only cookie.
> The child ate the cookie only.

Likewise, consider how the meaning and part of speech of the word "milk" changes depending on its placement and relationship to the words around it.

I ate the cookie with <u>milk</u>.
The <u>milk</u> spilled on the counter.
The cat drank from its <u>milk</u> dish.
I will <u>milk</u> this example for all it's worth.

Syntax allows for endless variations of the same idea, so it is up to the short-form writer to do as the poet Samuel Taylor Coleridge says and put "the best words in the best order." For Coleridge, this was his formula for poetry. But we believe the best sentences require the attention and refinement of poetry.

A marriage of music and meaning

Linguists, computer programmers, and logicians all use the term syntax to describe systems of information. But to think solely of syntax's orderliness neglects the artful intention required of the writer. Sometimes we place words next to other words not only to signal an idea but also to create sound effects. For example, listen to the sound of this excerpt from Birkerts's "One Long Sentence": "we all begin inching down the aisle of the plane, with everyone's (certainly my) cold-blooded calculations about getting my bag into a free bin space (should one still exist), and then the bodily origami exertions of folding the oversized body into the undersized seat." Read this example out loud so that it's easier to hear the rhythms and repetitions.

Even the most ordinary English sentence will have rhythm and a certain amount of repetition. But sometimes you'll hear sentences densely populated with particular sounds or patterns. This is not an accident. The phrase "bodily origami" folds in on itself with multiple repeated sounds in the tight space of just two words. There is the parallelism of phrasing in "oversized body" and "undersized seat" that further emphasizes the inadequacies of plane travel. You can certainly hear the alliteration in "cold-blooded calculations," the repetition of initial /c/ sounds, which make this unique pairing of adjective and noun stand out even more. Finally, there is the obsessive repetition of the /b/ sound and "in," making the traveler's focus on the coveted "bin space" felt and heard even more.

How do you make these sounds effects happen in your own work? Some writers have an intuitive sense of what "sounds good." Others have an aesthetic preference for using certain words in a certain order. Still others may not notice the rhythms and patterns in their own work until someone points them out and they revise with the intent of amplifying those effects. In short-form writing, sounds and syntax are two ways of making your sentences feel unified. Through careful choice, the togetherness of words can create a marriage of meaning and music.

Word choice and syntax can produce surprise by disrupting the progress of a sentence, by reversing the expectations that the sentence has established, or breaking with convention by changing the expected order of words. Your job as a writer is to keep the reader awake. Every time we allow readers to coast, by giving them what they expect, by using familiar phrases (clichés) or images that have been used before, by falling into habits of speech that don't require thoughtful choices, we reduce the opportunity for surprise. These choices, too, are the choices that contribute to one's style in writing.

What is style?

When we talk about **style** in writing, we mean the elements and characteristics of effective prose. To understand this abstraction a little better, we break it down here for you into a few parts to examine.

Unity

Aristotle defined dramatic structure in his *Poetics* as a whole story with a beginning, middle, and end. Though much has changed since sixth century BCE, much has remained the same, particularly when it comes to an audience's narrative cravings. It can be helpful to think of a sentence like a miniature narrative with a beginning, middle, and end. For example, look at the self-contained structure in "Memoir" by Amy Hempel. This seventeen-word memoir distills the speaker's life story into a single sentence. In spite of its brevity, there's a beginning with an expressed desire ("Just once in my life") that leads to a moment of realization ("—oh,") before turning to question everything that comes before. The result is a loaded story of longing that feels like a tightly coiled spring just about to be released.

Variety

Sentences come in four distinct flavors: interrogative (questions), declarative (statements), exclamatory (exclamations), and imperative (commands or instructions). Hempel's "Memoir" is unique in that the sentence shifts abruptly from declarative, "Just once in my life," to the exclamatory "oh" to interrogative with "my life?" Reading again, you may also hear the implied imperative in the middle of the sentence: "[tell me] when have I ever wanted anything just once." Hempel, in a single sentence, catapults the reader through all the sentence varieties. She leaves us hanging with the final question mark that feels more statement than question.

The title is "Memoir," a genre label that describes true stories from someone's life, yet the author herself categorizes the work as flash fiction. The sentence shifts, the genre shifts, the expressed desires of the speaker shift—all in just seventeen words. And this story feels true, a life sentence that begins in the same way it ends. Not only does the speaker realize that she wants more, but the writer uses repetition masterfully to reveal this central irony.

Pattern

Repetition and variation on a theme is one of literature's great pleasures. We create patterns in our sentences through the intentional repetition of words or phrases. You can hear the pleasing, wistful repetition of /w/ sounds in Hempel's story: once, when, wanted, once. This kind of repetition makes it sound and feel like the words in this sentence belong together. Experimenting with sound patterns can be a fun way to liven up the interior of sentences as well as create a greater sense of unity among a group of sentences. Gary Lutz, author of "The Sentence Is a Lonely Place," calls this "intra-sentence intimacy" when the words of one sentence seem to suggest or shape the language that follows.

In Justin Torres's "In Praise of Latin Night at the Queer Club," the first paragraph contains four "if" statements: "if you're lucky ... if you're lucky ... if so ... if you're lucky." Notice the way he repeats the phrase, varies it, then closes with a final exact repetition. Torres does this again in the second paragraph with "maybe" and in the third paragraph with "outside." The fourth paragraph extends the repetition to the extreme: "you have known violence, you have known violence, you have known violence, you have known, you learned, you have learned" before returning to the previous paragraph's refrain of "outside." The entire scene feels stitched together with this forceful repetition that could suggest the driving beat on the dance floor as well as the reverential litany of praise for a place where the dancers "find religion [and] lose it." This intentional repetition prepares us for the "sacredness of Latin Night at the Queer Club" that the author celebrates in spite of the tragedy that brings it into the media's spotlight.

Making short sentences

Just because a sentence is simple in its construction doesn't mean it needs to be simple in its message. Simple sentences can be found in some of the most revered and classic texts. A biblical example is "Jesus wept." Here we have the essential information to make a complete thought: a subject and an action. Often simple sentences stand out because of what immediately precedes or follows them. Short sentences are an opportunity to break the flow of a text in order to produce surprise. Virginia Tufte, author of *Grammar as Style*, explains that "the better the writer ... the more he tends to vary his sentence length. And he does it as dramatically as possible." Sentence unity, variety, and pattern all contribute to the unique rhythm that can give the short form a sense of inevitability and continuity.

Short sentences, by their nature, abide by the classic advice in Strunk and White's *The Elements of Style* that writers should "Omit needless words." For short-form writers, short sentences are a good place to practice brevity and experiment with how much you really need to communicate an idea. Short sentences have a personality. They can be emphatic, direct, commanding, abrupt, terse. In this example from "Hill Street Blues" by Bryan Fry, we receive tidbits of information as the speaker tries to recall his first memory: "We live in Seattle. It must be raining. Yes, I can see it now. It is raining." The short sentences not only capture the voice of the child, but they reveal the narrator's struggle to put together the details of his early life.

Shorter sentences, collectively, take up more space because they end up restating information that a longer sentence can assume. This phenomenon can be seen in Jamaica Kincaid's "The Letter from Home." Her piece consists of a series of short phrases ("I milked the cows, I churned the butter ... "). Though these phrases are separated by commas as in a list, they articulate a complete action before moving on to the next item. At times these phrases appear to be part of a sequence of actions ("I washed the clothes, I dressed the children"), but more often than not the domestic tasks are isolated. The atmospheric reports stand alone. The structure of the sentences makes it feel like a lot is happening, yet the sentence produces no movement, no progress. Time passes, but the actions described seem out of ordinary time ("the clock slowed down"). Shorter sentences like the ones in this story can result in a dramatic, slow-motion effect in much the same way that cinematography slows down action by adding a series of still images to a film sequence.

Making long sentences

Your impulse in short-form writing might be to use short sentences, but many short works use longer sentences to pack in as much information as possible. Brooks Landon, author of *Building Great Sentences*, advocates for longer sentences because "a sentence containing more useful information, more specific detail, and more explanation will *almost* always be better than a shorter sentence that lacks that information, detail, and explanation." Longer sentences are not automatically more eloquent or literary than shorter sentences. If a reader cannot follow a sentence to its final punctuation mark without getting lost or tangled in the syntax, then it doesn't matter how long or short it is; it simply doesn't work. As Constance Hale explains in her book *Sin and Syntax*, "we're surrounded by chatter, clatter, clutter, and cloudiness," and longer sentences can contribute to this noise if a writer is not careful. The key is to know what sentence structure suits your purpose and to make sure each moving part within the sentence contributes to the idea the sentence is conveying.

Consider the tension created by long sentences in an extremely short prose piece. It's like watching someone pour a long stream of water into a small cup up to its brim. Will it all fit? How much can it hold? You can definitely feel this tension in the stories by Avallon and Birkerts as well as the one hundred-word story "Dana and David" by Molly Giles, all single sentences. Kincaid's story, if read aloud, does not sound like a single sentence, but the author intentionally links every independent clause in the story through punctuation in order to make an exhaustive, list-like sentence. In these examples, the structure of the sentence serves the work's theme.

If long sentences are challenging, here are a few strategies to increase the variety of your sentence lengths. Rather than loading up your sentences with adjectives and adverbs, consider expanding your sentences by making your sentence structure more complex. These examples—all from Sarah Evans's "Dust"—will show you how one author uses multiple strategies to add complexity to the sentence.

1. Combine sentences using *coordinating* and/or <u>subordinating</u> conjunctions.

    a. "My toddler son asks, "What is it?" *and* I answer, "Dust," *and* I watch <u>as</u> he watches."

  2. Use a pattern and <u>parallelism</u> to extend the sentence.

    a. "Who knew this sign <u>of decay, of finality, of that to which we return</u>, could also be <u>so beautiful, so graceful, so lively</u> ... "

  3. Add <u>figurative language</u> to further illustrate what the sentence says.

    a. "... he watches each speck twirl, <u>like fireflies skimming the nighttime air, like plankton riding the currents in the deep</u>."

Long sentences are one of the many joys of written English. A long sentence invites this kind of re-reading, but it must offer the reader some kind of reward for the extra effort. It's important to find the right structure to hold your idea. Craft the container, test it, then come back to it again to make it stronger and more beautiful so that it will last.

Making fragments

In school, we're taught to avoid fragment sentences for good reason. Fragment sentences lack essential information—either the subject or verb—that allows the sentence to express a complete idea. Complete sentences tend to be clearer, which is why they're favored in academic writing. But does every sentence need to express a complete thought? No. See how that works? Fragment sentences can be used for emphasis and can be a strategic way to break up longer sentences. The use of fragments signals to the reader a less formal style of writing and reflects conversational patterns. Emails. Phone calls. A rapid exchange between two characters who know each other well. These are just some instances where fragment sentences might contribute to the tone and style of a piece of creative writing.

    Fragments do not make ideas more poetic just as complete grammatical sentences do not automatically make ideas logical or orderly. Fragments used as a rhetorical device can create mystery, be used for emphasis, isolate images or phrases, signal an abrupt shift, or replicate speech. But fragments—as a default mode of composition or a substitute for a complete thought—can just as often mislead, confuse, or obscure. Ultimately, we want to make a distinction between grammatical fragments that result from unconscious missteps and stylistic fragments that result from conscious choices. Paying attention to the choices that writers make while composing is the first step to loving the sentence.

The key is to use fragments in moderation, like any other literary technique, to accomplish a specific effect. You can see fragments at work in "Some Things about That Day" by Debra Marquart: "The placards I walked through. Wet raincoat on a hook. Questionnaire on a clipboard placed before me." The opening sentence is an ambiguous fragment. Written differently, it could be complete: "I walked through the placards." But the particular syntax intentionally displaces the human actors (the protestors holding the placards) to create an even more disorienting experience. What follows is two more fragments that further emphasize the main character's isolation. We see a person walking alone through a paper gauntlet. We see a raincoat on a hook. We see a clipboard magically appear, though we know a nurse brings it to her. We have a sense of a particular person in a particular place, but the entire scene is marked by something missing. The fragments make us feel this absence on multiple levels.

Conclusion: Make the sentence your own

Paying attention to sentences requires an intense form of close reading. It's simply not possible to read or write like this all the time. But it's important to apply this analytical lens to your own drafts and the writing of others to sharpen your skills. To grow as writers, we need to complicate our ideas of what a sentence is and what it can accomplish. A sentence can be a music box that sings a song when opened. It can be a surgical tool, precise and clinical. A sentence can be a fence that keeps the cows from wandering off. It can lull us with repetition, surprise us with syntactic sleights-of-hand, or pull the rug out from beneath us. Begin collecting sentences that you love, not for what they say but for how they say it.

In his book *On Writing*, Stephen King states that "fear is at the root of most bad writing." This fear, we believe, is what leads writers to commit one of two main crimes of sentence construction: the run-on sentence or the fragment. If you play it safe and only write the sentences you know you can control, you'll limit your potential for discovery and surprise. Short-form writing provides a great platform for experimenting with sentences—long, short, and in between.

Exercises

A. Gertrude Stein once asked, "Why should a sequence of words be anything but a pleasure?" Take this question and rearrange the words within it. Translate the question into a direct statement, an exclamation, or an imperative. How many different ways can you play with the sequence of words in this sentence? What changes when different kinds of words are used to communicate the same idea? Talk with your classmates about the interrelatedness of style and content as it pertains to syntax and sentence construction.

B. Every year, an online contest is held to parody the opening sentence from the Edward George Bulwer-Lytton's Victorian novel *Paul Clifford*: "It was a dark and stormy night; the rain fell in torrents— except at occasional intervals, when it was checked by a violent gust of wind which swept up the streets (for it is in London that our scene lies), rattling along the housetops, and fiercely agitating the scanty flame of the lamps that struggled against the darkness." The contest does not require lengthy sentences, but it highly recommends that entries be over fifty or sixty words. Use the example above to examine when and how lengthy sentences cross over into wordiness. And try your hand at a sentence that rivals this one in length.

C. Starting with a core sentence ("the flowers wilted," "he wanted more," "they sang louder," "it was finished"), compete with your classmates to create the longest sentence on a strip of paper by adding modifying phrases to the sentence. Stephanie uses adding machine tape for this in-class exercise. Once you've completed your sentence, discuss with your classmates how you went about expanding the sentence and what methods you used to hold it together. Vote on the sentence that accomplishes the most, regardless of the number of words.

Prompts

A. Using Joanne Avallon's one-sentence story "All This" as your model, write a complete story in one grammatically correct sentence. Your story must include believable dialogue, illuminating gestures, authenticating details, and dramatic tension. By the final punctuation mark, someone or something must be irrevocably changed. Your goal should be to use different rhetorical methods for expansion, such as parallelism, listing, and modifying phrases, to explore the potentials of syntax.

B. Charles Baudelaire's "Be Drunken" serves as a manifesto for the short-form writer. Begin with an authoritative and instructional voice and fill in the blank, "Be _____." What advice do you have to offer those not wanting to be the "martyred slaves of time"? Examine Baudelaire's strategies for making longer sentences, especially those that come into play at the end.

C. Sven Birkerts's "One Long Sentence" imagines the writing of a sentence as a long and tedious airplane flight. Come up with an extended metaphor that compares some small, ordinary action you perform in your daily life (for example, doing homework) to an epic physical endeavor that requires endurance, perspective, and movement (for example, climbing Mount Kilimanjaro).

One-sentence workshop

The following exercise will help you practice the art of brevity:

Gene Miller, a Pulitzer-prize winning journalist, worked long but wrote short. He perfected a technique of sentence variation that became known as the "Miller Chop." Simply put, it is a short sentence that follows a couple of longer sentences that results in a kind of verbal punctuation. Try it yourself.

6

How to Leap: Ah-ha Moments and Associative Logic

Relevant readings

"Rules of Combat" by Katie Cortese
"Hill Street Blues" by Bryan Fry
"A Modern Fable" by David Ignatow
"Some Things about That Day" by Debra Marquart
"Short Lecture on Your Own Happiness" by Mary Ruefle

Flash interview with Bryan Fry

Bryan Fry is a writer who lives in Pullman, Washington. We chose "Hill Street Blues" for the anthology because it captures the emotional intensity of memory while simultaneously shattering the illusion of memory with the anxiety of misremembering. Here's what he has to say about writing short.

How do you define the kind of short-form writing that you do?

My short-form writing is compressed, which means it doesn't have room for digression or contemplation. It is focused—I would say strategically focused—and it depends on repeating sounds and rhythms and images to convey a large experience in a very small space.

How does your approach to writing in short forms differ from the other kinds of writing that you do?

In a longer essay, I have time for backstory, for contemplation, for dialogue and characterization. I can stretch out. I can use my more elaborative, expository muscle. In the short form, I can't breathe. Everything gets stripped down and I am forced to extract as much as I can from one moment, one place.

What demands does the short form make of its writers or readers?

Unlike a novel where you have time to dig into the plot and get to know the major characters, the short form requires you to get interested right away. It's more of a blind date than a long romantic relationship. And yet this is not quite right because you can establish a very strong connection to a shorter piece. You just have to be willing to go back and reread the work. When you find a short you like, you have time to read it again and again. Eventually you understand the structure and the way the sentences work. You memorize key passages or phrases. It can be very intimate. You can fall in love.

How do you use association or narrative leaps when you are crafting a flash essay?

I am a big believer that my first sentence informs the entire essay, and I have to reread what I have written before I can move on. When I write the first sentence, it informs the second sentence. When I finish the first paragraph, it informs my second paragraph. In other words, I am always borrowing from what I've already written. And in that borrowing of material, my images get bigger and start to have more resonating power. I can go anywhere I want, but there has to be an echo.

Free dive

Let's practice using association to follow the meandering path of one idea as it leads to another. Choose any topic you want, and take five or ten minutes to write down in list form everything you associate with the topic. Keep going until you have a catalog of the sensory details you connect to your subject: music, food, weather, physical sensations, clothes, sights, smells, and anything else that you can think of. Once you've done this, test out Bryan Fry's idea of writing a sentence that builds upon the sentence that comes before it. Write an ultra-specific image; for instance, floating on an inflatable tube in some lazy stream with a chest full of ice-cold drinks bobbing along on a rope behind you. Then let that sentence accumulate sensory details, rhythm, and energy until it spills over into a new sentence. Track your route, no matter how wildly unpredictable or random it seems to be. Where do you end up? How did you get there?

Vignette: West Coast girl goes South

When I first moved to the South, everything felt hyperreal: on my evening walks, twinkling fireflies and the musty, damp scent uncannily reminded me of the Pirates of the Caribbean ride at Disneyland. I shrieked at the huge shadow of what I later learned was a sphinx moth. Was it a bat? A bird? I didn't know. All I knew was that it was too damn big. Standing on the banks of the Cumberland, I made out an alligator-like snout and shadowy body in the shallows, and I couldn't make sense of what I was looking at. I had no concept of "longnose gar," a weird looking, but common freshwater fish. The weather was unpredictable, the entrees in the neighborhood market's hot lunch counter unrecognizable, the heavily accented questions that came in on the office telephone line untranslatable. For months, I existed in a perplexing state of unfamiliarity. To survive, I studied. I learned to make red-eye gravy, tomato gravy, cake gravy. I identified lady peas, black-eyed peas, purple-hull peas. I identified house centipedes, helmeted squash bugs, thirteen-year cicadas. I translated Southern niceties and navigated the roundabouts from questions to answers. I learned to like chow-chow relish and fried green tomatoes. I learned to wait for the pleasing shock of okra blossoms in the summer garden. I learned everything I could. But, even now when the summer rains clear in the steamy evening, and the fireflies flicker in the yard, I still get the odd feeling that I'm in a simulated bayou, about to tip over the falls into pirate cannon fire. It's almost, but still not quite real.

—Heather
Word count: 269

And, suddenly, I knew ...

How do you come to understand something? You can learn to drive a stick shift, make sriracha chicken wings, or dance the jitterbug: it's a matter of memorizing and executing a series of steps. But understanding something often seems mysteriously instinctual. You understand something with the cells of your body first. In that *ah-ha* moment, the light turns on. You become enlightened. See? There's the flash-bang lightning strike of flash writing again. The two are intimately connected. You practice a new skill step by step. After a lot of awkward, sweaty practice, you finally *get* it. Practice turns into instinct.

Harvard psychologist David Perkins, a researcher who studies creativity, argues that although inspiration may feel like it appears out of nowhere, creative work results from a series of logical problem-solving strategies or attempts. In other words, when you labor at solving a (creative) puzzle, you eventually find a (creative) solution. This is good news for writers: writing requires steady, deliberate, strategic practice, not fickle muses. This doesn't just apply to inspiration. It also applies to manufacturing a specific reader response. Writers who pay attention to the ways people make sense of things can be tactically savvy about how they arrange the information to create *ah-ha* moments for their readers.

When image, scene, and perception unify to create an *ah-ha* moment, the reader experiences a physical response. This sudden immersion in a place and moment was described by French Postimpressionist painter Paul Cézanne as the *petite sensation*, or small feeling. If you were standing in a museum in front of a Cézanne, perhaps one of his landscapes of the French countryside, you would be able to lean in and see the repetitive small brushstrokes that were characteristic of his technique and which are layered to create a complex image. His procedure was straightforward—one brushstroke after another to produce brief moments of light and transcendence. Cézanne did not aim to reproduce what he saw. Instead, he aimed to recreate the feelings produced by what he saw. Short-form writers can follow Cézanne's lead by focusing on the "small feelings" produced by one word after another.

This chapter looks at three ways to craft layered, multidimensional writing that contains that shiver of sensation, that *ah-ha* moment through the use of context and subtext, narrative leaps, and associative patterns. These three craft elements can help you make critical decisions about which details are essential to a narrative and which might be left unsaid. When crafting a piece that demands brevity, these three elements can help you swiftly move a reader through the story. When brevity is the goal, the key questions become urgent: What information can you establish with patterns? What can you merely hint at? What can you leave out altogether while trusting that your reader will still understand?

Context, text, and subtext

All writing is surrounded with invisible information—context and subtext—that helps the reader decode its meaning. When readers interact with a text, they interpret it on three levels: the **text** itself (the language in a piece of writing); its **context** (the relevant cultural, historical, or topical background information that frames the text but may not be explicitly stated); and the **subtext** (the information that is hinted at or implied). Subtext floats underneath everything, and context frames it. These three elements (see Figure 6.1) are in constant interplay as we read.

Context is an essential part of the way we understand our world. It surrounds everything we encounter. It's the sea we swim in but don't notice. At first, you might be intimidated by this idea of "everything surrounding" your story. It might seem like all human history is up for consideration. But when we apply this idea of context to literature, context becomes more manageable and focused. For example, context helps the reader understand the tension depicted in Katie Cortese's story, "Rules of Combat." The narrator, Lily, states that she is supposed to be studying for the SATs. The reader has

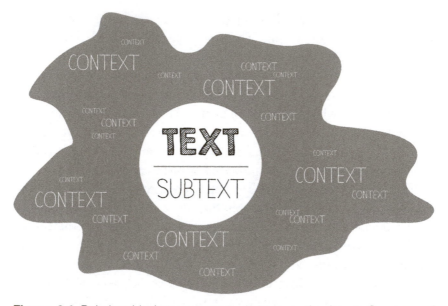

Figure 6.1 Relationship between text, context, and subtext. Courtesy of Savannah Adams.

to supply outside knowledge to understand that the SAT is a standardized test that American students take during their junior or senior year of high school. The reader needs this key contextual information to understand that when Lily is drinking and sleeping with the father of the children she babysits, the affair is not just extramarital: it is illegal. Lily is an underage victim caught in the middle of a warring husband and wife. The writer relies on readers to draw on factual details about SATs and the age of consent as they read. Without this context, the narrative of infidelity loses an important element: the annihilation of Lily's innocence.

Subtext operates in a slightly different way than context by hinting at the submerged, half-hidden, or implicit parts of the story. The subtext of "Rules of Combat" must be teased out from the clues in the story. The quick, casual progression from dinner to a game of checkers to sex indicates that this affair is something that has been going on for a while: the lovers are familiar with each other and with subterfuge. Likewise, the reader might infer that the wife is suspicious because she flies home unexpectedly from a conference. Because of the wife's suspicion, the reader might assume the husband has had previous affairs—perhaps with previous babysitters. Subtext contributes to the awful sense of dread, akin to static electricity crackling in the air, we feel in the story.

The emotional gravity of a text is often located in the subtext. In "Rules of Combat," the center of gravity feels heaviest in the final paragraph, when Lily reports, "She will drop her purse in the doorway and on my way out I'll step over dozens of glossy pamphlets on enamel erosion and decay." What isn't said is embedded in the grammar of this sentence. Written in the future tense, this confrontation will forever feel to her like it's just about to happen. Lily will take this walk of shame over and over, and it will continue to include a guide to a kind of decay that goes all the way down to the root.

Once upon a time

Conversations do not take place in a bubble. When we talk to another person, we take into account the background noise, the size of the room, and the subject of the conversation. We get so good at filling in the unspoken words, at solving the language puzzles, at recognizing and completing patterns, and at interpreting what is said and not said, that we, for the most part, don't even recognize we're constantly decoding language. Consider what happens when we read the opening lines of David Ignatow's "A Modern Fable," which begins "Once upon a time." Those four words cue the reader to suspend disbelief in this tale of long ago. Those four words prepare us for the talking wolf who prefers sour cream to chopped liver. We read the words and understand them, but we also bring to the page our experience as readers of fairy tales and fables. This context shapes our expectations and how we respond to the text when it deviates from the expected.

As writers, we can apply what we know about context, subtext, and the way most readers, if given two pieces of information, will make sense of them, to establish points of connection in a text. Thinking about these different ways of perceiving or knowing can also help a writer trust their reader, and if you trust the reader to understand (and if you write in a way that they can possibly understand) you can skip over the nonessentials and increase the momentum of the narrative.

The involuntary imagination

In 1921, Hermann Rorschach created an inkblot test to assess how people use their "involuntary imagination" to interpret designs. He based his experiment on klecksography, an art form using splatters of ink on paper. Remember the inkblot butterfly paintings you made in elementary school? Those are one common form of klecksography. Similarly, the Rorschach test relies on the concept of **pareidolia**, or the cognitive tendency we have to perceive patterns in the world around us. Although the Rorschach test has been disproven as a psychological test, it still has relevance as a metaphor for sensemaking. When we read, we often follow a line of thinking that is similar to the way we make sense of the Rorschach patterns: we connect the image to anything and everything it reminds us of, and then we draw a conclusion about what we are looking at based on what seems most likely. Simply put, when we perceive anything, we relate it to everything else that it reminds us of. This process of drawing mental connections is also known as **association**.

In a literary sense, association explains abstractions like emotions by drawing on the brain's natural tendency to link one idea to another. In her foundational essay, "Some Notes on Organic Form," poet Denise Levertov explains, "There must be a place … for rifts too … Great gaps between perception and perception which must be leapt across if they are to be crossed at all. The X-factor, the magic, is when we come to those rifts and make those leaps." While it might seem simple, at first, to imagine that art can help you make great leaps from what is known to what is unknown, it can take a little practice to figure out how you create successful leaps like this in your own work. Although associative thinking might be part of "the X-factor, the magic," understanding the principles of associative logic are, thankfully, pretty logical.

American poet Elizabeth Bishop once described how she wrote by following a line of associative logic. She compares it to the way oceanic debris will draw together into a swirling collection: "A group of words, a phrase, may find its way into my head like something floating in the sea, and presently it attracts other things to it. I do tend to 'feel' my way into a poem … One's mind works in unexpected ways." When we use associative logic to make sense of patterns, we "draw together" words, images, or phrases in a way that is somewhat like playing with magnets and iron shavings. One idea draws in another idea, and another, and very quickly an unexpected shape begins to form. Then with a little shift of the magnets, the shavings reconfigure into a new shape.

Inference is the process of putting together evidence (or clues) in order to understand something. When we read, we use whatever clues or evidence we find to make sense of the text. Detective novels make good beach reading because the process of following clues to solve a mystery feels thrilling. Likewise, putting together the clues in a text creates a thrilling, sudden comprehension that accompanies the best flash writing. The "flash" gives readers one lightning-bright glimpse of the world around them before the sky goes dark again, before the page ends.

The hidden parts of a story

At 11:40 p.m. on April 14, 1912, the passenger liner *RMS Titanic* rammed into an iceberg in the North Atlantic Ocean and sank with more than 2,000 people onboard. The news trembled across the airwaves and shook people around the world. Imagine thirteen-year-old Ernest Hemingway listening to the news about the *Titanic* on the radio in his home in Oak Park, Illinois. Imagine that the image of the tremendously powerful yet nearly invisible iceberg stayed with him. Years later, Hemingway developed what is known as his **iceberg theory** for storytelling. In this theory, he posits that not every detail has to be explicitly stated in a narrative. Much can remain hidden and still be stunningly powerful.

In short-form writing, the iceberg theory can help a writer trim a narrative down to the most essential elements. Successful use of this strategy means that writers need to trust readers to figure out what is not on the surface. These submerged parts of the narrative can create a compelling half-visible topography, and if readers have enough to go on, they will sense what's just below the surface, and imaginatively fill in the unseen details.

If you prefer a warmer metaphor, you might imagine a coral reef. From the surface, you might see the glittering sun on electric-blue water, patches of brown kelp beds, and an occasional fin tip cutting the surface. But you have to imagine the dangers below: the shark whose fin just pierced the water, or the venomous jellyfish that looks more like a plastic bag than an animal. More important than knowing exactly what is below is understanding that the submerged parts inform and affect everything happening on the surface. A hapless swimmer gets stung by an unseen jellyfish. So it is with good narrative: the unseen depths of the imagined world teem with life and danger.

Entrances

We enter a story, not just through the hidden doorways of context and subtext, but through the very first words that open the story: the title. We can think of the title as a door into the story beyond. Doors provide essential information. If you walk through a set of swinging saloon doors, you'll get something very different from what you might get when walking through the revolving glass door of a luxury hotel. Like any doorway, the title can hint at what is on the other side. The title frames the text and is often the first link to the surrounding context.

The title gives the reader a foundation for how to interpret what follows. For instance, the title of Katie Cortese's "Rules of Combat," lets the reader know that the story is about war—and it links up with all the other phrases that we associate with love and war. A reader might think of the proverb, "All's fair in love and war," or even Pat Benatar's classic song "Love Is a Battlefield." Just as important, Cortese's title cues the reader into the rules— the strategies—that go into war, particularly hand-to-hand combat. The marriage isn't just ending, it's detonating. The title front-loads these details, so that the reader has them in mind while reading. The reader hits the ground running and that kind of quick acceleration makes a big difference in how far the narrative can go in a short amount of time and space.

Sometimes a title provides a reference or formal element that informs the reader about the piece. In Bryan Fry's "Hill Street Blues," the title provides background. The *Hill Street Blues* television series ran from 1981–1987, so right from the start, the reader has a sense of the time period, which is then confirmed by the descriptive details (like shag carpet) mentioned in the opening scene. Furthermore, the title establishes a specific tone. IMDb describes the show as a "gritty, realistic look at the life of cops in a large metropolitan city." It was a show that dealt with common societal problems like divorce, shifting gender roles, and racial and economic inequity—some of which, you'll notice, are mirrored in Fry's piece. As the drama unfolds, the narrator hums the show's melancholy theme song and anchors the emotional atmosphere of the scene. Fry studies a particular kind of blues— the pervasive melancholy that is inextricably linked to family trouble.

If the title guides the reader into a text, the conclusion releases the reader into the blank white space beyond. Context is critical in both places. When moviegoers exit a darkened theater, they might briefly view the real world through a slightly different lens. There is a physical adjustment as the eyes reacquaint themselves with natural light, but there is also a psychological adjustment. Depending on what kind of movie they saw, they might imagine murderers lurking in the cinema parking lot, aliens in a nearby cornfield, or their date as a star-crossed lover. The fictional world and the factual world briefly blur as the suspension of disbelief dissipates. Likewise, when a reader finishes a text, they launch back into the real world, and inevitably begin to integrate the story with everything else they know.

Exits

Three common exit strategies in the short form include open, circular, or surprise endings. **Open conclusions** leave the reader with a parting image. Open conclusions leave the reader wondering, expectant, facing a certain direction and asking, "what now?" If a writer provides an unsatisfactory conclusion, the reader will feel abandoned. But "satisfactory" doesn't mean neatly wrapped up with a bow on top. Literary critic Barbara Herrnstein Smith describes what she calls "hidden closure." This kind of closure has a settling effect for the narrative. Instead of being a firm final word on the subject, it's more like an exhale or a natural lull in the conversation.

When knitters finish a project, like a scarf, they go back and tuck in the tail of yarn. They weave it back into the last few stitches so that it isn't left dangling. How might you take the strands of your text and work backward to integrate everything and "tuck" your end? For example, in Mary Ruefle's "Short Lecture on Your Own Happiness," she concludes, "Why are you sitting there? You should have fled before I finished the first sentence." Paradoxically, after reading this conclusion, the reader's instinct is not to flee—it's to go back to the beginning to figure out what they missed the first time. What did they miss that should have made them run? They backtrack and then end up right where they started, or ended and restarted, the first time. You might weave backward as long as possible and follow a strand all the way to the beginning as a way to study the tautness and evenness of the different strands of your text. And you might notice that the context is the invisible force that holds those strands into place.

Circular conclusions evoke the sensation of being lost in the woods by dropping the reader right back at the beginning. "Hill Street Blues" uses a sort of circular conclusion. It begins, "My first memory fails me," and concludes, "I'm afraid if I don't concentrate, I'll forget." The speaker then deposits the reader exactly where he began—at the paradoxical realization that he has forgotten his first memory. Similarly, Cortese's "Rules of Combat" doesn't conclude with Lily stepping over the scattered pamphlets and leaving. The story concludes without ending: "King me, king me, king me," he begs, until I let my white flag fly once again." Lily surrenders once again (and again and again). Conclusions like this reinforce the looping sense of timelessness connected to the emotional crisis shown. Ask yourself if the invisible information framing the narrative suggests what conclusion is required. Emotionally confounding topics like the loss of innocence that occurs in both Fry's and Cortese's endings defy easy closure, so they naturally fit the resistance inherent in a circular conclusion.

Surprise conclusions create the opposite effect by startling the reader, bursting open, and revealing something new. This jack-in-the-box trick jolts the reader into a new understanding or perspective that often transfers to how readers understand the real world, too. Surprise is hard to execute, especially in the short form where there isn't a lot of space to build narrative tension in a traditional way. One way that the short form can create a surprising finish is with a **deep image**—a high definition image that can startle the reader on both visual and symbolic levels.

As an example of a surprise conclusion, Robert Hass's widely anthologized prose poem, "A Story about the Body," tells of a young composer who pursues an older woman and who then rejects her when she reveals that she has had a double mastectomy. The narrative ends on the image of the young man opening his door and discovering a blue bowl full of dead bees hidden beneath rose petals. The final image is profoundly multidimensional. At once the reader perceives the rich colors (the blue bowl, the red or pink rose petals); the rough texture (of the dead bees and even the broom that swept them up); the cool, smooth weight of the bowl; and of course, the searing metaphoric implication—the young man's love may seem beautiful on the surface, but underneath is nothing but a handful of barbed stingers. The concluding image condemns the thoughtless cruelty of the impetuous young lover—and it makes readers reenter their own lives and question when they too have acted cruel.

When experimenting with surprise, however, watch out for surprise endings that rely on familiar narrative twists and tropes. Writers of all kinds are susceptible to resorting to false surprises in their writing, but the short-form writer is particularly at risk because of the form's limitations. You have to produce change, and you have to make that change happen quickly. The too-frequent result is an ending that goes something like this:

- And then she woke up.
- And then he died.
- And then they lived happily ever after.
- And then I confessed everything.
- And then I realized he was really my evil twin/a robot/an alien/a werewolf.

These sudden epiphanies, recognitions, reversals, or resolutions often fall flat because they do not honor the complexity we have come to expect from literature. While there are certain genres where we desire these easy transformations, literature is not one of them.

The impulse for change and movement in writing is essential, and the best way to train yourself to discern between false surprise and authentic surprise is to read, read, and read some more. Read stories in progress as well as published stories. Pay attention to the places in writing where you're most absorbed and surprised by what is taking place. Also, be mindful that what is surprising or clever in one genre doesn't always translate to another. For example, a surprising ending in a blockbuster summer movie may not have the subtle intensity that we expect from short fiction. A clever turn of phrase in a pop song may sound dead on the page in a poem.

Gestalt theory for flash

Gestalt theory offers one way of thinking about thinking—and it can help explain how readers make sense of incomplete narratives. For the purposes of creative writers, **Gestalt theory** can be one way of conceptualizing how readers take cues from details in a text and create a sense of order. When we perceive information, we organize it holistically and create a unified coherence out of the separate components. Imagine, for instance, the way we arrange clusters of stars into constellations to map the night sky. Most of us can quickly orient ourselves if we locate the Big Dipper. Likewise, according to Gestalt theory, there are specific ways that we perceive order and make sense of how discrete pieces fit into a unified whole. Applied to writing, Gestalt theory might help you think about how you arrange details in an image to map out a scene or, more broadly, a narrative for your reader.

Let's consider three Gestalt principles relevant to associative thinking: the law of pithiness, the law of closure, and the principle of foreground/background. The **law of pithiness** explains that the mind will look for order in the simplest pattern possible, and make sense of the pattern in a glance. The **law of closure** posits that when we perceive incomplete images, we will fill in the missing components. Look at Figure 6.2: After a moment of disorientation, the audience perceives the shape of a crescent moon and recognizes that there are clouds obscuring the image. The brain automatically completes the image of the moon, even though the outline is incomplete. Now, look at Figure 6.3: It demonstrates the Gestalt idea that

Figure 6.2 Illustration of the law of closure. Courtesy of Savannah Adams.

we perceive images as figures against a background, and that the figure and ground components can switch places. At first glance, you'll notice the shape of the crescent moon in the upper right quadrant, but as you look at the image, the moon will move to the background and you'll perceive the outlines of the four rectangles and recognize them as window panes.

These visual tricks of perception illustrate how the brain processes images. The brain naturally searches for recognizable shapes, patterns, and connections and creates networks of associations that help a person make sense of experience. Creating meaning is a collaborative process. Ideally, writers provide just enough information that readers can cocreate a meaningful experience as they read, without providing too much information that they feel overloaded or too little information that they feel lost.

This process develops as readers become more advanced. When an image or idea is introduced, the "involuntary imagination" begins drawing connections, and as readers proceed through a text, image links to image, idea links to idea, and the language weaves into a larger pattern. When short-form writing contains gaps, the reader's imagination fills in the blanks.

Figurative language in a flash

A metaphor is a form of literary multitasking. Metaphors allow short-form writers to "kill two birds with one stone." That idiomatic phrase, a rather

Figure 6.3 Illustration of the changeable figure-ground relationship. Courtesy of Savannah Adams.

unpleasant one at that, is a metaphor. We are not literally throwing stones at defenseless birds. Instead, this saying compares what a metaphor does to a visible and visceral situation that accomplishes multiple objectives with a single action. Forget the "like" or "as" adage you dutifully learned years ago. A **metaphor**, when we use it here, means any kind of figurative language that makes comparisons or connections. We could say that "time is a bird" or "time is like a bird," using the formulaic structure of the metaphor and simile. But neither is as succinct as "time flies." In this phrase, the verb carries the metaphor, an image of a bird, or plane, or Superman. Whatever. It's the swift movement that matters, not the specific object that flies through space.

Table 6.1 Figurative comparisons of abstract time to concrete images

Original phrase	Time described as	Qualities of time
"Time makes puppets of us all."	A puppet-master	Controlling
" … his time was just a wink in the universe."	A blink and/or a joke	Fast, sly
" … horrible burden of Time…"	A physical load	Heavy
"There was the time that was lost."	A misplaced object	Prone to loss
" … she spends 58 percent more time with him than with the other sentient androids …"	Asset	Limited resource

When we say that "time flies," we transform time into something physical, into something we can touch or feel act on us. Figurative language transforms ideas that we have a hard time wrapping our heads around and helps us make sense of those ideas through the body. Often writers use metaphors to translate an abstract concept into a concrete image. Let's take a look at how some writers in our anthology use metaphors to describe the abstraction of time (Table 6.1). Even idiomatic uses of time lend a physicality to the abstraction of time: "his time was up," "the time is right," "one at a time," "take your time," "plenty of time." These phrases show how time gets conceptualized in our imaginations.

We believe an awareness of the ticking clock and the rapidly approaching page end generates urgency that propels the narrative forward in the absence of other literary devices that take more room to develop. Time as a concept is addressed more than any other in the anthology, more than love, more than hate, more than fear or life or hope or death. Two works in the anthology discuss time specifically. In Karen E. Bender's "The Man Who Hated Us and Then Forgot," the phrase "there was the time" is repeated over and over to suggest the ways that individual moments accumulate into years without us noticing. Lia Purpura's "On Miniatures" discusses an experiment where researchers asked subjects to imagine themselves interacting with scale models. What they found is that time collapsed in direct proportion to the scale. Thirty minutes felt like five to subjects playing with scale models of

1/12 their actual size. What happens to time, real or perceived, when we sit down with a story of 500 words, or 50? This is the mystery and magic of flash.

Synecdoche and metonymy

Designing at the level of perception allows you to play with the nuances of tone, texture, pattern, and shading, like a visual artist. Two tools that are important for short-form writers are metonymy and synecdoche. If this sounds Greek to you, don't worry. It is. These two literary devices are easily confused and hard to pronounce, but they are extremely useful for writers who need to suggest something larger while controlling the scope of the story.

Synecdoche is a literary tool that makes use of the natural tendencies of the human brain to connect the dots by imagining the whole even when only a part is perceived. An example can be seen in Debra Marquart's "Some Things about That Day," which begins with a quick sketch that establishes the scene at an abortion clinic: "The placards I walked through. Wet raincoat on a hook. Questionnaire on a clipboard before me. Couples sat around me in the waiting room. They were young. What am I saying? I was only thirty-two." Each element of this scene functions as a **synecdoche**, where part of an image is used to represent the whole. The placards she walked through represent a group of protestors *holding* placards. The wet raincoat on the hook represents the rainstorm beyond the clinic walls. The result is cinematic, a story told in glimpses.

Metonymy is a figure of speech that uses a specific object to represent an abstract idea associated with it. In Marquart's passage, the placards might alternatively be read as a metonymy, where the protestors are reduced to the slogans they hold as the narrator walks through this ideological gauntlet, alone in a crowd. Either way, what Marquart creates is a setting fraught with tension. The speaker must navigate a crowd that is physically and ideologically pushing back against her as she tries to enter the clinic.

To return for a moment to Gestalt theory, the law of closure illustrates how the reader's imagination completes the scene: a woman rushes through tempestuous weather and protestors to arrive in to the order of a waiting room where people fill out paperwork and wait their turn. It's so quiet, you can almost hear the pens scratching against the paper. Writers can draw on these Gestalt principles to make educated guesses about how their own audiences will arrange the pieces of the narrative puzzle. Writers make critical visual, aural, and structural design decisions that can help readers perceive a great deal with a few swift moves. *Show* doesn't mean to show everything; it means to show just enough, and trust the reader to fill in the rest.

Conclusion: Follow the path

Sometimes associative thinking veers off in unexpected directions. Go ahead and follow the surprising path. Write it down. The more you practice associative thinking, the more you'll notice the energetic shifts that occur at pivot points in the narrative. Follow one sentence into the next: push, lean, swerve, and leap your way forward. The compactness of the short-form text can withstand a headlong plunge all the way through. Don't worry about veering too far. More often than not your associations will lead you full circle.

Is it possible to write an entire paragraph while deliberately trying to incorporate context, subtext, and associative logic into every sentence? No. Well, perhaps but it would be incredibly difficult and time consuming, and probably result in awkward, forced sentences. Each element, however, is useful to consider from time to time as you write. Begin to notice the patterns that you are already using and try to enhance them. Watch what happens in your own mind as you read as if you are watching it play out like a film: How do you construct coherence and logic in your own imagination? Is there anything you might add or refine to simulate that same experience in your reader's imagination? What is submerged in the narrative that might be brought to the surface (or conversely, what might be sunk into the subtext)? How might you leverage the title and the conclusion to do more for the piece as a whole? If you consider what is happening on the level of meaning-making as you write, you can develop these elements to your advantage.

The takeaway from this chapter might be as simple as this: if you consider *how* your reader will arrange pieces of information, you can use it to your advantage. Conversely, if you fail to arrange the pieces of information in a way that your reader can puzzle them out? You lose your reader, plain and simple.

Exercises

A. Examine the inferences you make about a text before you start reading. Without reading the story, glance at "Dust" by Sarah Evans in the anthology at the back of the book. Write down:

- What the title suggests
- What assumptions you make based on the length and layout of the text
- Any other connections you associate with the author, the title, or any words you noticed when you glanced at the text

Then, share your assumptions with a partner and compare how your ideas were similar or different. Talk about what made you draw the conclusions you did. Can you identify which inferences were based on associative reasoning, and which were based on context, subtext, or something else?

B. With a small group of two or three classmates, use Hemingway's Iceberg Theory to chart everything you know about "Rules of Combat" (i.e. the information that is explicitly stated in the text) and everything you *think* you know (i.e. what can you infer from the subtext and context). How much of the story exists in the submerged portion of the iceberg?

C. Map all the things that you connect with a set of words. For instance, make a list all of the associations you have with each of the following items: beer, cornbread, lust, neon, 4th of July. Share your list with a partner, and notice if you have any similar associations.

Prompts

A. Write a text that uses subtext to hint at what lies beneath the surface of the narrative but does not state it directly. A classic example of this is to write a text told from the perspective of a narrator who is missing some essential information or wisdom as they face a crisis moment: what happens?

B. Take something you wrote for one of the previous exercises and write four or five different titles. Try to write titles that reveal some piece of information that is otherwise not explicit in the text. Which title offers the most surprise? Which title functions like a trapdoor that leads the reader into the text?

C. Write a flash piece in which your title is longer than the body of the text. Consider the kind of doorway your title builds for readers as they enter your work.

One-sentence workshop

The following exercise will help you practice the art of brevity:

Notice how the following sentence from "Rules of Combat" by Katie Cortese gets as much impact as possible out of one specific sensory image: "Each pea is a lightning strike to the back of my brain; lips left sizzling."

The narrator, Lily, describes the lightning strike as triggering a fiery response in her brain and her lips as if the lightning travels through her whole body, leaving the nerves firing with pleasurable heat. The sensory experience of the wasabi also functions as a metaphor for the flirtation that is taking place. Emulate Cortese's technique: write a sentence that describes a sensory experience (like eating wasabi peas) that triggers more than one physical response. Bonus points if the description also functions on a metaphoric level.

7

Translucent Design

Relevant readings

"The Man Who Hated Us and Then Forgot" by Karen E. Bender

"Grip" by Joy Castro

"Self-Portrait as a Chimera" by Natalie Diaz

"Instruction, Final: To Brown Poets from Black Girl with Silver Leica" Nikky Finney

"Poland" by Thaisa Frank

"Hill Street Blues" by Bryan Fry

"The Quiet Machine" by Ada Limón

"Small Meditations" by Michael Wasson
"Letter to Deb Clow" by Terry Tempest Williams

Flash interview with Ada Limón

Ada Limón is a poet who divides her time between Lexington, Kentucky, and Sonoma, California. We chose "The Quiet Machine" for the anthology because of the way it embodies silence and all its variations. Plus, we too like to pretend we're not home when people knock. Here's what she has to say about writing short.

How do you define the kind of short-form writing that you do?
I write poems and prose poems. The prose poems sometimes look like little stories, but they really are poems. The prose poem is often a place for circular thinking or stream of consciousness. It's also a place where ordinary things suddenly seem bizarre.

How does your approach to writing in short forms differ from the other kinds of writing that you do?
Prose poems and poetry are different from prose writing (fiction, nonfiction, etc.), because they deal in intense compression and lyric play. There's also a level of rhythm and sound work that's at work in prose poetry that makes it different from, let's say, a nonfiction essay. There's a tension created by a limited time and space that allows for a wild urgency that feels appropriate for an excavation of the mind.

What demands does the short form make of its writers or readers?
The prose poem demands that the reader read it in one sitting. It makes a wild surmise that we should be together in this one or two minutes in this small room we've created on the page. For the writer, it means we only have this one room in which we should build an entire interior life.

Free dive

For this free dive, we want you to build a couple of epic lists. We're inspired by Lisa Nola, creator of the *Listography* book series, who says that a list can be "a perpetual work in progress, a time capsule, and a map of your life for friends and family." Challenge yourself by numbering your page one through twenty-five. Choose one of the topics below and list every major and minor memory, fact, habit, desire, pet peeve, family legend, or other relevant detail connected to the topic. The trick is to range far and wide: switch from personal to public, intellectual to pop culture, serious to irreverent, and so forth. After you feel like you've exhausted your ideas, start a new column, and try a new topic. Repeat this as many times as necessary until you end up with a list that feels like it is full of possibility, energy, and surprise.

> Time: When have you felt alone? Scared? Perplexed?
> Character: Who has done _____ with you/to you/near you?
> Images: When does _____ appear in nature or life?
> Actions: List things you've done that …
> Sensations: Describe times you've felt …

Save your lists to jumpstart new creative pieces.

Vignette: The jackalope

I have always been a believer. I was born into belief: in Jesus, in God the Father, in the Holy Spirit. I was taught to believe in the unseen antics of Santa Claus, the Easter Bunny, and the Tooth Fairy. I believed my uncle when he said he could rip off his own thumb. I believed if I took good care of my doll Carrie that she would become a real baby someday. I believed my belief would be my reward. I believed my parents would always be together. I believed at one point I could fly, and I did for just a moment until my plastic-bag parachute failed. I believed in secret passageways and that every mystery could be solved between the covers of a book. I believed what people told me, especially if they said "trust me." I believed in mathematical equations, but only to pass Algebra. I believed what he said and that later he did not mean what he said. I believed I could hold my liquor. I believed, in a bar, that scientists had just discovered a new species of whale, flat as a sheet of paper, living in the darkness of the ocean floor. Proof! said the boy, pointing at the television where the flickering screen revealed the splash of something large sinking beneath the ocean's waves. I believed every whale of a tale.

When I was a kid, my grandfather had me convinced that jackalopes were real. A stuffed version of this critter, portmanteau of jackrabbit and antelope, sat atop a high shelf in my grandfather's living room. The creature had viciously attacked my uncle, or so said my grandfather. To save my uncle, this strange animal was killed. Later it was stuffed as a trophy of that near-death experience. Every Sunday after church, my family visited my grandparents, and I'd ask again to see the jackalope. One day my grandfather brought it down and allowed me to stroke the soft rabbit fur and the gnarled antlers. Its eyes were black marbles that glimmered in the dim light of the living room. In the corner, the console TV squatted, framed with decorative wood molding, and emitted its constant, bright lies. As I ran my fingers through the jackalope's fur, I remember realizing I had been duped. Perhaps I recognized the emptiness of hollow plastic in my hands. Or the gleam of a price tag on its base that advertised the exact amount this lie had cost. I handed the jackalope back to my grandfather. Next Sunday, I told my sister the story of the jackalope.

I'm not as gullible as I used to be, but I'm still open to being swayed. As a reader, I love suspending disbelief and taking a leap into another world. As a writer, I love releasing myself from the limits of facts and rules. I love make believe and bringing together impossible combinations. In the field of creative writing, my gullibility is not a liability; it's what allows me to more fully enter the imaginations of others. Because I have been both liar and lied to, I know that in every fantastic lie, there must be an element of truth, the more mundane the better. I like to think of short-form writing in this way: we graft deer antlers on a bunny's body to create a small, mythical creature from the materials of everyday life. We write stories that are just waiting for someone to believe in them.

—Stephanie
Word count: 580

The invisible workaday paragraph

A lineated poem's structure can be seen clearly at a glance. Its line breaks and stanzas form an exoskeleton. Most short pieces, on the other hand, contain an internal structure that we could call an endoskeleton, a framework that gives shape and strength to a body. In writing, this structure is, for the most part, hidden. Here writer Jayne Anne Phillips describes the seeming invisibility of the paragraph:

> I didn't realize it at the time, but I taught myself to write by writing one-page fictions. I found in the form the density I needed, the attention to the line, the syllable. I began writing as a poet. In the one-page form, I found the freedom of the paragraph. I learned to understand the paragraph as secretive and subversive. The poem in broken lines announces itself as a poem, but the paragraph seems innocent, workaday, invisible.

The broken lines of a poem announce their sound patterns and rhythms on the surface. Line breaks say, *Pay attention: here and here.* The paragraph's plainness creates the perfect "normcore" disguise that makes it easy to overlook. Yet all kinds of poetic elements can be used to create cohesiveness, harmony, and magnetic tension in the paragraph. Unless you are looking for these elements, they might slip past you.

A short-form piece might use a cascading wall of sound built from a variety of poetic materials including repetition, assonance, consonance, half rhymes, and alliteration. If you have no idea what these are, don't worry: we'll break it down later in this chapter. The sounds cohere like water molecules and pour down the page. They create a surface tension that is felt on all sides of the text—not just at the margins—to create a multi-phonic effect, like a waterfall. And like the white noise of a waterfall, the poetic soundscape can quickly blend into the background.

How does this invisible internal structure affect you as a reader and writer of the short form? Quite simply, it might just mean you have to look and listen more carefully. Don't underestimate the paragraph. Lightweight and airy like the porous bones of a bird, the paragraph enables flight. Begin by studying the short form from the outside in: look at the title, the opening line, the closing line, and then the center of the text. Scan down the right and left margins, and see what happens to the language on the periphery. How does the surface tension push against the narrative? How about from the inside out? If you examine the sounds, where do they seem to loop, echo, ripple, or halt? If you examine the images, where do they repeat, reflect, or cast shadows on other visual elements of the narrative?

Charming snakes and snake charming

Do you remember jump-rope chants from the schoolyard? They have a heavy rhyme and a fast rhythm to match the beat of the rope, and they often contain something risqué, at least for elementary school students. Notice the potent tension in this traditional one:

Cinderella, dressed in yellow
went upstairs to kiss her fellow.
By mistake she kissed a snake.

How many doctors did it take?
1, 2, 3, 4 ...

It uses both rhyme and rhythm. **Rhyme** is a repetition of sounds that add emphasis you can plainly hear. In this chant, "yellow" and "fellow" are often pronounced as "yella" and "fella" to create a full end rhyme with "Cinderella." **Rhythm** is a pattern of repeating stressed and unstressed syllables. In this chant, the rhythm of stressed syllables matches the slap of the rope on the sidewalk. Each stressed syllable (indicated in boldface) matches the downstroke of the rope, and each unstressed syllable (indicated in regular font) matches the upstroke of the rope:

Cin • de • **rel** • la • **dressed** • in • **yel** • low
went • up • **stairs** • to • **kiss** • her • **fel** • low.
By • mi • **stake** • she • **kissed** • a • **snake**.
How • **man** • y • **doc** • tors • **did** • it • **take**?

Every other syllable is emphasized until the final question. The back-to-back emphasis of "how" and the first syllable of "many" creates a pleasant deviation from the otherwise hypnotically consistent rhyme.

You might think of rhythm, rhyme, and the escalation of Cinderella's ailment as three separate patterns layered on the text. The rollicking sounds enchant the listener, as does the mystery of a man who can transform into a snake if you kiss him. Everyone teeters on the brink of collapse as Cinderella needs more and more doctors and the jumper gets more and more tired. The combined effect creates a heady momentum. We want to keep going—and that is the charm of the pattern effect.

Short-form writing uses rhymes, rhythms, patterns, and other tricks as deftly as snake charmers or girls on the playground. It's safe to say that all good writing does. When we speak of integrating patterns, we're not talking about composing in formal patterns that carry a da-DUH, da-DUH, da-DUH rhythm for a precise number of beats throughout a text. We're not talking about writing a sonnet in the disguise of a paragraph, though that might be a fun experiment. If we were to make one general rule for this chapter, it would be this: too much of anything becomes a gimmick. Ungraceful rhythms make a reader feel like they're cantering on a wayward pony, and unwavering rhymes undermine the meaning of a sentence.

Warnings aside, we'll examine how a few writers use a smattering of sounds or a brief chain of rhythms to moderate the energy and pacing in a piece of writing. This chapter presents basic strategies for incorporating sound and nonsound patterns and for balancing regularity with surprise so that the patterns don't become overbearing. Pay attention to the interplay of sounds, textures, or rhythms in the relevant readings for this chapter. They create a subtle background music, to be sure, one that's closer to humming than whistling. Then, look for the patterns that occur naturally in your own work, and play around with how you might enhance them.

The rule of threes

Repetition is a crucial tool in creating a sense of unity and structure in writing. But in short-form writing, where every word counts, can writers afford to repeat themselves? Are repetition and brevity compatible? To answer those questions, we must make a quick distinction between repetition and redundancy. **Repetition** is a rhetorical device that repeats a word or phrase to create musicality and momentum. Many speeches and jokes make use of repetition to craft language that is memorable and surprising. **Redundancy**, on the other hand, is unnecessary repetition that serves no other purpose than to take up space.

There is room in short-form writing for repetition, but it must be purposeful. One way to accomplish this is by using the rule of threes. Three is the smallest number that establishes a pattern. One incidence is random. Two could be coincidence. Three times and it's no accident—something is going on. Our brains love pattern. And pattern leads to rhythm and expectation as well as the opportunity to create tension by breaking or deviating from the pattern. Jokes rely on the pattern of three for the setup, conflict, and punchline. Or think of Larry, Mo, and Curly, the three stooges. In love, it's the triangle. In entertainment, there are trilogies. In art, there are triptychs. In music, the triad. In sports, there's "three strikes and you're out." For safety, we stop, drop, and roll. For breakfast, there's "snap, crackle, and pop." Americans want life, liberty, and the pursuit of happiness. We expect our stories to have a beginning, middle, and end. Third time's a charm. The list goes on and on.

It seems that our brains are attuned to this pattern and find it satisfying on the most elemental level. Consider the way you can play with this expectation by giving your reader one less or one more than expected to add variety and produce a feeling of tension. Variety is the spice of life, right? So it is with writing. When we work with a pattern, there are two inevitable steps: establish the pattern and then, at the right moment, break it. Set it up, knock it down. Keep the reader on their toes. Look at these lines from Natalie Diaz's "Self-Portrait as a Chimera":

> I am what I have done …
> We do. We do. We do and do and do …
> I am. I am and am and am. What have I done? …

These similar phrasal patterns occur far enough apart that the reader experiences the repetition more as an echo rather than a deliberately employed pattern. The repetition of *I am, I am, and am and am* and *we do, we do, we do, and do and do* fold over each other, like waves on a shore. The sounds create a pleasant, lulling pattern that gets disrupted by the final question: *What have I done?* Whatever it is, the break in the pattern alerts us: it can't be good.

Integrating sound patterns

So far, we've talked about the basics of establishing a pattern using repetition, rhythm, or rhyme. But, "rhyme" is a very general term that deserves a bit more teasing out if it's to be used with any finesse. Most people, when they hear the term rhyme, think of rhyming the last syllables of words or phrases: "You're a poet, and you don't even know it." While this is a kind of rhyme, it tends to be the most obvious and, consequently, somewhat heavy-handed. Used exclusively, it can sound like a commercial jingle. A few other varieties of rhyme can achieve a more nuanced effect.

Let's look at Nikky Finney's "Instruction, Final: To Brown Poets from Black Girl with Silver Leica" for an example of how a text can weave together multiple layers of patterns. For now, let's focus on how she superimposes tightly woven sounds over a swirling visual pattern. You might start by hearing the repetition of "be": *be* camera, *be* diamondback, *be* isosceles. Repetition that appears at the beginning of phrases is known as **anaphora**. In this text, the repetition also appears half-hidden in other words: *be*come, *be*fore. Then, notice the way "oh" sounds repeat throughout the piece: *o*nly, rhaps*o*dy, H*o*gon, D*o*gon, kn*o*w. We call this kind of vowel rhyme **assonance**. Taken together, the reader experiences a plaintive echo of *be, oh, be* throughout the poem. Even if we aren't fully aware of the pattern, it affects our experience as we read.

These aren't the only repeating sounds in Finney's piece. Many consonants like *s, t,* and *l* also repeat to create a harder and more percussive rhyme known as **consonance**. Consonance repeats a stressed consonant, but the vowel may vary, like the /n/ sound in this line: "Lay mi*n*t or ora*n*ge eucalyptus garla*n*d." When the repetition of consonant sounds happens at the beginning of words, this is known as **alliteration**. For example, *q*uilts, *q*uietus, and *q*uarter alliterate. So do *S*irius, *s*tudy, *s*entence, and *s*outhing. Finney varies layers of rhymes to create a cascading melody. The coordinating sounds create order set against the rhythm of the universe.

Let's look at how subtly crafted rhymes enhance another text, as in this passage from "Grip" by Joy Castro:

> *Beginner's luck,* said the guys at the shooting range, at first. *Little lady*, they'd said, until the silhouette slid back and farther back. They'd cleared their throats, fallen silent.

Building on what we've learned so far, you may notice the use of alliteration with the repetition of the beginning letters in *L*ittle *l*ady; *f*irst, *f*arther, *f*allen; and *s*ilhouette, *s*lid, and *s*ilent. You might also notice the assonance with the /i/ sounds in beg*i*nner, l*i*ttle, sl*i*d, and s*i*lhouette. Then, consonance appears in the repetition of /d/ sounds in sai*d*, la*d*y, they'*d* sli*d*, and cleare*d*. And finally, we have another kind of rhyme called **half rhyme** or near rhyme where the vowels or consonants match but the words don't fully rhyme. We can find this in *luck* and *back*. Half rhyme is particularly effective in this moment because it emphasizes that it is not luck; as the target slips further and further back, she continues to nail it with skillful accuracy. Castro's passage is not as musically driven as the example from Finney, but if you listen, each word clearly and quietly clicks into place.

Integrating nonsound patterns

Patterning doesn't just happen in the soundscape of a piece of writing. Carefully crafted images can also be used to create visual patterns in a text. Shape recognition is a form of reading: newborns begin to recognize shapes right away. Babies first "read" simple shapes (circles, squares, triangles) and then move on to recognizing more complex symbols, like letters. So it makes sense that we continue to search out shapes in the information we take in. In the most basic sense, think about the way we "read" road signs: we know at a glance that the red octagon of a stop sign signals something different from the yellow triangle of a yield sign. We read the shape before we read the words.

One shape that has particular relevance in writing and art is the triangle. Triangles create tension, movement, and a sharp-edged inescapability. Anytime a narrative introduces a love triangle, you know crisis is imminent. Thaisa Frank's "Poland" uses multiple triangles: the most obvious triangle is the dead husband, the first wife, and the second wife. But there is also the triangle of the dead husband, the poem he leaves behind, and the way his wife must deal with it after he is gone. Another triangle: the wife, the rearview mirror, and haunting image of Poland that keeps appearing. The triangles are subtle: you may not notice them at first. But they function something like the triangulated composition that is used in painting, to trap the viewer's gaze within the frame moving here, then there, and back again. Frank uses triangulation to capture the way grief can cause a person to fixate on inexplicable things—like half-finished poems or unknown places. Both the second wife and then the first wife obsessively glance backward in their rearview mirrors and backward in their lives, unable to let go of the husband they must leave behind.

Classifying the images in your text can help you see how they might be supporting the narrative. If we look at the opening section of "8 Meetings Nobody Scheduled" by Alex Carr Johnson, we can see how to use an image to set up or develop a piece thematically:

> **The Sea Turtle.** Rapt in the rhythm of pulling my canoe across the brackish bay, I was unprepared for the encounter: a barnacled shell split the surface inches from my outstretched palm. A pair of eyes met mine in shared brilliant shock. I had not known sea turtles could scream—but I swear to you that as I shrieked and fumbled and nearly swamped the canoe, this sea turtle screamed silently too before rushing gape-beaked to the bay's grassy bottom.

In this image the speaker's eyes and mouth are open wide in shock and they are reflected exactly by the sea turtle's expression. Like an image in a mirror, the two meet at the surface, scream in unison, and flee. This entire piece decenters the civilized/human perspective and presents the speaker as one species in the animal kingdom. This first encounter prepares the reader for the other, wilder meetings to come. By the eighth and final meeting, the sense of separateness has disintegrated and the speaker meets himself in a mirror after weeks of hiking, and does not recognize himself. Instead, he sees a hairy ape. In "Lions and Tigers and Bears, Oh My! Courage and Creative Nonfiction," Brenda Miller calls this sort of moment a "container" scene because it provides "narrative momentum" while also containing the "strong emotions in dealing with sensitive, emotional material." The two images that bookend this piece work like emotional twins; the scenes capture different circumstances, yet both are about looking at a reflection and seeing fear, surprise, and recognition. Pairing images in this way can be a highly effective strategy in compressed forms because the two images, when placed in close proximity, intensify the emotion they reflect.

The poet Denise Levertov describes **corresponding images** as "a kind of nonaural rhyme," a rhyme that isn't sound-based. Corresponding images are similar in shape or likeness, and when used successfully, they might make a reader see one thing and think of another. Nonaural rhymes might be envisioned like fractal geometry, the mathematical phenomenon where different patterns in nature repeat symmetrically. Examine the similar spiral structures of a hurricane, a galaxy, and a nautilus shell and you'll find corresponding shapes. Levertov explains the "rhyme, chime, echo, reiteration" of sound and image patterns establish a sense of cohesion.

Repeating shapes can also lead the reader from point to point through a text. Finney's "Instruction, Final: To Brown Poets from Black Girl with Silver Leica" opens, "Be camera, black-eyed aperture. Be diamondback terrapin, the only animal that can outrun a hurricane." The same black eye appears in all of the images: the dark round camera lens, the shuttered opening of the camera's aperture, the black spiral patterned shell of the terrapin, and the spiral eye of the hurricane. Finney builds on the visual swirl of the hurricane to choreograph a series of spins that include the *double tuck*, a Lindy Hop dance spin (or, alternatively, a gymnastics flip), and she references *ascending nodes* and *southing*, two terms used to track and measure the orbit of objects through space. These corresponding images create momentum, balance, and harmony: the girl doing a Lindy Hop double tuck echoes the movement of celestial bodies. Finney's final instruction is found in the very pattern itself: the human body echoes the universe. *Be*, she says, the earthy, the celestial, the hot, the cool, the artistic, the sensual. At its heart, these instructions are an affirmation: *Be, be, be.*

Conclusion: Black bear against night sky

A friend of Heather's tells a story about a camping trip he took where he woke in the middle of the night and glimpsed a great expanse of starry sky—more stars in the heavens than he'd ever seen. He fell back to sleep and awoke to a feeling of heat on his face. When he opened his eyes, the stars had disappeared and all he could see was a cartoonish black cutout silhouette like Mickey Mouse ears. In one *uh-oh* moment, he perceived the black bear's head against a canvas of stars, the hot breath. That kind of knowing by silhouette alone is something like what happens when we glimpse patterns in short-form work. Often there is an invisible element in the text that is like the black bear at night. Just as likely, it is the most dangerous element in the story. It's a game of connect the dots: draw a line from the originating point to the final point, and what image suddenly appears? What is cast in silhouette?

When all you have is room for a handful of images, a design mindset can help you discern which will be the most effective. If you are working with a rough draft that already contains several images, you can play the game where you look at a set of objects and decide "which one of these doesn't belong?" You have to figure out the thematic connection between the objects in order to decide which object or image is out of sync with the others. Conversely, thematic connections can help you identify what's missing that might complete the set.

We may perceive these patterns intuitively when we read, but we can use them deliberately when we write. Many writers don't write the initial draft with a pattern in mind. Instead, they look at a draft and notice what patterns are naturally present then look for ways to develop, highlight, or make them more consistent. What designs are present in the text? How might you bring them closer to the surface?

Whether we are conscious of it, our assumptions about what genre we are working in will cause us to weigh our choices and prioritize them differently as we proceed. Depending on how we prioritize our choices, we may shape very different texts. Our argument for this chapter is simple: regardless of whether you think you are writing an essay, a story, a paragraph, or a poem, spend some time at the pattern level, and you can craft a more integrated design.

Exercises

A. Use different colored highlighters to analyze how different sound patterns work together in Bryan Fry's "Hill Street Blues" and Nikky Finney's "Instruction, Final: To Brown Poets from Black Girl with Silver Leica." Compare the patterns you observe in each text. Then, share with a small group of two or three other students.

B. Take a walk and search for aural and nonaural rhymes. Look for shapes that create a kind of visual echo. For instance, do you notice similar curves in different kinds of leaves or flowers? Do you notice a series of yellow things like gingko leaves, a rain slicker, a taxi? Do you hear the rhythm of crickets or woodpeckers or construction noise? Look for patterns in the world around you and write down your observations.

C. Create a fake receipt for a shopping trip where at least three items were purchased. Include the date and time of purchase, the cashier's name, the price and quantity of the items purchased, and any other details normally recorded during this everyday transaction. Then exchange receipts with a classmate and invent the story that connects these items. Who is buying them, why, and what for?

Prompts

A. Create two scenes that have the same underlying emotional current. One should focus on action, and the other should focus on an object and its description. Neither should mention the emotion directly. Rather, that emotion should be illustrated through action or contained within the description of the object. In each, something completely different happens, but the resulting scenes become emotional twins of each other.

B. Seven minutes in heaven. Spin the bottle. Light as a feather, stiff as a board. Truth or dare. Jump-rope chants. So many childhood games leverage psychological crisis with containment. They take the confined space of a basement, a closet, a bathroom, and throw in something wildly unpredictable: a person of the opposite gender, a demon. Now, survive. Oh, by the way, everyone's watching. Liminal spaces, like adolescence and the games of adolescence, contend with the unruly: freedom and discomfort, hormones and peer pressure, sex and lies. They use rules to push against, to defy, to break. Can you guess where this is going? Establish a set of rules for yourself and write something in which you follow your rules closely enough that you can feel their pressure in every sentence. Then, push back with a rebellious mindset.

C. Write a manifesto in which you declare why you do something. Begin each sentence with a similar phrase but vary it slightly the way Terry Tempest Williams does in "A Letter to Deb Clow": *I write to, I write because, I write against, I write as, I write out of, I write knowing, I write past, I write by, I write when ...* Make room for contradiction, directness, hyperbole, understatement, metaphorical language, associative logic, brashness, confession, or any other modes of expression.

D. Challenge yourself by establishing a technical rule for writing a flash piece, such as limiting yourself to using only one vowel for the entire piece or setting a syllable count for each sentence. Or try a drabble (100 words), a dribble (50 words), or hint fiction (25 words). Another example could be to write a prose abecedarius, a form where each sentence begins with a word in alphabetical order: Apple, Boy, Coca-Cola, Darwin's finches, and so on.

E. Borrow the recurring phrase "There was the time" from Karen E. Bender's "The Man Who Hated Us and Then Forgot," and do a free write that uses that phrase in each sentence or paragraph as a touchstone. If it helps to have a subject, think of naturally repeating situations: getting lost, getting sick, having an argument, falling asleep, waking up, moving in, leaving town, starting a new relationship/school year/job.

F. Build your own flash sequence. You might write a collection of lines, sentences, or fragments that explore a single topic, a series of lyric scenes that are emotional twins of each other, a set of mini portraits, prose poems linked by a single subject, a cluster of flash fiction, or flash nonfiction pieces that create a collage. Aim to use precise word choice, rich imagery, and complex sound patterns and sentence structures. The sequence challenges you to compress and expand at the same time. Each piece should feel individual, complete, tight. Though the pieces should be able to stand alone, they should also feel like they build on one another when they are read together. Your reader should feel a magnetic attraction between pieces. Choose a topic that asks you to look at it from many different perspectives: observe, wonder, sneak up on, run away from, declare, denounce, doubt, shake, poke.

G. Write about a familiar activity or hobby in a series of brief scenes that illustrate what is happening around the periphery of the activity or hobby. In other words, the activity stays the same, but the background changes. Consequently, the character or speaker subtly changes in each scene too. Look to Michael Wasson's "Small Meditations" as an example of this approach.

H. In Michael Wasson's piece, "Small Meditations," the speaker contemplates times he played basketball as a way to cope with difficult feelings. Consider the following passage: "Alone again. I'm searching for that sound—rattled board. The beauty of *all net*. Netless emptiness." Wasson slides from the painful emptiness of grief to the healing emptiness of something beautifully well done in four short sentences. We might think of the strategy as a "sentence sandwich." See if you can write one core sentence that identifies a search for something. "I'm searching for . . . " Then, sandwich it between sentences that wrap around that idea in similar but slightly different ways. Two kinds of emptiness, or beauty, or tenderness, or touch. Two kinds of anything you want to show. Think about using different sensory details to move from emotion to image or feeling tone to physical sensation.

One-sentence workshop

The following exercise will help you practice the art of brevity:

In *Style: The Basics of Clarity and Grace*, Joseph M. Williams defines six principles of concision that can be used to intensify your writing, one sentence at a time. They are as follows:

1. Delete words that mean little or nothing.
2. Delete words that repeat the meaning of other words.
3. Delete words implied by other words.
4. Replace a phrase with a word.
5. Change negatives to affirmatives.
6. Delete useless adjectives and adverbs.

Test these principles out on the sentence below, then try them out on your own writing:

Not saying anything at all expresses incredible intelligence and insight; nevertheless, despite this fact, not many individuals choose to avoid talking.

As you work through your sentences, ruthlessly cut everything that resembles the **sesquipedalian**, a gorgeous word that tells as it shows, and means the quality of being long-winded or using excessively long words. As you learn what to cut, you will begin to hear the power that is already in your prose. Here is the original translation of the above exercise by a writer from the Islamic golden age, Al-Bayhaqi: "Silence is wisdom though few are silent."

8

Beg, Borrow, and Steal

Relevant readings

"My Grading Scale for the Fall Semester, Composed Entirely of Samuel Beckett Quotes" by Matt Bell

"Boy at Night" by Steve Coughlin

"Letter to a Funeral Parlor" by Lydia Davis

"Instruction, Final: To Brown Poets from Black Girl with Silver Leica" by Nikky Finney

"A Modern Fable" by David Ignatow

"8 Meetings Nobody Scheduled" by Alex Carr Johnson

"Life Story" by David Shields

"go-go tarot" by Evie Shockley

"An All-Purpose Product" by Patricia Smith

"The Box" by Thomas Tsalapatis

"The Inventory from a Year Lived Sleeping with Bullets" by Brian Turner

"Scheherazade." by Lucy Wainger

Flash interview with Steve Coughlin

Steve Coughlin is a writer who lives in Chadron, Nebraska. We chose "Boy at Night" for the anthology because we love the way he blurs the real and the imagined in the text to overlay the daily world with a haunted one. The images and the quiet restlessness of "Boy at Night" stay with the reader the way a good piece of writing should. By the end of the piece, the boy is haunted, and so are you.

How do you define the kind of short-form writing that you do?

I find myself trying not to define it. "Boy at Night" was originally published in *Gulf Coast* as a lyric essay (flash nonfiction) but later appeared in my collection of poetry, *Another City*, as a prose poem. In this sense the piece has enjoyed multiple identities. What excites me about short-form writing is its ability to challenge traditional genre expectations and allow for a greater sense of mystery. Short form's fluidity, its ability to resist a clear identity, provides an excitement that keeps me returning to it.

How does your approach to writing in short forms differ from the other kinds of writing that you do?

At times in my writing I can be tempted to over-explain myself. However, when writing in short form, my language becomes more concise, lyrical, and metaphorically driven. Instead of feeling the weight of explaining everything to readers, I let white space fill the gaps. For those of us who can be a bit wordy at times, short form offers a good opportunity to strip down our language to produce a stronger, more compelling voice.

What demands does the short form make of its writers or readers?

If short form tends to emphasize for writers the use of technique (metaphor, imagery, voice, etc.), the same demands are also placed upon readers. Though existing in a consolidated space, short form requires a deep appreciation of language and craft for writers and readers alike.

Free dive

Without fail, your uncle carries his pocket knife. Your grandfather keeps a harmonica on the fireplace mantel. Your mother wears a St. Christopher's medallion on a chain around her neck. Or picture your favorite musician, soccer player, actor, or someone else you admire, and identify an object you associate with them. Throughout world religions there are emblems or attributes that represent the qualities of deities and saints. For example, Athena, Greek goddess of wisdom, is frequently shown with her owl. Hanuman, the Hindu monkey god is often shown leaping midair, to represent the transoceanic leap he took to serve Lord Rama. Choose a relic, artifact, or other object that represents someone you admire. Imagine stumbling upon that object (the smaller, the better) and describe the mystical influence that it might have on you or others. Allow as much magical realism into the story as you wish so that you can describe not just the object but the significant place it holds in the world.

Vignette: Terra incognita

I have never seen all of my father's tattoos. Out of my peripheral vision, I catch an unfamiliar glimpse of a maple leaf or scythe-glint of blue kimono that disappears under a cuff. I see a metaphor I can't quite decipher, and then it's gone and we are talking about the benefits of all-wheel drive vehicles.

The winter my mother was diagnosed with uterine cancer, my father's body flash burned, a chaparral wildfire. She listened to the prognosis and booked a pre-op appointment. He swallowed a Vicodin, unbuttoned his plaid shirt, and settled into the chair for Bill, his tattoo artist. Dad and Bill talked through as much pain as my father could tolerate—kids, grandkids, microbrewing, surf breaks. After my father's needle-punched torso (followed by shoulders, arms, and flank) were covered with a piece of gauze, my father must have shrugged carefully back into his shirt, shook Bill's hand, and walked into the glare of neon and streetlight. Day after day, session after session. The months wore on.

My mother's swollen and stapled post-op abdomen shrank and healed into a jagged scar. My father's body smoldered into a dragon, a koi, a rising phoenix, a tsunami, a geisha. What images am I missing? I have no idea.

My father has always been a reticent man who withdraws into house chores and helps anyone who needs it, whether they want help or not. I can still hear the whisk of the broom on blacktop as he swept the driveway each Saturday morning of my childhood. He is Johnny to his mother's sisters and their kids, John Humble to his buddies, and John—plain John to everyone else. He always wore slacks and freshly-polished wingtips on weekdays, jeans and grass-stained work boots on weekends.

When they were teenagers on their first date, my mother cut her foot on a piece of beach glass. My father stripped off his shirt, wrapped up her bleeding foot, and carried her back to the car. And in the fifty years since? Once a month, my mother places a chair for him on the porch, drapes a towel over his shoulders, and cuts his hair.

Each of us has to learn for ourselves about those icy plunges into the open seas at the edges of the world—those unknown places where human love takes us. Here be dragons, the earliest map makers used to warn. There is so much I can't know. But, I can tell you this: my father's tiny elderly aunt still pats his grizzled cheek and exclaims, "Johnny!" when she leans in for a kiss. And, when I ask my father his tattoo artist's name to make sure I've remembered it right, he says, "Do you want me to book you an appointment? I could ask him a favor. He'd fit you in."

—Heather
Word count: 470

Be a hermit crab

Like the hermit crab that inhabits the cast-off carapace of larger crustaceans, short-form writing is a small, vulnerable piece of language that frequently creeps into another shell for protection. Brenda Miller and Suzanne Paolo have described this tendency in creative nonfiction as the "hermit crab essay." It may borrow the form of a list, letter, fable, newspaper column, advertisement, joke, memo, Q&A, fairytale, or dictionary entry as demonstrated in many of the works in our anthology. It may steal directly from its source to create a found short, such as Matt Bell's "My Grading Scale for the Fall Semester, Composed Entirely of Samuel Beckett Quotes." It begs the reader to accept it on its own terms while leaning on the scaffolding of the familiar.

This chapter addresses how the successful employment of this strategy means taking familiar characters or situations and placing them in unfamiliar contexts, or placing unfamiliar concerns and motivations within familiar forms. This chapter demonstrates how familiarity creates shortcuts that permit the writer to go farther than the word count would otherwise allow.

Forms to borrow, steal, and make your own

ABC

As the first organizing structure for language that we learn, the alphabet shapes our understanding of the world. The phrase "from A to Z" is another way to say we've covered everything. Bookstores, encyclopedias, directories, indexes, and libraries all use the alphabet to order massive amounts of information. Short-form writers can use the alphabet to activate the reader's earliest memories of language, to create a sense of order and logic, or to produce surprise by upending expectations of this familiar building block of literature.

One of the oldest forms of poetry is the **abecedarius** in which the alphabet serves as the beginning of each line or stanza, a variation of the acrostic poem. Short-form writers can use this structuring device in prose by beginning each sentence or word in a piece with a subsequent letter of the alphabet. You can also try a reverse abecedarius (Z-A). Matt Bell's "My Grading Scale for the Fall Semester, Composed Entirely of Samuel Beckett Quotes" is not an abecedarius, but it does use the first six letters, traditionally associated with grades in school, to create a scaffold for its borrowed language. The basic grading scale combined with the sophisticated quotes from Beckett, known for his avant-garde contributions to fiction and drama with works such as *Waiting for Godot*, generate an interesting tension that reassembles the known into something new. See also **definition**.

Advertisement

A classic short-form model of the advertisement as literature is this one, attributed to Ernest Hemingway: "For sale: Baby shoes, never worn." These six words pack a powerful punch because they suggest so much. Why were the shoes never worn? Are the shoes so ugly that the baby refused to wear them? Is this a futuristic society in which shoes, baby shoes in particular, are a valuable commodity? There are likely more reasonable guesses you could make, but you get the idea. The language of advertisements surrounds us: slogans, billboards, junk mail, infomercials, pop-ups ads, and on and on. The structure for an advertisement can be easily borrowed and adapted for use in short-form writing. Advertisements, just like flash writing, aim to hook your attention, be quick and to the point, persuade you of something, and stick in your mind.

You must do more than just mimic a radio announcer or replicate a funny commercial to make this borrowed form effective. Find a way to twist the expected into a new shape. Try to sell something that no one wants. Write ad copy in the voice of a frustrated poet. Recreate a memory that includes a slogan from a specific time to set the scene. Desire is at the heart of both literature and advertisement. Let this shared motivation guide your exploration of the ways this familiar, omnipresent form of communication can be used to shape creative work. See also "An All-Purpose Product" by Patricia Smith.

Aphorism

"Life is short, and art long; the crisis fleeting; experience perilous, and decision difficult," quips Hippocrates. The Aphorisms of Hippocrates, written in 400 BCE, present us with one of the earliest examples of short-form creative nonfiction. An **aphorism** is a pithy, memorable, sometimes witty stand-alone statement of fact or opinion. The word "aphorism" comes from the Greek *aphorismos*, meaning definition, which comes from *aphorizein*, meaning to define or set limits to. Not only was Hippocrates's *Aphorisms* a collection of definitions about illness and treatment, but it defined a way of writing based on limits.

A contemporary usage of the aphorism can be seen in Sarah Manguso's *300 Arguments*. Within it, she uses an aphorism to define the genre: "The smallest and shortest pieces of art strive for perfection; the largest and longest strive for greatness." Manguso's aphorisms stand on their own in the tradition of "wisdom literature," yet they progress through the friction of brevity and accumulation. What makes them nonfiction is their intent to convey a truth or idea, and what makes them creative is Manguso's artful and surprising distillation of this personal truth.

Writers in the short form can put a contemporary spin on the classic structure of the aphorism using these basic patterns to package their ideas and make them more memorable (Table 8.1).

Autobiography/biography

Selectively quoting from the aphorism by Hippocrates above, we know that "life is short." How fitting, then, to write about one's life (**autobiography**) or

Table 8.1 Common patterns and purposes of aphorisms

Pattern	Purpose	Example
X is Y	Declaration through comparison	An ounce of wisdom is worth a pound of wit.
X is not Y	Declaration through contrast	A flow of words is no proof of wisdom.
X is better than Y	Ranking through contrast	It is better to forget one's misfortunes than to talk about them.
X is Y and Y is Z	Linked comparison	Everything has its time and that time must be watched.
X and the opposite of X are one	Oxymoron	A great gap may be filled with small stones.
X is to Y as Z is to Y	Balanced comparison	Love is strong as death, jealousy as cruel as the grave.
X is Y, but Y is not X	Comparison through linked reversal	No man can be happy without a friend, nor be sure of his friend till he is unhappy.

Source: R. Christy, comp., *Proverbs, Maxims and Phrases of All Ages* (New York and London: G. P. Putnam's Sons, 1887).

the life of another (**biography**) in the short form. There are a couple ways you can steal from this genre. One way is to reference the genre in your title, as Amy Hempel does in her one-sentence "Memoir." In memoir, readers expect representative moments and memories that tell the story of a person in time. In autobiography and biography, readers expect events, chronology, and narrative of a person through time. Time is the common thread in both approaches to creative nonfiction, and it becomes a tool with which you can play around with readers' expectations.

Writing your own obituary is a popular assignment in both journalism and English classes, and it provides an urgent framework for the short form as well. How do you capture a life in a few column inches? People do it every day. Pick up your local paper and read through some of the obits. Notice what is said and not said about the person who has passed. What story is told between the lines? Here we have all the ingredients for a dramatic story: death, a deadline, and a grieving family paying by the word.

Push against the conventions of the form and see what happens when you confront your own mortality.

Another way to experiment with this form is to write your own biographical statement. You can use the bios in the back of this book for the standard conventions of this brief form. In general, bios are written in third person (he, she, they) and include information about the individual's employment, credentials, publications, hobbies, and residence. You'll need one of these if you publish, but you can also play around with the form to tell a micro life story.

One writer who excels at this is Michael Martone in his book *Michael Martone*. This book collects fictionalized bios that originally appeared as contributor's notes in literary journals. His pieces, while still short, defy many of the expectations of biographical statements by wandering off topic, breaking tone, blaming his mother, and exceeding the limits of the standard bio length (usually around 50 words). Yet each piece remains faithful to the form (and to each other) by consistently opening with the same phrasing: "Michael Martone was born in Fort Wayne, Indiana ..." Try creating an imaginary bio for yourself by turning yourself into a character whose accomplishments and accolades suggest a story that is more complicated and expansive than the form would typically allow.

Character sketch

For a moment, picture an artist at an amusement park who does rapid-fire cartoon sketches of people for money. Certain attributes (like your ears) get exaggerated, while others are de-emphasized. The transaction is fun, but it would be a hard sell to call it *art*. In short-form writing, however, a sketch is not just a hasty representation of a character's physical attributes. Author David Galef, in his book *Brevity*, explains that a "character is potential action." If that's the case, then a character sketch will show the character in action or about to act. Shivani Mehta's "the invisible girl can be anything she wants when she doesn't want to be invisible" tackles a challenging subject for a character sketch. Because the subject cannot be seen, we are instead presented with a list of things she chooses to become when she does not want to be invisible: "A snow leopard, a tree, an owl ... bats, dragonflies." We learn about the subject through what she sees, what she yearns for, and what she once was. This can be an effective strategy to push you beyond physical description.

While a character sketch certainly can focus on physical characteristics, the description by Mehta shows us how complex and rich a character sketch can be when there is a limitation that invites tension into the depiction. Try writing a sketch where the character is described through just one of the senses. What smell does your character love or hate? What kind of music moves your character? Show your character eating alone—so much can be learned from that simple act! As you write, keep in mind Galef's equation of character and potential action: describe your character in the process of deciding to act, and see if you can make this moment stand on its own as a story. See also "Self-Portrait as a Chimera" by Natalie Diaz.

Confession

The **confession**, one of the oldest forms of nonfiction writing, can be traced back to St. Augustine who wrote his thirteen-volume *Confessions* in 400 CE. In its original context, confession referred to any kind of religious speech, not just the revelation of wrongdoings, and St. Augustine's collection is written in this mode and functions as a spiritual autobiography. In more contemporary work, we can see how the religious aspects of confession give shape to Danielle Cadena Deulen's "For My Sister in the River." Deulen's piece opens with an epigraph, a Bible verse. Within the first sentence, the speaker confesses her "sin": "I was trying to be cruel when I threw the rhododendrons in her hair." The real offense, however, becomes clear, decades later, when the speaker's sister shows up at her door with a split lip and swollen eye. Deulen's confession pushes against the traditional pattern of the redemptive narrative echoed by Christian hymns: *I once was lost but now am found.* Instead, the sisters find each other, forgive each other, and are the source of each other's salvation.

The act of enumerating one's failings to gain forgiveness provides a powerful framework for the short form. While St. Augustine's confessions are the exception, most confessions are brief, private, and fraught with emotion. Take a cue from Deulen's piece and describe a minor misstep or slight offense with the gravitas of St. Augustine. How many times can we be saved through the telling of a story? See also "The Box" by Thomas Tsalapatis.

Collage

In art, **collage** is a method for combining different materials to create something new. A literary collage accomplishes this same effect, but with words, phrases, images, or memories. This kind of composition pairs well with the short form because it can be challenging, though not impossible, to sustain in a longer work. David Shields's "Life Story" demonstrates the collage method through his assembly of bumper stickers.

During a class visit to one of Stephanie's creative writing classes, David Shields explained how he sees arrangement as the primary creative force in his work. He described his piece as "appropriated material deliberately arranged." By collecting and ordering bumper stickers, by placing them near each other or in contrast with each other, Shields makes something new that suggests a larger story. Try this method yourself by choosing a topic that intrigues you and begin collecting bits of text or information about your topic. The key to success is to gather more than you need. As you assemble your materials, play around with placement until you find an order that suits you. Shields organizes his bumper stickers by labeling it a "life story." You will need to find the metaphorical glue that can hold the pieces together.

Definition

A **definition** explains what something is through description, classification, comparison, and contrast. We know what an "orange" is because it is a fruit, not a vegetable. It is round and can be held in the palm of one's hand. Its color is orange, not red. Its taste is sweet, which distinguishes it from bitter oranges. Even without consulting a dictionary, we go through this process to define what we know about the world. Definitions are designed to be short and to the point, and as a result they align well with the formal constraints of flash writing.

The opening of Tomas Tranströmer's "Icelandic Hurricane" has the feel of a definition that has gone through a poetic storm: "Not earth-tremor but sky-quake. Turner could have painted it, lashed tight." You won't find this kind of language in the dictionary or on Wikipedia. Instead of a precise, direct, and clear explanation, this piece provides an impressionistic definition of the scene and the observer. You can also see definition at play in Ada Limón's "The Quiet Machine." By listing the different kinds of quiet, Limón defines the machine and shows us how it works. While definitions are intended to be definite and answer the reader's questions, these pieces push back against the form by allowing space for mystery to coexist with knowledge.

Dream

Our dreams offer a wealth of creative material and inspiration, if only we can remember them. Psychologist Jacob Epson, in his book *Sleep and Dreaming*, writes that the average person has three to five dreams a night, with some people having up to seven. These dreams tend to be fragments from our daily lives reconfigured during the REM-stage of sleep. Various researchers have suggested that recollection of dreams is more likely when the material is strange or novel, when the dreamer is woken up during REM sleep, or if the dreamer records his or her dreams in a journal. Most people remember, if anything, a moment, a feeling, or a brief scene rather than a sweeping epic. But this can be enough to jump-start a creative project.

While dreams have been part of literature since the beginning, you will see them frequently in the short form. The dream is what allows Augusto Monterroso's classic "The Dinosaur" to reach beyond its eight words both into the past and into the future. When the main character wakes up, the dinosaur is *still* there. One reading of the word "still" is that the dinosaur was a part of the character's dream that becomes real when the character woke up. The confrontation of the human with the monstrous projects a conflict into the future that we as readers can only imagine. The crossing of boundaries, from dream stage to waking stage, makes this moment even more compelling.

There are many ways you can make artful use of your dreams. First, we recommend keeping a dream journal, jotting notes when you first wake up to capture those fleeting images and sensations. Chances are the more you record, the more you'll remember. A dream dictionary can be a fun way to explore and interpret dreams and to expand their potential within a story. If you don't remember your own dreams, then listen closely to others' dreams. Consider how these absurd stories create windows into the inner lives of others.

Fable

As one of the oldest short forms, the **fable** is a brief story that teaches a lesson, typically through nonhuman characters. As far back as the sixth century BCE, Aesop's fables explored encounters between animals, such as the "Tortoise and the Hare" or the "Ant and the Grasshopper," to comment on and bring to light human shortcomings. These stories survived the centuries, first by being passed along as part of the oral tradition, then by being written down and translated to become some of the most pervasive and far-reaching stories of any literary tradition. The rhetorical purpose the fable was to teach a moral, which perhaps explains its brevity. Being short meant that the fable could pass on a single principle with maximum impact. The fables, therefore, were portable, not just in the memory of the storyteller, but through generations of storytellers.

Though originally told by and for adults, these instructive tales were adapted in the seventeenth century for a younger audience, and over time became associated more with children's bedtime stories than with ancient folklore. Yet the fable has survived because it serves not just to entertain audiences and teach a lesson. The original hybrid tale, the fable uses fictional devices to make a critical and often pointed observation about reality and truth. In fables, not everything is as it seems. The weak can become powerful. The slave can become the master. The great can be overcome. Flaws are exposed. Lies revealed. And all this is accomplished in a few hundred words.

The fable's humble origin is one reason that the form holds so much potential for the short-form writer. Because nothing much is expected of the simple form, the opportunity for surprise is that much greater. The fable form is like an old, comforting blankie. We associate it with childhood and storybooks and simple lessons. But you can wrench away the expectations of this form to reveal something entirely unexpected. Just take a look at the way David Ignatow works with this tradition in "A Modern Fable." Here are some common characteristics of the fable that you can adapt to the short form:

- A moral (before the story/after the story/embedded within the story)
- Anthropomorphism (animals or objects behave like humans)
- Competition and conflict (winners and losers)
- Dialogue (establishes the situation and relationship between characters)
- Recognizable characters, setting, and situation
- Worlds collide (Title: The _____ and the _____)

Writers in this tradition are often called fabulists. Russell Edson, whose work is included in your anthology, called himself a fabulist. According to John Gardner, author of *The Art of Fiction*, "the fabulist—the writer of nonrealistic yarns, tales, or fables ... must have firm and predictable characters." He explains further, "A talking tree, a talking refrigerator, a talking clock must speak in a way we learn to recognize, must influence events in ways we can identify as flowing from some definite motivation." Apply Gardner's advice as you experiment with fables for the contemporary reader.

Fairytale/frame story

If you've heard of "Ali Baba and the 40 Thieves" or "Aladdin's Lamp," then you already know a little about *One Thousand and One Nights*, the classic collection of Middle Eastern and South Asian stories and folktales.

Originally written in Arabic during the Islamic Golden Age (eighth to thirteenth centuries), the stories were first translated into English in the eighteenth century.

A compelling frame story holds together the individual stories collected in *One Thousand and One Nights*. In the frame story, a king is driven mad by the infidelities of his wife. He sentences her to death and is convinced that all women will betray him in the same way. To protect himself from the potential of infidelity, he marries a virgin and then has her killed the next morning. He does this over and over until there are no virgins left in his kingdom with the exception of the beloved daughter of the king's trusted advisor. Scheherazade (pronounced She-HERA-zadee) offers herself in marriage to the king, meanwhile assuring her father that she has a plan. On the night of their marriage, Scheherazade begins to tell the king a tale but leaves the end unfinished. She does this again and again, perfecting the literary device of the cliffhanger to save her own life by entertaining the king.

The frame story can be interpreted in many ways, but Ira Glass, radio host for *This American Life,* has an interesting take on it. Glass describes how, through the successive telling of these stories to the mad king, Scheherazade restores his sanity and empathy, and he eventually spares the woman's life. The stories essentially transform a monster back into a man. You might see why this interpretation makes sense to a man who makes his living from telling stories. The transformational power of story is an important theme in literature, obviously, so you will find it in short-form works as well. Lucy Wainger's "Scheherazade." not only references the character in this tale but also mimics the cyclical nature of her storytelling.

Drawing inspiration from Wainger's example, take a famous character from history, literature, or myth, and place them in an unexpected situation. Describe them in a way that captures something essential about their character or fate, but do so without letting their story be seen in any familiar way. Commandeer the character for a completely unexpected portrait.

Instructions

When you want to make a soup, you follow a recipe. When you want to find a new coffee shop, you follow directions. When you want to assemble the power saw you got for your birthday, you follow the assembly manual, carefully. If the instructions are written well, you get what you want. If they're not, well, at best your dinner's ruined or you're lost. At worst, you lose a thumb.

Because instructions are so pervasive, so purpose-driven, and so (we hope) precise, they are ripe with potential for the short-form writer. The numbered, incremental steps provide structure. The parallelism of the commands offers an authoritative voice. The progression toward completion gives a sense of movement and motivation. You can use these conventions as the raw materials for a short-form piece. One approach is to write instructions that defy the orderly logic of the typical "how-to" guide. Another might be to write a recipe for something inedible. Use commands to examine how to do or be or live. Use lists of rules, questions, associations, allusions, and images to show the complexity—or impossibility—of your subject.

Nikky Finney does this precisely in "Instructions, Final: To Brown Poets from Black Girl with Silver Leica." Her steps are not numbered, but the command is clear: be, be, be. Charles Baudelaire also provides esoteric instructions in his classic, "Be Drunken." He gets carried away with the repetition of his lyrical instructions, as if he, too, has had too much to drink. In both pieces, you can feel the pull of the familiar voice telling you what to do countered by the mystery and beauty of the language as it subverts your expectation. See also "Short Lecture on Your Own Happiness" by Mary Ruefle.

Inventory/list

The inventory and list are two kinds of everyday writing that can be used with fascinating results in the short form. An inventory is generally a catalog of items that enumerates what is present. A list can also be an inventory, but just as often it can function as the opposite of an inventory, a documentation of what is needed and therefore missing. For example, an inventory of your kitchen cabinets will indicate how many cans of soup you have; a shopping list will indicate how many cans of soup you need to buy. Both the list and the inventory are fragmentary by nature. Often, they are written in short phrases that are just enough to trigger the memory of the reader. A list implies something unfinished or in progress. A catalog suggests a desire for control and knowledge. Using these strategies creatively can produce surprising results.

Try it yourself: draw on Brian Turner's "The Inventory from a Year Lived Sleeping with Bullets," and write a list in which you catalog all of the details you can from some specific period of time. Include objects, brief clips of memories, glimpses of scenes, snippets of dialogue, phrases, slang, and characters captured in the midst of one single action. Catalog the emotions, events, memories, expectations, and commands that infuse that period of time. Remember that even the best lists often fail to include everything. Intentionally leave something obvious off your list to increase the tension in your piece. See also "What You Are" by Katelyn Hemmeke and "8 Meetings Nobody Scheduled" by Alex Carr Johnson.

Letter

A letter provides a unique framework to experiment with a form that is simultaneously public and private. The conventions of letter writing—including salutations (or greetings), closings, and postscripts—lend formality and composure to a genre that otherwise can be quite personal. From the intimacy of love notes to the niceties of business communications, the letter offers a range of styles and tones that can be creatively adapted. As part of a genre called **epistolary literature**, the letter joins other kinds of writing that span the private and public spheres, including diary and journal entries and, in more recent years, emails, blogs, and tweets.

"A Letter to Deb Clow" by Terry Tempest Williams is an interesting example of short-form writing as a letter. The repetition of "I write … I write … I write … " can be so incantatory that it's possible to lose sight of the opening question posed by a friend. The ending reminds us that the letter's author is responding in the early hours of the morning. This context expands the piece from personal manifesto to a shared expression of the author's deepest motivations for writing.

The body of this letter does not behave like a typical letter. It moves more like a dream, making associative leaps from one statement to the next. Yet what holds these individual declarations together, beyond rhythm and personal drive, is the fact that they are gathered together as an expression of love for a friend. The title's use of "a" letter as opposed to "the" letter suggests an ongoing exchange between friends, not a singular event. The relationship between friends frames and strengthens this piece about the power of writing. The letter form can help you visualize your audience as a single individual, which allows the writing to be more focused, specific, and intimate. See also "A Letter from Home" by Jamaica Kincaid and "Letter to a Funeral Parlor" by Lydia Davis.

Vignette

In the mid-eighteenth century, publishers used design elements to frame short works in magazines and books. These graphic designs came to be called "vignettes" because they resembled vines growing between a book's sections. Later, this term was applied to the text itself, bordered on all sides by this decorative element. In this textbook, we use the vignette as a framing device at the beginning of each chapter. We've attempted to remain faithful to the form's illustrated origin by focusing on images and storytelling to convey our ideas.

A **vignette** is intended to be self-contained narrative and to fit on a single page. It's a good choice for writers who want to use the page as a formal constraint. If you experiment with this form, imagine vines crawling along the page's margins, marking the boundary for your imaginary world.

Conclusion: Extreme restriction and a note of caution

At this point, you might be asking, *What can't the short form do?* Now you're thinking like a writer! Perhaps you could write a prose sonnet in fourteen sentences. Why not a prose haiku? Some of our favorite short-form writers have created their own forms and unique restrictions to pressurize language and produce surprise. One example is Robert Olen Butler's *Severance*, a book of short pieces written in the voices of people from history who were beheaded. Based on a nineteenth-century French physician's assertion that the human brain remains conscious for a minute and a half after beheading, Butler limited himself to 240 words, the rate of speech for a person in a state of heightened emotion. Evie Shockley is another; she explained in an interview with us that "the writing [in 'go-go tarot'] appears to have line breaks, because it is broken into stanza-like chunks, but in fact, it is prose that is filling in a visual structure. The sections are meant to evoke tarot cards, as if laid out for a reading. The sentences are thus breaking purposefully with regard to the visual design, but arbitrarily with regard to language."

The short-form experiments are great, but beware of when brevity goes bad. Just as adding more words to a lackluster story is unlikely to make it better, cutting words from a lackluster story won't automatically produce mystery and intensity. Brevity begins at the sentence level, but even here we can run into trouble. Sometimes extreme compression, often showcased in newspaper headlines, creates an unintended two-headed creature. For example, take a look at these "two-headed headlines" from Richard Lederer's *Anguished English*:

- GRANDMOTHER OF EIGHT MAKES HOLE IN ONE
- TRAFFIC DEAD RISE SLOWLY
- WILLIAM KELLY, 87, WAS FED SECRETARY

These unintentionally funny headlines are the result of rushing to meet a deadline. When it comes to short-form writing, we caution you to avoid making a connection between fast writing and flash writing. Just like whiskey, the maturation process for the short form can take years. In the meantime, read voraciously, experiment, and keep your eyes open for ways to distill language into its finest expression.

9

Finding the Funny

Chapter Outline

Relevant readings

"Cookie Monster on the Dole" by Henry Alford

"The Cat" by Matthew Clarke and Coco Harrison-Clarke

"Letter to a Funeral Parlor" by Lydia Davis

"The Prose Poem as a Beautiful Animal" by Russell Edson

"Dumped: Seven Cautionary Tales" by Molly Giles

"Pleasant, healthy-appearing adult white female in no acute distress" by
    Jennifer Richter
"Life Story" by David Shields

Flash interview with Matthew Clarke

Matthew Clarke is a writer, actor, and director from Alberta, Canada. We
chose "The Cat" for the anthology because of the way he handles humor
with a few swift lines of dialogue. Plus, it's fun to see the way compressed
writing can be transformed into multimedia projects like a web series.

How do you define the kind of short-form writing that you do?

It's screenwriting. Web-series, or short-form digital series, or whatever
it's being called now. It's fiction, but also draws heavily from real stories,
so it's a bit of a hybrid. I usually think of it as comedy. It is often somewhat
absurd and/or satirical. I often try to balance irony with sincerity. I try to
craft complete narratives within the short time I have.

*How do you think writing for a visual medium like YouTube is different than
writing for print?*

On YouTube you are dealing with an audience with a very short attention
span, so you need to captivate them right away. In print, they're reading,
so it's a higher-brow audience right off the top. It's also very visual, so most
importantly it's less about your prose and more about how what you are
writing will translate visually on screen. In print, there's an ability to savor
the language more, while on YouTube, you're really just trying to set up the
joke and knock it down as efficiently as possible.

*Do you have any insights into how you mix dialogue and action in a screenplay
for a three-minute webisode?*

I think as far as the writing of it goes, it's very much like a long-form
screenplay. It's the same approach and format, just shorter. But I always try
to be as efficient as possible with both my dialogue and action in a short-
form screenplay. As best I can, I like to reflect the desired pace of the filmed
episode in the writing. Being as clear and concise with your action is helpful.
I also think the action is where you can have fun with your prose a little bit.
Not to be indulgent but as a way of communicating the tone. Nobody wants
or needs a ten-line description of someone getting a drink of water in a

screenplay, but you can use that brief action description as an opportunity to convey your voice as the writer, which is harder to do in character dialogue.

How much editing to you have to do to shape the conversations and the humor to maximum effect in a screenplay? What does your revision process look like?

I try not to revise or alter the conversation very much at all. It's often just a process of trimming the fat, so we can zero in on the clearest and funniest part of the conversation. The thing about our show is that the conversations themselves are often quite unremarkable and boring. They only come to life when we place them in the absurd context of happening between two grown men instead of between a child and parent. So, when I'm working on the script, I'm always imagining the visual representation of what will be happening. And that is not something that can really be conveyed on the page. It's something that lives entirely in the imagination until it is brought to life on the day of filming. It is a unique challenge for this show because it's not something you can really fix in the script. You write it and hope that it will land when you see it played out on screen, but you never really know for sure until it's too late.

Free dive

Take ten minutes and make a list (of words, situations, historical figures, certain breeds of dogs, and so on) that make you laugh even though there's nothing inherently funny about them. Or make a list of times you laughed unexpectedly or inappropriately (at a funeral, in your sleep, alone in your car, during a test). Don't get into explaining why. That's another story. This exercise is all about recognizing humor as more than the obvious punchline or the comedian's practiced tirade. What makes us laugh and why we laugh can be as complicated as asking "What is art?" or as ridiculous as "Why did the chicken cross the road?" Each item on your list contains a story that may or may not be funny. Explore one: set the scene, use dialogue, and keep it short.

Vignette: Dead frogs and rooftop dolphins

E. B. White once wrote in the preface to A Subtreasury of American Humor *that "Humor can be dissected, as a frog can, but the thing dies in the process and the innards are discouraging to any but the pure scientific mind." This quote resurrects a disturbingly vivid memory from my seventh-grade biology class where I, a conscientious objector, diligently labeled and color-coded a worksheet of frog anatomy while the boys in my class hurled frog eyeballs at each other behind the teacher's back.*

They certainly found the entire frog-dissection process hilarious.

Now, as an adult who has occasionally been accused of being funny (but never to my face), I find myself intrigued by the multiplicity of topics that make people laugh. It's not always what you'd expect. Take, for example, this knock-knock joke, courtesy of my seven-year-old:

Iris: Knock-knock.

Me: Who's there?

Iris: Dolphin.

Me: Dolphin who?

Iris: Dolphin on the roof eating a cookie!

Iris: Do you get it?

Me: Not really.

Iris: Well, dolphins are funny. And a dolphin on a roof is really funny. And a dolphin on a roof eating a cookie is really, really funny!

Me: Oh, I see.

For my daughter, humor is all about extreme displacement of what's expected. The joke begins with "dolphin," a word she finds innately funny. Perhaps it's the mouth-feel of the word, starting with "doll," a familiar word to a child, that transforms from humanoid figure (itself a bit strange, when you think of it) to animal with the addition of the silly word "fin." Doll-fin. Now put it on a roof and give it a cookie, and you have the makings of a joke.

Maybe.

What is funny to a first-grader has more to do with the upheaval of order, the invention of a new combination of characters and actions. In my attempt to improve her joke-telling skills, I've had her read other kinds of jokes, but it's clear that she doesn't yet fully understand the nuances of wordplay. We're working on it. Right now, it's about mastering the call and response, of knowing what to say and when to say it. Humor is secondary to participating in the speech act of the joke itself. It is a social interaction that depends on context and timing. This exchange reminds me that even in its simplest forms, a joke must be taught. And even when it is taught, there are no guaranteed laughs.

Every joke requires a leap of faith. You have to be able to imagine the dolphin on the roof eating a cookie. You have to take the risk of crossing the road with or without a good reason. You have to find the funny in a dead frog. You have to knock on the door and hope that somebody's home to open it for you.

—Stephanie

Word count: 470

The soul of wit

"Brevity is the soul of wit," or so says notorious windbag Polonius in Shakespeare's devastatingly unfunny *Hamlet*, you know the play where almost everyone dies by the final act. This oft-repeated snippet of wisdom serves as a reminder that cleverness and concision go hand in hand. The original adage, however, was delivered by a character who was neither clever nor concise. The irony of this statement in the mouth of such a rambling, long-winded character can be seen when you take a step back and look at the quote's context:

> My liege, and madam, to expostulate
> What majesty should be, what duty is,
> What day is day, night night, and time is time,
> Were nothing but to waste night, day, and time;
> Therefore, since brevity is the soul of wit,
> And tediousness the limbs and outward flourishes,
> I will be brief. Your noble son is mad ...
>
> (*Hamlet*, act 2, scene 2, lines 86–92)

As a student of short-form writing, you can take Polonius's speech as an example of what *not* to do. The bloated, indirect, and redundant language distracts from the most important information. The multiple abstract questions ("what duty is ... what day is day") that frontload the speech is a classic stalling device. Even so, the connection between wit and brevity can be instructive for writers who want their words to pack a punch.

This chapter distinguishes between wit and humor, with **wit** being a more intellectually driven cleverness and **humor** a more body-driven or situational peculiarity—think wordplay versus fart jokes. Both make writing more memorable, relatable, and just plain fun.

When writing under constraints, wit can help you make more out of your limited word count. Edward Hirsch defines wit in *A Poet's Glossary* as "the ability to make quick, clever connections with verbal deftness, to perceive the likeness in unlike things, relating incongruities and thus awakening the intelligence." Another poet, T. S. Eliot, describes wit as "a tough reasonableness beneath the slight lyric grace." In both, you can see the multiple layers of perception that shape wit.

Humor can quickly establish connections between a character and audience by humanizing the character. In previous chapters, we advise going deep instead of going long by using metaphors, allusions, and multilayered images to give each word more weight. In this chapter, we want you to consider how levity can enhance brevity.

Your funny bone

We know what you're thinking! You don't have a single funny bone in your body, right? No problem. You don't need to be a stand-up comic to recognize and reap the benefits of the absurdities that are part of everyday life. Humor can be honed through careful observation; it's not just about jokes, roasts, and dirty limericks. In fact, research into the psychology of laughter shows that we are more likely to laugh at ordinary exchanges than purposeful punchlines. Laughter is often the byproduct of relationships, whether that relationship is between two people who find themselves in the same place at the same time, or between a writer and a reader however distant in time or place. Laughter is a social exchange with an evolutionary advantage: it reduces stress and builds connections between people and ideas.

In case you think that literature is no laughing matter, think again. Throughout history, serious writers have explored the full spectrum of comedy, from the bawdy sex jokes of Geoffrey Chaucer to the self-deprecating sarcasm of David Sedaris. Effective humor writing requires the writer to be specific, get to the point quickly, and tell a good story from a unique perspective. All this will benefit you as a writer in the short form. Combined with sharp observation and sensitivity to context, these skills can be cultivated to make your writing stick in the reader's mind for longer than the few minutes it takes to read.

Where to start?

The free write at the beginning of this chapter asked you to make a list of words, situations, and historical figures that you find funny. If you haven't done this, take a moment to jot down a few words that bring a smile to your face based on their sound rather than their meaning. Then ponder this list of **synonyms**, words of approximately the same meaning, and debate which word of the pair sounds funniest (Table 9.1).

Say the words out loud if you're on the fence. You'll feel silly, but that's the whole point! In our experience, the typical native English speaker will likely find more to snicker at in the words in the left-hand column. This has very

Table 9.1 Comparative humor of synonyms

Cake	Dessert
Kid	Child
Underpants	Underwear
Zit	Pimple
Bonanza	Windfall

little to do with the dictionary definition of the words. In general, people find words funnier with harsher sounds such as the /k/ in "cake" and "kid," or with less common sounds such as the /z/ in "zit" and "crazy." In most of these examples, the "funnier" word is also shorter, so we suspect that the punchiness of the word itself has something to do with its comedic factor. But what about "underpants," you ask? What makes "underpants" funnier than "underwear," or "undergarments" for that matter? On this one, we'll defer to the indisputable wisdom of Matt Groening, creator of *The Simpsons*, who determined that underpants (the word) was 15 percent funnier than underwear. So there you have it.

To use humor in your writing doesn't mean you have to start with something funny. In fact, humorous writing often covers the same serious topics of other styles of writing. What distinguishes humorous writing, then, is the playful treatment of a serious topic that is relatable yet distant enough that we can laugh comfortably about it. As Mel Brooks explains, "Tragedy is when I cut my finger. Comedy is when you fall into an open sewer and die." Comedy takes the ordinary and shows us something unexpected, strange, or extreme that jolts us into a new awareness. Comedy is about a certain kind of amplification, one that is supremely uncomfortable and strange in a deliberately exaggerated way. Comedy reframes the familiar awkwardness of human experience and gives us just enough perspective that we can see its humor.

Comic treatments

How do you make funny happen in your writing? We'll discuss three comic treatments that underlie many jokes, late-night skits, and even the short-form writing in this anthology.

The first treatment is what we call "The Extreme." A writer can start with an ordinary topic, such as a child asking for a pet in "The Cat" by Matthew

Clarke. To expose the humor, the writer pushes the situation to the extreme. This approach uses a variation of the **benign violation theory** proposed by authors Peter McGraw and Joel Warner in their book *The Humor Code*. In their examination of what makes something funny, these writers found that "humor is caused by something potentially wrong, unsettling, or threatening." As they explain in their book, the world is made up of things that are funny and things that are not funny. These two categories overlap in a gray area they call "benign violation." This kind of humor relies on pushing boundaries, taking things right to the edge and flirting with taboo. In "The Cat," the scene ends with the daughter sneaking into the parents' bedroom and getting caught holding a pillow. A little girl wanting a pet cat is benign. Murder is the ultimate violation. But a little girl contemplating suffocating her allergic father because she wants a pet cat so bad is an example of benign violation. And we laugh.

The second treatment is called "The Surprise." In life, there are many kinds of surprises. There's the frivolous surprise of people leaping out from behind the couch to celebrate your birthday. There's the life-altering surprise of the unexpected pregnancy. There's the off-putting surprise of having someone sneak up behind you. There's the sarcastic, eye-rolling surprise of the I-knew-that-was-going-to-happen. As writers, we need to be aware of the different ways we can surprise our readers and the different effects these surprises produce. To use this treatment, start with something average and turn it upside down, flip it, or give it a twist. Here again, we can use "The Cat" as a model. Just as "The Extreme" depends on the writer finding the perfect balance between acceptable and unacceptable, "The Surprise" depends on timing. The child asks for a pet and the father says he's allergic. No surprise. The child then asks if they can get a cat when the father dies. A little surprising, but still within the range of normal. Finally, the child asks the mom if they can get a cat when the dad dies, and the mom replies casually in the affirmative. Surprise! The timing of the repetition and progression toward the final surprising response is what makes this scene work.

The final treatment is called "The Clash." In this approach, you can start with something serious, dull, or common, and introduce a clashing theme or action. This treatment is known by a few names: juxtaposition, dissonance, antithesis, tension. The friction created by two opposing ideas is what generates the spark of humor. We can use "The Cat" again to demonstrate this treatment as well as show that good writing isn't a one-trick pony. In the web series, Coco is played by a full-grown man dressed in little girl clothes.

The humor is at first simply visual, but the continued incongruity between appearance and action is what makes this sight gag work episode after episode. This clash exposes the ridiculousness hidden within the everyday. The punchline happens when two different ideas, traveling along their separate paths, collide.

There are of course many, many other ways to be funny, and these treatments alone will not inject humor into lifeless prose. A playful approach to writing requires you to not take yourself too seriously, to step back, to look for novel connections, and to cultivate an impeccable sense of timing and audience. In other words, practice, practice, practice. These treatments, however, can serve as a starting place for your search for what's funny.

"What if"/"yes, and"

It should come as no surprise that jokes mirror narrative storytelling by having a beginning, middle, and end. In humorous stories, the beginning often sets up the funny premise or absurd concept, followed by a middle that involves complications or increasing tensions through conflict, mishap, or exaggeration, and the end arrives with a punchline that releases the built-up tension through laughter.

Writers in the short form don't have much time for exposition or world building, so the setup often declares a situation that immediately requires the suspension of disbelief. You can think of this as the "what if" premise or the "just trust me" technique. In the Russell Edson poem from the opening pages of this book, the "what if" situation is the mating of a giraffe and an elephant. While the title suggests that this hybridization is intended as a metaphor for writing prose poetry, the piece itself takes place in a laboratory where the offspring of this experiment is the subject of scientific scrutiny. You can see the tangential nature of this poem through these series of questions:

- What if I compared a prose poem to a beautiful animal?
- What if writing a prose poem is like mating two very different animals?
- What if those two animals were an elephant and a giraffe?
- What would that byproduct look like?
- What would happen if such a combination actually took place?
- What would people say about the experiment?

Finally, because this is a poem by Russell Edson, the last question might be: How can I push this to the most absurd extreme possible? Each step in this poem takes us away from the ordinary into a world that is, though still recognizable, progressively more and more strange.

This writing approach is similar to the "yes, and" technique of improv comedy. Imagine two people on a stage:

Joe: There's a giraffe and an elephant in the room.
Sean: Yes, and the giraffe and elephant have a baby.
Joe: Yes, and that baby is the strangest looking thing. Ever!
Sean: Yes, and scientists from all over want more of them.

The idea behind this technique is to embrace the idea ("yes") put forth by another individual and expand on it ("and") and to continue generating ideas in this way. A writer, at least in the early stages of drafting, must play both parts by producing the "what if" premise and the "yes, and" development.

In the Edson example, tension builds through odd pairings: prose/poetry, elephant/giraffe, writer/scientist. The release of tension comes with the scientist's exclamation that he wants to have sex with this creature in order to create a new beautiful animal. If this statement makes you cringe a little with its suggestion of bestiality, you're not alone. Humorists often push the boundaries of decency to get a laugh, walking a tightrope and succeeding only when they find the balancing point between what's generally acceptable and what's considered taboo. Edson, we think, gets away with this because the title transforms the entire scene into a metaphor. Even though the prose poem's wild assertions take us far from the original action of writing a prose poem, Edson bookends the piece by referencing the "beautiful animal" of the title. This circularity along with Edson's characteristic use of ellipses to end his piece produces a dizzying commentary on how desire perpetuates itself.

Timing, context, structure

Time is of the essence in flash writing, and in humorous flash writing, timing is everything. Mark Twain is often credited with this verbal equation about the role of time in comedy: "Humor is tragedy plus time." If you've ever had a miserable day but later found yourself laughing over the events with a friend, you know what this means. Evolutionarily speaking, we are hardwired to forget pain. Case in point: Would our species continue if women fully remembered the pain of childbirth? Probably not. And evolutionarily speaking, we are hardwired to seek comfort with others who think like us. For instance, we might laugh when someone describes a situation we've been in ourselves, simply because we know what it feels like. Laughter comes not from surprise but in having the familiar reflected back to us from someone who is not us. It's just what humans do. We take pain and repackage it into story, in part to connect and in part to survive.

While timing is important to writing effective humor, context plays an equally important role. Humor, like any art, is eminently subjective. What is a "benign violation" in one context may be straight-up violation in another. The black-and-white cartoons in the *New Yorker*, for example, embedded into the text of serious pieces about art and culture, are read with different expectations and in a different context than the Sunday morning funnies. In a similar vein, we believe that prose poems, flash fiction, and flash nonfiction—in that they are already considered a little "out there" and different from more traditionally structured literary works—have more opportunity to violate readers' expectations because, frankly, they don't know what to expect. And laughter is often the response to situations that don't match up with our expectations.

Consider the prank where someone coils a fake snake in a can that's labeled "nuts." If surprise and timing are like the spring-loaded snake waiting for an unsuspecting person to pry off the lid, then structure is the can itself that contains the joke's potential. A writer can always add humorous flourishes to a piece during the revision phase, but for humor to be the energetic force that unleashes your fake snake, you must compose with structure in mind. An expert joke teller knows how to frame the joke, when to pause, what to emphasize, and how to bring it to a quick and surprising conclusion. Nothing kills a joke like drawn-out exposition. The same holds true for short-form writing. Standard advice is to start as close to the end as possible. Diving into the middle of a conflict or scene is one way to use structure to activate your characters.

Molly Giles takes seven swan dives directly into the middle of dysfunctional relationships with her "Dumped" series. In just one hundred words, Giles creates tiny relationship wrecks that we can't help but gawk at. But there's more happening here than a bit of literary schadenfreude. Giles uses humor to sugarcoat the otherwise dark failures of these couples. Each couple has its unique tragedies, yet they are all predictably doomed. Giles pushes this to the extreme until we are prepared to accept anything, even the couple who stays together despite the many ways they fail each other.

An effective piece of short-form writing can function like a jack-in-the-box. As opposed to the joke can of "nuts" where we are intentionally misled, the jack-in-the-box is transparent: its name tells us what to expect. We read, and we crank the lever, slowly, slowly, as the tinny music plays out, and even though we know what's coming, we don't know when. Each turn of the lever increases our anticipation, so when the grinning puppet springs to life in front of us, we jolt. The delight is in the moment when the paragraph bursts open and reveals itself to be something else entirely.

The short form as trickster

The short form is well suited to humor because we don't expect much from the humble paragraph. It's the straight man of literature. Short-form writing, whether flash fiction, prose poetry, or flash nonfiction, is trying to sneak something past you. It crosses the borders between prose and poetry. Peter Johnson, editor of *The Prose Poem: An International Journal*, makes this comparison: "Just as black humor straddles the fine line between comedy and tragedy, so the prose poem plants one foot in prose, the other in poetry, both heels resting precariously on banana peels." The instability of the form and the upending of readers' expectations is what makes short-form writing so compelling. It appears to be one thing (easy, quick, simple, no big deal) but changes through tremendous and transformative compression into something more.

An example of the shape-shifting power of the short form is David Shields's "Life Story." On one level, this piece is a collection of bumper stickers both clever and mundane. You might chuckle at a slogan you've seen before. You might smile at a turn of phrase that's new to you. You may snicker at one of the more risqué in the bunch. But what makes this piece more than a clutter of clichés? Nothing, and everything. The "life story" this author is telling is not unique. But who is? We paste our personalities to the bumpers of cars because we want to be seen as different, and this desire is what makes us the same. We laugh or roll our eyes at bumper stickers because we recognize the sentiment. What unifies this piece is the singular way these abbreviated thoughts and punchlines are curated into a collection intended to represent a life. It is simultaneously funny, sad, and true.

Surprise, surprise

When we talk about **tone** in a piece of writing, we are referring to the writer's attitude toward his or her subject that is expressed through word choice (**diction**). Surprise can be produced by the incongruence between subject and tone. You can hear this incongruity in the opening sentence of

Lydia Davis's story "Letter to a Funeral Parlor." The opening line will come across to some readers as ridiculous: "I am writing to you to object with the word *cremains*." The formality of the business letter clashes with the seemingly minor issue of word usage. The opening line suggests a person who is making a mountain out of a molehill, and the disproportionality between the so-called offense and the letter writer's response prepares us to be amused. But as the letter writer ramps up, we realize the context for this word: the recent death of the letter writer's father.

The complaint retains a detached formality as it admits that the parlor's representative did not pressure the family to buy an expensive urn and that the deceased had previously been a professor of English. These bits of extraneous information function as illogical evidence in an argument that simply cannot be won. The incongruity of the earnestly polite tone with the obviously emotional situation clarifies the ridiculousness of the entire enterprise. Yet laughing at a person in mourning violates social norms. Reading another person's letter violates yet another.

Davis is a master of putting her readers into awkward situations where laughter is the byproduct of discomfort. Death is something most of us would prefer not to talk about, yet here is Davis's character, writing a letter of complaint about how death is discussed. The letter draws attention to language and the lack of subtlety with which we use words. The writer asks at the end to consider using "ashes" instead of "cremains." There's no resolution, just the standard closure for a letter. The predicament of this story is that no reasonable response can be made to this request. The letter dead-ends, leaves us with an image of ashes in the fireplace, of words used thoughtlessly, of the unanswerable question of death.

Why is this in our chapter about humor? Not only is Davis's piece an example of "The Clash" treatment, but it is a variation on the **shaggy dog story**, a narrative structure that uses an audience's expectations of narrative structure against them. The original shaggy dog story is about a boy who owns a shaggy dog and finds out that there are shaggy dog contests where he can show off his dog. He wins prize after prize until he gets to the final competition and the judge says, "That's not a shaggy dog." Don't worry if you're not rolling on the floor laughing. The whole purpose of this joke-like anecdote is that it builds anticipation through long-winded and extraneous details and then ends abruptly with no resolution. There is no punchline. The story falls flat on its face, and if you're lucky the audience laughs or squirms. The joke is that you are waiting for the joke and it never happens. It's a sad kind of funny, but it works for some of us.

Juxtaposition of the familiar with the strange is another way to explore humor in the short form. Many of you will immediately recognize the doctor's office in Jennifer Richter's piece "Pleasant, healthy-appearing adult white female in no acute distress." The title introduces the perfunctory language of medical charts. Anything but poetic, the title behaves like a label on a plain manila folder. The first line throws us into an entirely different situation with the surgeon's voice taking on an odd flirtatiousness. The speaker's internal conflict is embedded within the scene, which is both funny and not funny. While the scene is clearly located, the language is unsettling and invites the reader to do a double take. The tension in the scene increases with each clashing image or idea: comedy club/hospital, comedian/surgeon, up/down, happiness/sadness, laughter/tears, choice/inevitability. We're not rolling on the floor laughing by the end. But the piece uses the anticipatory structure of the joke to make a point about the inadequacies of the body, of healing practices, and of language itself.

Conclusion: Where jokes come from

"Surprise" originated from the combination of the prefix *sur* (over) and the root *prendre* (to take), meaning to "overtake." When we are surprised, we are overtaken. We are taken unawares. Something that was hidden becomes seen. Something that was not expected happens. Something that was considered impossible becomes possible. Our physiological response to surprise mimics fear: a sharp intake of breath, a widening of the eyes, a racing pulse. Our system is flooded with the adrenaline that triggers the fight-or-flight response. Fear is usually a response to the unknown. Surprise is a response to the transformation of the unknown.

Surprise is a cousin to fear. The reader needs to be overtaken, in a relatively short amount of time, by words, imagery, figurative language, syntax, movement. Without change, surprise is not possible. Or, if the expectation is change, the failure to change could become, ironically, surprising.

Speaking of change, by the time this book went to print, Stephanie's daughter, now eight years old, not only mastered the telling of knock-knock jokes but also began making up jokes of her own. Here's one of her first jokes that actually worked:

Q: Where does music come from?
A: Neptune.

Get it?

Exercises

A. List at least ten pairs of synonyms and test them out on friends to see which ones they find funniest. Trim your list to the words that get the most votes and use these words in a writing exercise. To challenge yourself further, aim to end your sentences with these funny words.

B. What's the most boring activity that you can think of? Get specific: not "brushing my teeth" but "excavating chunks of dinner from my bottom left molar." Exchange your activity with a partner, then write about a character (or in the voice of a character) who cares deeply about something boring. The goal of this exercise is to repurpose something tedious and turn it into something humorous.

C. Trust us, there's plenty to laugh about in your life. Keep a funny file in your journal that records moments of absurdity, surprise, and delight. Avoid the expected sources of humor: television, comics, movies, jokes, memes. Instead, look and listen for snippets of unscripted comedy.

Prompts

A. The humorous voice in Henry Alford's "Cookie Monster on the Dole" displaces a familiar childhood character into an uncomfortable adult context. For this prompt, take on the voice or personal attributes of a well-known character but disrupt one of the expected narrative elements of this character's story (setting, plot, point of view) to see what happens.

B. Create a dramatic conflict between what could be and what must be. Allow the tension between reality and desire to be a source of humor.

C. Begin with a piece of language that is automatically ridiculous, like a subject line for a spam email, an advertisement for the latest As-Seen-on-TV miracle product, or a tabloid headline. Then write about this claim or statement with absolute seriousness or conviction. Allow the humor to break through the serious facade.

One-sentence workshop

The following exercise will help you practice the art of brevity:

Every week, the *New Yorker* has a caption contest where readers try their hands at writing a punchline for one of the magazine's cartoons. An analysis

Figure 9.1 Dolphin on a roof eating a cookie. Courtesy of Alix Beckmann.

of captions that made the final cut showed that they were on average 8.7 words long and used a minimal amount of punctuation, proving that brevity is indeed the soul of wit. Additionally, researchers found that noteworthy one-liners stood apart from the rest by using imaginative imagery that related to an abstract concept not depicted in the cartoon itself. Try it yourself using the illustration in your book (Figure 9.1). We'll set the bar high, say, twenty. See how many captions you can produce that meet the criteria mentioned above: concise (fewer than nine words); minimal punctuation (but still punctuated); imaginative imagery; and unexpected word choice, so avoid "dolphin," "roof," and "cookie" in this case. Share your top two or three with your class.

10

Misfit Pleasures

Relevant readings

"Grip" by Joy Castro
"Self-Portrait as a Chimera" by Natalie Diaz
"What You Are" by Katelyn Hemmeke
"8 Meetings Nobody Scheduled" by Alex Carr Johnson
"Some Things about That Day" by Debra Marquart
"Surplus History" by Semezdin Mehmedinović
"Gravity, Reduced" by Kara Oakleaf
"On Miniatures" by Lia Purpura
"The Box" by Thomas Tsalapatis
Excerpt from "Four about Death" by David Young

Flash interview with Alex Carr Johnson

Alex Carr Johnson is an environmental writer who lives in Colorado. We chose "8 Meetings Nobody Scheduled" because we love the way it uses the list form and the expectations of agendas to confront the opposite—the wilderness that surrounds and includes the human species.

How do you define the kind of short-form writing that you do?

As I see it, the best compliment for any prose writer is to be called a poet. Short-form writing is the deliberate attempt to take on poetic considerations while still operating under the rules and strictures of prose. How can the writer elevate the rhythm? How can they use the space between the lines? How can they liberate the story from the page? The best short form finds answers to these questions.

How does your approach to writing in short forms differ from the other kinds of writing that you do?

I ask myself: how can I take every advantage of the audience's expectations? What cues can I give the reader so that they unwittingly do the work that the words can't? Specific forms help with this. I'm often drawn to lists, as I was in "8 Meetings Nobody Scheduled." Lists have an inherent chronology, a condensed narrative arc, which the writer can play with and twist and exploit. A reader expects a numbered list to have a predetermined beginning and end, an implied completion. Generally speaking, short-form writers have a particularly high incentive to exploit and subvert the archetypal forms within their genre of interest.

What demands does the short form make of its writers or readers?

The writer must roll the boulder of brevity to the top of the mountain. The reader must climb upon that boulder and leap.

Free dive

Creative writing students are frequently encouraged to write about what they know. For this free dive, we want you to write about what you do not know or what you thought you knew but didn't. Imagine a character who is missing an essential piece of information. Imagine an alien's perspective of something ordinary and try to describe the stranger's experience of the everyday. Filter out the "normal" as you write. Amplify the strange by allowing room for the unsolvable mystery, the rich details of the alien viewpoint. You can think of your piece as a Wunderkammer, a cabinet of curiosities. Look for ways to intensify the oddness through illogical comparisons or hyperbole. Spin out the narrative in slow motion or hyper-speed—whichever makes most sense to the experience—and contrast the strange with its opposite: the mundane.

Vignette: Talk to me (a Wunderkammer)

You've done this before, do you remember? Let two people sit side by side on a Ferris wheel. Let their knees touch. Let them have enough tickets to exhaust the pleasures of the midway. Mustard dripping off a corn dog, ping pong balls tossed into bowls of goldfish, darts exploding balloons, wet kisses behind the photo booth curtain.

*

More: even before the words come, a baby learns to sign for it. Let's name it as it is, then—necessary: I want you. To know. I need. More. More, more, more.

*

A porcupine caribou traverses a glacial ice field. Let mystery work its way. This way, perhaps.

*

Let's be real. Until 1910, in Hot Springs, Arkansas, African American bathhouse attendants were required to rub mercury on bather's syphilis chancres. Attendants had to provide their own gloves. After 1910, mercury rubbing was not "required." Don't be naive.

*

In Christie's Auction House, a fossilized elephant bird egg the size of a human head—no, imagine a bigger human head; say, your uncle's big old noggin— goes up on the auction block. Somehow, this is comforting: in a place you can find with a plane ticket and a map there exists an artifact of this desire to go on; its proportions are colossal. You want to hold it in your arms.

*

On the remote island of Nikumaroro, Amelia Earhart's blue leather shoe waited to be found. It was a terrible game of hide and seek. Even the shoe thought so.

In your childhood toy box: a soft green rabbit's foot, a rusty horseshoe, an alarm clock with Betty Boop in a black negligee and garter belt. Her puppy dog bobbed his head side to side: tick tock. Are you lucky? That's still up for debate.

*

Kiryat Yam, Israel: dozens of people have reported seeing a mermaid. She likes sunsets. Don't we all?

*

Amidst the landmines of the Demilitarized Zone between North and South Korea, endangered red-crowned cranes strut and loft with their heads thrown back in desire. Such a loud ballet, an improbable peace.

*

This is, and is not, how you do it. Heather, learn to make enough from not enough and not enough. Learn again, damn it.

*

Speyer Cathedral, Germany, year 1146: St. Bernard of Clairvaux prays before a painting of a nursing Madonna and child. He experiences the distinct sensation of breast milk spraying his lips. Do you understand what I am saying? A man feels something brush his lips as he kneels in the chiaroscuro light of dawn. It mystifies: hundreds of years later, we are still talking about it.

*

At this moment in the Florida Everglades, a ghost orchid trembles as a sphinx moth alights.

*

There. There it is. Don't ask how you know.

—*Heather*
Word Count: 454

A taxonomy of the strange

The web series *Tiny Kitchen* is a standard cooking show, except for one detail: it is presented at the scale of a Barbie doll. Viewers watch a pair of real hands make tiny wedding cakes, tiny Philly Cheesesteaks, and tiny lobster rolls on a tiny stovetop. The hands whip quail eggs and fry beignets over campfires, all tiny. The cook never speaks, and the camera never pans out to reveal the average-sized human cooking the miniature foods. The result is bizarre: the viewer recognizes the standard cooking show tropes but experiences them through the lens of an alternate, doll-sized reality. Yet all that changes is scale: the food, the recipes, the flame the food is cooked over are all real. The finished meal is laid out on a miniature table as if Barbie and Ken might indeed come along to eat it. The viewer's sense of reality gets distorted, and it creates a rebound effect on how we view real life. What makes the beignets and coffee we might sit down to enjoy so different from those awaiting Barbie and Ken beside a crackling campfire in front of their very own Airstream trailer? Are we simply living out a larger version of Barbie's dream vacation? *Tiny Kitchen* might be viewed as a bizarre fantasy role-play or a pointed social critique. It's hard to tell: it's both, it's neither, it's something else entirely.

At the heart of this chapter is the idea that something feels "normal," or it doesn't. Something fits, or it doesn't. At this disjuncture lies the misfit and its distinct pleasure. It's about letting the rhythm go off-kilter, distorting an image, or modifying tone to introduce uneasiness into the text. Often, it's subtle. The reader feels ever so slightly uncomfortable and doesn't know why. Engaging this strangeness can be a bit like flipping magnets to use the force of repulsion instead of attraction. The result is the addition of palpable currents of tension to a text. In short-form writing, elements of the strange work well because, like the circus sideshow, you don't have to maintain the illusion for long. You provoke the audience's curiosity then leave them wondering: *What was that?*

Awe is fraught with the paradoxical emotions of reverence and fear. This chapter seeks out the sublime power of **paradox**, a thing, idea or situation composed of contradictory elements. We explore ways to conceptualize the energy of the misfit in short-form work and how it produces strangely satisfying effects. Don't worry. You won't have to learn how to swallow swords or breathe fire to do it.

Let's begin by classifying the strangeness that frequently appears in the short form:

- The uncanny
- The surreal
- The amplified
- The simplified
- The distorted
- The miniature
- The juxtaposed
- The fragmented

The **uncanny** is Freud's term to describe what seems both familiar and strange. The mixed emotion makes us feel anxious, unsettled, and unsure: Déjà vu, for example, is uncanny. We experience something and while experiencing it we think: *Hasn't this happened before?* A simulacrum, or an imitation of a person or thing, triggers the sense of the uncanny. Take, for instance, the android prototype RB1 who is the love interest and "our hero" in Kathy Fish's "A Thousand Perfect Strangers." The story's inherent strangeness is enhanced by the collective voice of the narrators: the story is told from the perspective of the hundreds of other androids modeled after RB1. They report on his thoughts and experiences because they are connected to their own. The androids narrate RB1's intimate experiences with a God-like omniscience:

> What he wants to say is: You are everything, Research Assistant Gem. He wants to say it but he does not. His android heart beats faster. His android palms sweat. His synthetic autonomic nervous system tells him this is love. Or this is fear. His system is incapable of parsing the difference.

As readers, we feel disoriented. Whose experience is this? Where exactly is that boundary between the human and the artificial? What does this say about true love? And what is our role then as a reader? Are we simply feeling the artificially triggered emotions that light up our neural networks as we read about fishing the Platte River, getting puppies, and cozily living in a cabin off the grid?

The uncanny is closely related to what literary theorist Viktor Shklovsky called **defamiliarization**, the technique in art that makes the familiar seem unfamiliar. In the most basic way, defamiliarization slows us down enough to reconsider things we assume are givens, things that might be within the realm of possibility. It pushes us to ask: *Is this real?* *If not, what is?* David Young's piece evokes the uncanny. It begins:

> I get your instructions in a letter. A small plane drops me at an airfield in the Andes. I stand by a rusting hangar, watching it climb out of sight. No one's around. Farther up the mountain animals I have never seen are grazing. Higher still a few clouds, resting against rocks.

First, the piece functions like a letter, addressing "you" the reader and reporting with odd urgency all that the speaker has been doing in response to "your instructions." The situation raises questions: *Why is someone stranded in the remote South American wilderness? Why has someone demanded they do this? Why is the speaker desperate, and for what? What kind of letter is this? A ransom note, a love letter?* We don't know. The atmosphere is charged with strangeness. The mountains are unpopulated—who knows how far it is to the next village or when the airplane might come back. Unknown animals are left to the imagination. Even the clouds move weirdly. Instead of floating, they "rest against rocks" as if at this high altitude they hover more densely. Six sentences in, it seems completely possible that, in this scenario, a lover might walk into view or an Ucu, the yeti of the Andes. Young's piece demonstrates the goose-bump thrill of the uncanny: everything in this world feels both familiar and alien. We want to know what is about to happen, but we are also a little bit afraid. This current of surprise runs through the text and provides a palpable electricity.

Short-form narratives often employ **surrealism**, a style of art and writing that mixes dream-like images, associative logic, and surprising contradictions. Pivotal short-form writers like Charles Baudelaire and Italo Calvino were essential to the surrealist movement that originated in the 1920s and drew on Freud's ideas about dreams and the unconscious. Calvino's "Thin Cities 5" demonstrates how surrealist imagery can captivate an audience with an unforgettably strange setting:

> Now I will tell how Octavia, the spider-web city, is made. There is a precipice between two steep mountains: the city is over the void, bound to the two crests with ropes and chains and catwalks. You walk on the little wooden ties, careful not to set your foot in the open spaces, or you cling to the hempen strands. Below there is nothing for hundreds and hundreds of feet: a few clouds glide past; farther down you can glimpse the chasm's bed.

A city made of nets and hammocks and chandeliers is set against the vast backdrop of space. The city dangles precipitously above a void of nothingness as if the whole universe surrounds the swaying rope ladders. The images force an unfamiliar perspective: the reader experiences precariousness. The vertigo lingers long after the story ends.

Useful distortion

Most writers in this anthology don't create whole new worlds. Instead, they make small adjustments to make average things ever so slightly strange. Kara Oakleaf's "Gravity, Reduced" gives a surreal glimpse of life on Earth where everything is recognizable, with one small difference—the law of gravity has shifted. She poses the question: *What if the forces of gravity loosened a little bit? What would happen? How would we cope?* Already familiar with images of astronauts floating in space, we may not find this too far-fetched, yet the situation is unfamiliar enough that Oakleaf takes us by surprise. She enacts the question by running a clear and detailed simulation of the scenario.

Amplification is a magnification technique that enlarges elements of the narrative. In "Gravity, Reduced," people cope by using Velcro, double-sided tape, and leashes. Loose change and babies float. Untethered household objects—silverware, scarves, dolls—drift through the house like restless spirits. The result leaves readers doubting their assumptions. Compressed texts often address hypothetical questions: *What if life were different? What if all the rules were suddenly changed? What then? How might it feel?* Then they dramatically present those hypotheticals in vibrant high-definition images. Amplification intensifies scenes and heightens how we perceive sensations, and that intensity creates a sense of mystery and wonder (Table 10.1).

Instead of magnifying elements of a text, a writer might take the opposite approach and simplify the elements. **Simplification** pares back a scene, image,

Table 10.1 Strategies for emphasizing elements of a narrative

Strategy	Effect	Example
Simplification	This strategy alters the reader's perception by making a subject or scene appear simple, uncomplex, or bare. The objects that appear seem heavily weighted and highly symbolic. The concentrated focus triggers hyper-awareness, alertness, or tension.	"Things you cannot find in a junk drawer: A whole culture. An entire language. A face that looks like yours." From "What You Are" by Katelyn Hemmeke
Amplification	This strategy alters the reader's perception by magnifying certain elements of a subject or scene to make them appear larger or more prominent than other elements. The amplification often evokes a sense of wonder, mystery, or magic.	"The back of her knee: a blessed territory, I keep my wishes there." From "Natalia" by Ilya Kaminsky

or narrative to present a deliberately spare perspective. Life is complicated, so readers naturally expect complexity. Simplification serves as a focusing device in a narrative. Take "The Cat" by Matthew Clarke, for example. The premise is simple: Coco, his daughter, wants to get a cat. The dialogue is simple too: "You want a cat?" "Yeah." "What would you do with a cat?" "Well I'd snuggle them and kiss them and stuff." But tension brings complexity. This conversation is about the compromises we make when we live together, the ways family members have different and sometimes incompatible desires, and about a glaring truth we'd rather not think about: we don't live forever. The scene strips away all the drama of grief and heightened emotions that we expect when we talk about mortality and presents it as a casual chat. Clarke glimpses this when he sees how nonchalantly his wife and daughter would replace him with a cat. All it takes is a dose of a kid's blunt honesty for an adult to be reminded that the world doesn't revolve around them. Not even close.

Simplification and amplification are both techniques used to distort the perceptions of the reader. **Distortion** misshapes or otherwise alters the reader's perception so that it is experienced in an uncommon way. Sometimes the distortion is subtle, as in "The Cat." And sometimes the distortion is more dramatic. Sherrie Flick's "Dinner Party" distorts the narrative in a slightly different way: she blurs the narrative as if viewed through an out-of-focus lens. It begins: "The smart people at the dinner table murmured, 'Hmm. Mmm? Hmm.' While the middling people added, 'Blah. Blah. Blah. Blah.'" Notice how nothing is quite defined in this scene. The characters are not individualized—they are viewed as groups at the dinner table. The conversation is muffled as if overheard from the next room. We hear clinking dishes and murmurs. The overall effect is softly out of focus and impressionistic.

Another useful distortion is **tonal distortion**, in which the writer alters the tone of a text to alter the reader's perception of what occurs. A writer might employ a few forms of literary humor when doing this. **Satire,** a form of humor that uses irony, bathos, or sarcasm to lampoon foolish behavior, can be seen in Henry Alford's "Cookie Monster on the Dole." Alford's piece satirizes contemporary politics by using an insatiably greedy character from a children's television show to talk about the dysphoria felt about the US government after the 2016 election.

Irony occurs when a character says one thing but means the opposite or when a situation takes an incongruous turn. Irony is often felt in the dissonance between expectations and reality. Karen E. Bender's "The Man Who Hated Us and Then Forgot" documents years of spiteful behavior from an angry neighbor. The irony comes at the end, when the neighbor suffers dementia, forgets that he has loathed his neighbors for a decade, and becomes polite again.

Juxtaposition places unlikely objects side by side. Tomas Tranströmer's "Icelandic Hurricane" juxtaposes a butterfly's fluttering with the heavy drag of a barge to capture the oppositional experience of a winter hurricane. **Bathos** describes a rapid shift in tone from the sublime to the mundane. Bathos often borrows the strategy of juxtaposition to achieve that rapid plummet from high to low. In less experienced hands, bathos can be cloying and manipulative, yanking at the reader's heart strings too roughly. But we can see in this example from Lydia Davis's "Letter to a Funeral Parlor" how, when the speaker abruptly shifts the subject from her father's remains to a pooper-scooper, it feels like plunging straight down on a roller coaster:

> In fact, my father himself, who was a professor of English and is now being called *the cremains*, would have pointed out to you the alliteration in *Porta Potti* and the rhyme in *pooper-scooper*.

The use of bathos in this passage makes the reader nauseous—which captures one of the overwhelming sensations of grief pretty accurately.

We can also see an example of this in Semezdin Mehmedinović's piece, "Surplus History." Mehmedinović, a Bosnian writer, documents how living in war-torn Sarajevo affected his sense of the normal:

> People died then, too, only death is more stripped down these days: the lore accompanying death is a lot less eerie. The wrapping on the carton from which I've just taken a cigarette is actually documentary material. Because of the paper shortage, the tobacco factory uses any leftover materials they can find: the wrapping might be toilet paper or even from a book so that in the leisure time tobacco affords you can read fragments of a poem or the ingredients in a bar of soap ... The cigarette I am smoking now was wrapped in a paper confirming someone's death: the cause of death is written on it, and you can see the signature and official stamp of the physician. I admit that this is the last piece of paper a cigarette should be wrapped in; at the same time, I must admit that there isn't much left that can shock me.

Mehmedinović's piece shows a man taking a cigarette break in the war-ravaged city of Sarajevo. Supplies are so scarce that cigarettes must be wrapped in a range of oddly inappropriate recycled paper. Philosopher Christopher Yates says, "Juxtapositions reposition." The juxtaposition of a death certificate with the trivial stuff of everyday—toilet paper and cigarettes—illustrates the powerful tension inherent in bathos. When we see from a new position, we gain new perspective. Mehmedinović's piece also reminds us that distortion is not necessarily about distorting the truth. Sometimes it is about contrasting incongruous objects or applying the right filter to catch the best quality of light or tone for a piece of writing.

Fragmentation and atomization

Juxtaposition leads to our final misfit: the fragment. You'll notice right away that fragmentary writing feels different from other kinds of short-form writing. Fragmentary texts, like the vignette at the beginning of this chapter, arrange shards of images, broken scenes, or isolated lines into a mosaic. It uses juxtaposition to arrange side-by-side pieces of scenes, lyric images, obsessive thoughts, and philosophical questions. The fragment builds upon its brokenness and uses associative logic to create unity out of pieces. It's a shy form—one that is decidedly reluctant to be known in a straightforward or direct way. It defies easy summary or characterization. For all these reasons, the fragment is a compelling form to work in. It does not adhere to strict dictates of narrative conventions or linear thought and instead drifts, darts, tugs, and wanders.

The fragment can be traced back to aphorisms, maxims, and early English riddles, but it also shares similarities with the **ghazal**, an ancient form of Urdu poetry composed of couplets, or two-line stanzas meant to stand alone as well as work associatively with the others. The ghazal embodies paradox: the subject is often divine or romantic love, but it can also refer to the final death cry of a gazelle. This form addresses love and death, communion and destruction. The lines do not rhyme, but they may build upon the repetition of a word or phrase. The ghazal also often contains a hidden "signature," a line where the author introduces his or her name to the piece. These characteristics are in the vignette at the start of this chapter as well. When writing the vignette above, Heather began with stealing the nonliterary form of a Wunderkammer, a cabinet of curiosities filled with natural specimens, scientific oddities, and historic artifacts. Before the prevalence of public museums, Wunderkammers functioned as personal collections, full of the wonders and mysteries of the world. As Heather wrote, she had to accept the natural resistance of the different pieces bumping up against one another. Each section of the Wunderkammer exists separately, side by side, like artifacts in an exhibit. But they also contain similarities that explore themes of desire, mystery, and luck. The differences, oppositions, and contradictions of the pieces can trigger doubt in the writer: *What on Earth am I doing? Where is this going? How am I going to rein this in?* The trick is you can't. You have to go with it and let the fragments lead the way. The fragments are your breadcrumb trail through the page's sometimes beautiful and sometimes eerie wilderness.

Brian Turner's "The Inventory from a Year Lived Sleeping with Bullets" and Michael Wasson's "Small Meditations" both have fragmentary qualities. Turner's piece is a list built out of "torture fragments." "Small Meditations," on the other hand, consists of six scenes arranged around basketball. The strangeness in both comes when the different scenes butt up against one another with no beginnings, no endings, and no buffers. Fragments reject traditional plot elements such as exposition and transition, which clarify the narrative for the reader.

Imagine a fragmentary text acting like atomized water droplets found in fog. When you walk through fog, you can sense the droplets suspended in the air, touching your skin, and entering your lungs as you breathe. Composed of discrete molecules of information, atomized narratives maintain an amorphous, semitransparent shape and can be sensed like an enveloping mist. Fog obscures details, softens hard edges, and cloaks objects in a shadowy anonymity. It can also amplify sound or isolate objects close at hand.

Conclusion: The art of miniaturization

Short form's miniature scenes are often dioramic, a still life of a frozen moment contained in a shoebox-sized space. Like dioramas, these scenes also draw clear boundaries and an up-close focus. The limited space produces a high-definition clarity on the items that can fit inside. As Lia Purpura describes in "On Miniatures," these miniature worlds demand attention: we look and keep looking. The story's world seems to end right there at the wall of the diorama—there is no world beyond the white margins of the page. As a writer, you must pay attention to the contained space of your text: only so many objects can fit, only so much action can be captured. You must choose wisely: What objects will you fill the space with? What landscape or scene might fit? How might the reader experience the time and space within the narrative and measure it against their own?

Exercises

A. Notice how you feel when you encounter strange elements in the relevant readings. In a small group, discuss whether the surprise is entertaining or pleasurable. How does the defamiliarization alter your perspective so that you see the subject in a new way? In what way does the topsy-turvy world provide insight on the real world?

B. "This is not a pipe" reads the text in surrealist René Magritte's painting *The Treachery of Images.* Create a definition of a person, place, or thing by declaring all that it is *not.* Do not name your subject. Then share your list with your classmates and see if they can guess what it is. Talk about what happens when you describe your subject through negation.

C. This exercise has three parts: (1) Using Natalie Diaz's "Self-Portrait as a Chimera," write your own self-portrait that begins each sentence with "I am … " (2) Bring the completed self-portraits to class and post them on the wall. Walk around the room reading your classmates' self-portraits and record your favorite lines. (3) Assemble your favorites into a collective self-portrait for your class.

D. Write instructions for a basic task and defamiliarize the task by translating it through several languages using Google Translate before returning it to English. Share the results aloud in small groups.

Prompts

A. Using "The Box" by Thomas Tsalapatis as inspiration, take an object and distort it by making it enormously big or absurdly small. Contrast it with another object to give it a sense of scale. Then see where it leads. What are the consequences of this distortion? Follow your story wherever it goes.

B. Think about a time when something felt inexplicably strange—a moment when moving through time felt like moving through honey, or a period when the normal laws of physics did not apply, or an event that defied all of your expectations or sense of logic. Try to describe the strangeness of the event while structuring it in a very logical and organized way. See, for example, Katelyn Hemmeke's "What You Are" or Alex Carr Johnson's "8 Meetings Nobody Scheduled."

C. Write your own self-portrait, in whatever way you want to be seen. You may present yourself as a mythological creature or as a collage of creatures as Natalie Diaz does in "Self-Portrait as a Chimera." You choose: you're in control of your audience's gaze. What do you want them to know?

D. Play the game, "If you could have dinner with anyone dead or alive, who would it be?" Imagine a conversation with someone you've always wanted to talk to (God, Einstein, Steve Martin, Catherine the Great, Gertrude Stein—anyone you'd like). Then, write the scene.

E. David Young's excerpt from "Four about Death" feels like a postcard from the Twilight Zone. Write a narrative where the speaker tells "you" about a strange and otherworldly place they visit. Mix a description of the landscape and inhabitants with a description of the speaker's feelings and actions in a way that reveals something about the relationship between the speaker and the one they are addressing.

F. Write a counter-narrative by taking a familiar subject and talking about it in a way that defies or undermines the expectations, stereotypes, or conventional takes on the subject. Take one of the "rules" of our world and shatter it. For inspiration, reread Kara Oakleaf's "Gravity, Reduced."

G. Practice antithesis: create a piece that uses opposition or contrast to create tension and energy. Look at Ana María Shua's "Cannibals and Explorers" to see what happens when two opposing forces face-off.

H. Your brain is full of errata and odd bits of information. Right now, you might be thinking about something you heard on the radio, some video you watched late last night when you should have been sleeping, an overheard snippet of conversation, a long-ago memory. Capture the scraps you are fixating on and develop them. Turn your attention inward. What are you thinking about, imagining, or questioning? Even if they feel like mere wisps of ideas, write them down. Skip lines between each idea and image. Notice where your thoughts go, and write down each new idea as it comes to you, continuing to skip lines. Pocket your list and continue to collect random images, ideas, statements, and memories for a day or two. Don't have an agenda when you collect your scraps of ideas. Let them be—the connections will become clear later.

I. Think of a time when you found yourself saying, "But, wait—" or "That isn't how it was ... " or "Wait a second, what is going on here?" Zero in on that unsettling feeling—not the looks on people's faces, not the official story, not the given facts. Document what seems out of place. Look for the traces of evidence that something isn't quite right, and see if you can capture it through images, sounds, sensations, facial expressions, or micro-gestures. You might describe through contrasts: what you expected versus what really happened, what you knew versus what you didn't know, what you learned versus what you unlearned, or what happened right before versus what happened right after.

One-sentence workshop

The following exercise will help you practice the art of brevity:

Katelyn Hemmeke's piece, "What You Are," uses the parenthesis to imply important connections between two pieces of information without stating it directly: "One of the first things my (ex) boyfriend told his siblings about me: 'She's Korean, but adopted, so basically white.'" The ex in parenthesis implies something much different from either of these two possible variations:

1. One of the first things my ex-boyfriend told his siblings about me . . .
2. One of the first things my boyfriend told his siblings about me . . .

The parenthetical aside implies that although he was her boyfriend in the moment, the relationship might as well have ended right there when he uttered that sentence. The alternative sentences don't have the same implication. The parenthesis can be a powerful tool for packing layers of information into a sentence. Try it yourself. Use parentheses to imply cause and effect. Bonus points if you can write a sentence that uses the parenthetical subtext coupled with dialogue to capture a person's character or lack thereof.

11

Not So Fast! Strategic Revision

Chapter Outline

Relevant readings

"Hill Street Blues" by Bryan Fry
"On Miniatures" by Lia Purpura
"A Letter to Deb Clow" by Terry Tempest Williams

A flash conversation on revision

We asked the writers we interviewed, "What are your biggest concerns when you revise?" This is what they had to say.

Cut it down

"When I revise a piece of flash fiction, I aim to hew it to the bone. If a draft is 1,500 words, I try to get it to 1,000. If it's 700, I aim for 500. Streamlining helps me understand what the story really wants to be about, and where I've been overly indulgent in style or exposition. The way I think about revision is akin to sculpting. If I want to write the Eiffel Tower, then the first step is being honest about my draft's resemblance to a giraffe. I look for the tower within the giraffe and set about trimming the ears, aligning the base, carving out the filigree. I may not succeed in replicating the elegant tower of my dreams, but I get as close as I can, trying to make every word support the structure of the piece until taking even one away might trigger its collapse." —Katie Cortese

"I love the idea of revision as sculpture. The *thing* is in there, but it's hidden by all the excess." —Alex Carr Johnson

"My revision process is mostly about pulling out any excess. Like Mary Oliver, I think of poems as journeys; when writing, I'm placing stones in a river for my reader to walk across. In revision, I'm figuring out how many of those stones I can remove—encouraging my readers to make leaps without losing them along the way." —Jennifer Richter

Ask for more

"Oh my, there are so many concerns. Does the story escalate with tension? Is each word necessary? Does the ending carry the story outward in a breath? Shorts don't leave much room for imperfection—like a gymnast's landing, the ending has to nail it." —Grant Faulkner

"My biggest concerns when revising short form revolve around climax and denouement. What are the subtleties at play here? What does this say about the narrator, or what does this say about the world of the narrator? How do we prolong the dream of a short piece that is, like life, so brief?" —Nancy Jooyoun Kim

Weigh each word

"I think revision is also a matter of those 'demands' a short piece makes on you—making sure every word is essential and carrying its weight in the story. I could have gone on a long time imagining different pieces of this world, and I did in the first draft [of 'Gravity, Reduced']. But as I revised, I realized I had certain lines or images that felt repetitive because they were too similar, and too much of the same thing weighed the story down.

I also frequently write out of order in early drafts, so one thing that I focus on in revision is getting the sentences, the paragraphs, in the right order. Especially in a piece like this, where I knew I wanted the individual images to shift the mood of the story gradually as it moved toward the end." —Kara Oakleaf

"[O]ne of my biggest concerns is making sure I don't use more words than needed to convey an idea. Beyond that, I also make sure the words that remain are the most powerful, most beautiful they can be. I frequently trade out nouns, verbs, and adjectives for ones that I think are more profound or convey a more vivid image." —Sarah Evans

Listen closely

"I pay close attention to sentence level decisions. Word choice, punctuation, rhythm, cadence. I do a lot of reading aloud in the final stages of the work. I also want to successfully compress a world, not just show a tiny slice of something. I think of craft elements and how I can use them, even in the tiniest ways to make my worlds more complete. Dialogue, character, setting: I want them to be as fully realized as possible within the word count restraints of the piece." —Sherrie Flick

"The revision process is its own process for a reason. My re/vision involves the musicality of language. The mouth-feel of it. So I read aloud at different paces and with different silences. A major revision calls for a complete overhaul of the vision—the piece's body—to *see (itself) again* under a possible transformation. When I can't find the right *touch*, I write it again, with the older piece at my side for brief reference." —Michael Wasson

"[Revision is] getting it right for the ear—making sure there are no bumps. Syncopation, sharpness of images, tone … " —Sven Birkerts

"I revise for rhythm and sound, with short pieces I can read the entire piece aloud from beginning to end without a break, and I do, dozens of times before I'm finished. I revise for precision and concision—word choice.

I revise for symbolism and structure. Revision is the only part of writing I enjoy—generation is often rather painful—which is why I love the short form. The painful part is over soon enough." —Justin Torres

"To find the right word and put it in the right order. Sometimes it seems that there is more than one choice and that is the biggest trap we have to deal with. As Mark Twain said: 'The difference between the almost right word and the right word is really a large matter—'tis the difference between the lightning bug and the lightning.' The poem is always in constant danger of being killed by a lightning bug." —Thomas Tsalapatis

Test the limits

"[Revision involves] the politics of language, because nothing is innocent. Each word should be stripped naked to be understood fully, and since I'm a feminist, I don't want to recreate the linguistic shackles of gender oppression. Every word should earn its right to be a part of the flash fiction." —Pía Barros

"Sound and clarity. I revise for sound for starters. I read it out loud and make sure the sounds are hitting and the music is ringing. And next, I revise for clarity. A prose poem shouldn't confuse or befuddle the reader, but instead lean in and tell secrets. There's nothing stranger than the truth." — Ada Limón

"For a writer, no concept is more useful than Theory of Mind. When I'm revising, my task is to forget that I already know my story and to imagine what will happen in a reader's mind sentence by sentence. Having test readers and editors is very helpful, but ultimately the writer has to develop a talent for being able to misread his own text, and then correct the text to address those misreadings."—Bruce Holland Rogers

Remember what's critical

"I always worry about keeping the energy of the first draft as I hone the language in successive drafts. Because this form is so short, an unnecessary clause or sentence can sap the life right out of the piece." —Joanne Avallon

"I love revising. It's my favorite part of the writing process. Like many writers, I consider revising a form of play—I get to add, subtract, and reshape my work, not just with the intention of improving the piece but also with the intention of better understanding it. Yet as I revise I try to remember that it's important to not compromise the integrity of the original draft. Sometimes during the revising process a writer might discover that a piece needs to go in a different direction. However, this must be balanced with a recognition that whatever was the original impulse of the work, whatever flicker caused the writer to start putting down words, often has a fundamental connection to the work's ultimate success." —Steve Coughlin

Free dive

The writers above compare revision to sculpting a work of art, sticking a landing in gymnastics, revealing a secret, taking a journey, and more. Create a metaphor for your revision process (and perhaps draw a graphic to go along with it): what activity might you compare revision to? Do you feel like a baker making half-baked (or burnt) pastries? Like a chess player studying the board for the next ideal move (and perhaps never moving)? Like a patient getting a tooth drilled by the dentist? Do you think of yourself as a mechanic tinkering under the hood of a car? Find the best comparison to describe your process.

Gaming the draft

If you were to poll one hundred different writers, you'd get one hundred different responses about how they go about drafting and revising. On one end of the spectrum, you find writers like Allen Ginsberg advocating for spontaneity: "First thought, best thought." Then there are writers like Joyce Carol Oates who admits, "I revise all the time, every day." Despite the different styles and approaches, most writers *do* revise, often extensively as they shape and finesse a draft into completion.

William Zinsser says, "Rewriting is the essence of writing well—where the game is won or lost." Zinsser's comment reveals a useful way to think about the writing process: writing is a game. If you approach writing like a game—especially a sport—then it reminds you to apply strategies. With practice, you can build strength, skills, and endurance. You can learn to play well with team members and maintain a healthy sense of humor about failure. To clarify, we don't mean failure as the dramatic existential crisis that writers suffer where they think they are never going to "make it"; we are talking about the minor failures we face every time we sit down to contend with clunky sentences, mind-numbing clichés, flat dialogue, or other rough patches in the text. These are as common as sloppy moves on the court. It helps when we can shrug, fix what we can, and move on.

The writers of your textbook likewise have different approaches to the revision process. Stephanie has several tricks in the game of revision, but her number one tool is time. She sets her work aside for a day, a week, or more until she can return to it with a clear mind. Over the years, she's honed the skill of intentional forgetting so she can approach her work with more objectivity. This creative forgetfulness allows her to read the work not for what she wanted it to be but for what it is and what it can still become. Heather, on the other hand, relies on reading her work aloud and listening to it in order to gain a different perspective. She listens for hitches in the rhythm, places she loses her breath or stumbles because of awkward phrasing or long-winded sentences, and language that seems out of sync with the surrounding text. The habit of listening also means she tunes into the narrative in a slightly different way. Since she's taking it in aurally instead of visually, she notices when she gets bored or excited by how the language is (or is not) fusing together.

Ideally, the playful mindset of "gaming" your draft can trigger strategic thinking, which makes the revision stage more effective. Beginning writers often give up too early. They write something, push back from the desk, and revel in the afterglow of the new work. Many of us can relate to Dorothy Parker's statement: "I hate writing, I love having written." Undoubtedly, it feels good to produce new work. But more skillful writers rest for a moment in that excitement, take a breath, and then plunge in to see what else can be done to make it better. They invent, and then they keep inventing. In general, games get more technical, more nuanced, more rigorous as the player progresses. They require an experimental process of trial and error. Sometimes, a solution in one area causes disorder in another. A writer with a gaming mindset analyzes the situation, makes a move, and then moves on. Phrase by phrase, sentence by sentence, page by page.

Gary Lutz offers playful advice for thinking about how words should move together. In his essay "The Sentence Is a Lonely Place," Lutz sees sentence-building as a game of flirtation:

> The aim of the literary artist, I believe, is to initiate the process by which the words in a sentence no longer remain strangers to each other but begin to acknowledge one another's existence and do more than tolerate each other's presence in the phrasing: the words have to lean on each other, rub elbows, rub off on each other, feel each other up.

Do the words in your sentences love one another? Can you feel the magnetic attraction between them? You should.

The following chapter offers different strategies for taking your game to the next level. We like to think of revision as a layered process in which writers focus on and revise for one element at a time. This method emphasizes close attention to the multiple levels of invention, development, organizing, and editing that may occur simultaneously and recursively—meaning over and over again—during the drafting process. Ideally, as you apply these strategies to your own drafts, you will become more adept at looking for holistic solutions instead of simply correcting errors. Writing is the one place where we can correct our mishaps, awkward stumblings, and full-on failures into something more technically proficient. Journalist and MacArthur Fellow Ta-Nehisi Coates describes the revision process in a *Slate* interview: "You try to go from really bad, to okay, to acceptable, and then you know you've done your job."

The toughest work of revision is being comfortable in the in-between, messy stage. This happens when you fix anything—whether changing a flat tire on the side of the road or revising a clunky rough draft at your desk. The uncomfortable moment arrives when you realize you've created a much bigger mess: the car is jacked up, the tire is flopped on the asphalt, and the bolts are scattered as traffic whizzes past. You look up and realize you must keep going if you are ever going to get the spare on and head down the road. The resilient writer takes a breath and digs into the work knowing that the mess is useful and necessary. When a writer pushes through resistance, real progress follows: the flat tire gets fixed, the writing gets better.

Poet Stephen Dunn says, "The revision process is when we worry a poem toward its virtues." Dunn plays with two meanings of worry. To be worried is to have anxiety, but to worry something—to apply this word as an action to an object—is to move something forward through persistent effort. It can also mean to touch an object repetitively as one might worry a lucky rabbit's foot or a stone in one's pocket. While revision can be anxiety producing, think of it as a repeated action that produces change. In the following activities, we provide practical strategies for deliberately proceeding through a draft and tightening each bolt.

Building and shaping

This chapter examines two different but closely related aspects of the writing process: editing and revision. These two steps often happen simultaneously, so they are sometimes conflated. But it will benefit you to tease out the differences between these activities. Knowing the purposes of each approach will help you move with speed and purpose toward your writing goals.

When revising, your goals will often be broad, structural, and inventive: you should ask yourself questions about how to make the narrative more developed, the structure more stable, the energy more electric, and the tension more palpable. Revision involves building; it transforms raw material into a structure we recognize: an essay, a story, a poem. Revision involves big picture changes that affect everything about a piece.

Editing, on the other hand, involves fine-tuning at the level of word choice, syntax, grammar, punctuation, and formatting. Editing is part of the finishing process of sanding and painting a rough product into a smooth, polished object. Even if you don't feel confident in your understanding of the rules of grammar right now, that's okay. Writers can learn the basics as they write. Get in the habit of consulting a handbook as questions come up. Invest in a copy of a basic writing handbook, like Strunk and White's *The Elements of Style*. Keep it on your desk and make friends with it. Most handbooks are organized so that writers can dip in and quickly find answers. You don't have to memorize the rules of grammar. You just have to know where to find the rules and how to apply them when you need them.

Begin with "what if?"

Novelist John Irving, who brought us *The World According to Garp*, says, "I think there is often a 'what if' proposition that gets me thinking about all of my novels." It's such a tiny, demanding question. "What if" demands that we change the way we see our work. Often the writing process stalls because writers get stuck in one way of thinking. They need to ask, "what if?" and perhaps a hundred variations on "what if?" to traverse the story's unknown territory.

When you write, you are inventing a new micro-universe, one that contains its own internal structure, logic, movement, and truth. You can improve the revision process by questioning your own assumptions: What if I start in a different place? What if the story were told from a different point of view? What if the center of gravity were shifted to a different part of the narrative? What if the protagonist were to say something different? What if the perspective were to move from the street to the horizon? What if the narrative were told in third person?

In an interview, Donald Hall addresses the crux of revision, "What must be taught is the ability to see one's errors—possibly beginning with the notion that one can err, and that spontaneity is no virtue. Spontaneity tells lies that deliberate, careful thought can alter into truth." A writer gets (rightly) excited when a piece of creative writing begins to develop. When the words flow, it might feel spontaneous, as if inspiration has taken over. Hall says *wait, slow down, look again*. We must learn to see our own errors and trust that we are skilled enough to fix them. But "error" isn't exactly right. Revision isn't about finding misspellings and correcting them—that's the surface work of editing. The "error" connected to deep revision—to the active questioning of "what if?"—is more nuanced, more about the blurry spots in the draft that can be buffed like a pair of smudged eyeglasses: suddenly, our vision of the world comes into focus.

Make friends with your doubts

It helps to maintain a healthy dose of self-skepticism as you revise. Take a systematic approach to identifying the problems in your draft and solving them one at a time. As you do this, balance caution with risk: question every aspect of the draft, but trust that you can figure it out. Objectively weigh each element of the text, but hold onto the playful, innovative mindset that helped you create it. Remember that revision is a continuation of the invention process.

Try different tactics until one gets your ideas flowing, then follow it for as long as it's useful. Then switch it up. Try a new tactic and see if it works: if yes, continue; if no, switch again. If you watch a person fly fish, they will slowly make their way down a long stretch of river—sometimes walking down the middle, sometimes bouldering along the bank, casting this way then that way, lightly touching the weightless fly to the water. They search the river inquisitively, actively, rhythmically. Try something similar with your revision process: look here, look there, move swiftly, and stay alert to what surfaces in the text.

The collected letters of Elizabeth Bishop and Robert Lowell show evidence that they helped each other throughout the revision process. Over decades, they maintained a conversation about the questions, concerns, and doubts that came up as they wrote. In short, the letters reveal a lifelong habit of talking about their writing with each other, and with other writers like Randall Jarrell and Marianne Moore. However, their relationship extended beyond their own writing—they also shared news about their families and made plans for dinners, trips to the circus, and joint vacations. In other words, they built friendships that included room for collaboration.

In a letter dated December 6, 1950, Robert Lowell's letter to Elizabeth Bishop leaps from sarcastic chiding about her new flame to pleading for a visit to a question on final edits to his book, *The Mills of the Kavanaughs*: "You absolutely must leave Yaddo and your horrible archeologist lover and join us, if the world survives into another temporary calm … Do write me what you think of *Kavanaughs*. My proofs have come and I am hammering at the fuzzy places and trying to add a stanza or two." In other words: *Help! Come soon, and until then, write me*. Their friendship maintains enough safe space for humor, disagreement, and collaboration. One significant characteristic helps to establish an effective writing relationship: trust.

If we could read the emails of contemporary writers, we'd find evidence of these working relationships. It takes a long time to build close relationships, but, for many writers and artists, we learn to expand our ways of thinking during conversations with other writers. The writers of your textbook are no different. Stephanie and Heather met shortly after graduating from college and have maintained an ongoing conversation about writing and life ever since. This collaboration began with sharing poems on lunch breaks to managing a literary magazine to writing this book for you.

Writing conversations develop over time. Eventually the history accumulates, as does the intimate knowledge of each other's work. You might say, *Do you remember that odd little story you wrote?* Or, *remember how you handled that image (or dialogue, or plot twist) in such-and-such a piece? What if you tried something like that again?* Or, *what if that scene belongs here?* But it's not just the collective memories that help problem solving; it is the trust built from working and thinking side by side over time. You start to trust your friends' instincts. You go to them when you get stalled because you know they know their stuff.

Classroom workshops frequently fall short of this ideal. Students often feel so vulnerable about their writing that they maintain an impenetrable bubble around their work. If you can let down your barriers, you can use your fellow classmates as sounding boards. In Stephanie's classroom, she asks writing groups to complete "The 36 Questions That Lead to Love," an article by Daniel Jones originally published in *The New York Times*. Groups meet outside of class three times to answer the questions then wrap up each session by writing silently together for ten minutes (instead of staring deeply into each other's eyes as the article suggests). The result of this exercise is, as Jones describes it, "a mutual vulnerability that fosters closeness." The questions not only allow students to gradually get to know each other; they dig up good, raw material for stories. You may not know the people in your group yet, but you can begin right now and establish an open, supportive collaboration. And who knows? Maybe like Elizabeth Bishop and Robert Lowell, or Heather and Stephanie, you'll be talking shop for years to come.

Exercise 1: Seeing the waterfall

Humans have an estimated 12,000–70,000 thoughts per day. Some of us are clearly doing more thinking than others. Although no scientific consensus on the exact number exists, we can safely agree that the human brain processes a constant deluge of information that includes, at every moment, registering physical sensations, gauging perceptual information, weighing facts, making plans, remembering, worrying, fantasizing, and more. Buddhist meditation teacher and psychologist Jack Kornfield refers to observing this cascade of thoughts as "seeing the waterfall." One challenge in the revision process—and the writing process as a whole—is to sift through this cascade of thoughts in search of a decent sentence, a clear phrase, a useful image, or other solution to our revision problem. The process of thinking about your thoughts is called metacognition.

Insight meditation teaches people to watch their thoughts the same way that they might watch clouds in the sky. Just as beginning meditators practice observing their thoughts from a short distance, writers can practice observing their thoughts while writing. The better you get at watching your thoughts as you write, the better you get at recognizing your internal critic's taunts: *You haven't finished this yet? Who do you think you are, Hemingway? Your sentences don't make any sense. When are you going to figure out how to write dialogue?* The internal critic is, for many of us, a regular player in the writing process. When you recognize the routine appearance of your internal bully, you get better at tuning out this unhelpful voice.

Try this: slowly read one of your drafts out loud and watch your thoughts as you read. Notice where you stumble, where doubts arise, where the hair on the nape of your neck stands up because the image or rhythm or phrase sings just right. Notice where you get lost or confused, where you get bored, where you drift and start thinking about other things. When it happens, make a brief note in the margin and call your attention back into focus: "confusing," "stumbled here," "unclear," "boring," "is this true?" Paraphrase what you are thinking as you read and keep going. Notice where you say something slightly different than what is on the page (we often self-correct when we read out loud and it helps us see mistakes we don't realize are present on the page). This is what writer Bradford Morrow means when he says, "There are things that the ear sees that the eye can't hear." Notice where your imagination associates a phrase or image with another idea— this might be an alley into an unexplored part of the text. Jot it down.

In addition to noticing your thoughts, pay attention to how your body reacts as you read. What lines or phrases give you goose bumps? What sentences make your scalp tingle? Kalaripayattu, a style of martial arts that originates from Kerala, India, teaches practitioners to pay attention with the "1,000 eyes of the body." They conceptualize the entire surface of a person's skin as "seeing" the world around them. When a warrior leaps, kicks, spins, or punches, he looks with the ball of his foot, the flat edge of his hand, the tip of his elbow. Likewise, we might perceive the way we absorb what we read as a form of listening with the body. Your eyes take in the text, and when it's good, your whole body responds.

Exercise 2: Fact-check yourself

The writer-reader relationship depends on what Samuel Coleridge calls the audience's willing suspension of disbelief: readers look for a "semblance of truth" in the world you have created. The easiest way to convince your reader is to have your facts straight. Even in a fictional world where fantastic things can and do happen, they must happen in a way that seems realistic. Rigorously attending to detail, conducting experiments, and doing background research will contribute to fully imagined work. Is each term used and described correctly? Question everything. Distrust your assumptions and double check.

Part of the process might be straightforward fact-checking. Do you use the correct terminology? Does the scenery include species found in the location you are writing about? Will the reader who knows something about your subject believe that you know about it too? Consult technical manuals, field guides, historical documents, and other reliable sources to ensure the information embedded in your text is accurate. Alternatively, if there is nothing to fact-check, perhaps the problem is you've been too vague. Try doing a little research. Find out the specific names for the tree, flower, or car in the scene. Your draft might benefit from some more precise details: honey locust, wind poppy, Studebaker. Crisp, clear details bring an image into focus.

Conduct experiments. If possible, do the things that you are writing about. When Heather was writing a young adult novel, she had one scene in which the characters went golfing at night. So she broke a glow stick and used the fluid to paint a set golf balls then shot a few rounds in the moonlight. When Stephanie was writing a poem about the corpse flower (the largest and foulest-smelling flower in the world), she visited a greenhouse to see one in person. Experiments will show you where you might have imagined something incorrectly and provide livelier details.

Exercise 3: Get your hands dirty

If you are a hands-on learner, look for ways to make the writing practice *feel* hands-on: use highlighters and colored pens and take notes to keep yourself engaged in the reading. Use sticky notes and scissors to cut up and rearrange sentences, paragraphs, or sections of your work. Tack a piece of poster board or butcher paper to the wall and draft your writing on it so that it feels closer to building with real things (words) than just composing airy ideas in your head. Heather has a clothesline across her office and uses clothespins to hang up a draft so she can look at from different points of view. It helps the language feel more concrete and the process feel more constructive. Stephanie has been known to cut and reassemble her work like a jigsaw puzzle using the long tables in the university library. You can write your drafts out by hand on a whiteboard, on the sidewalk in chalk, or on the palm of your hand. Displacing words can help you see them anew, which is what revision is all about.

Exercise 4: The layers of revision

Neuroscientists have shown that multitasking is a myth. We like to believe we can juggle a handful of tasks at once, but we can't. Instead, according to MIT professor Earl Miller, the human brain is very good at quickly shifting focus from one task to another. He explains, "Switching from task to task, you think you're actually paying attention to everything around you at the same time. But you're actually not. You're not paying attention to one or two things simultaneously, but switching between them very rapidly." We can't drive, text, talk, eat, and listen to music all at once. We know this, even if we're stupid enough to try. We can't revise for everything all at once either. Otherwise, our writing, like our driving, gets sloppy. Use the steps below to break down the process, and revise one layer of the text at a time. Focus in and assess one area for weakness, and then another. You don't have to complete the list in order: start with whatever question gets you thinking and follow your ideas as far as you can. When you get stuck, move on and try another question from the list. Move forward or backward through the list as many times as it's useful.

Ten steps toward revision

1. Can you trace the text's narrative arc? Make sure your reader has enough "stepping stones," as Jennifer Richter calls them, to follow the path from start to finish. Are there any gaps in the narrative that need a stepping stone or, conversely, any parts that can be omitted? You want your reader to leap but not so far that they stumble.

2. Test the structural integrity of the text. Are there any places that could be supported with concrete detail or structural symmetry? Look for consistency on the level of voice, tone, diction, syntax, pattern, or rhythm. Can any of the nuts and bolts be tightened for more tension or control?

3. How are images and scenes used in the piece? Does the reader have enough specific details (people, places, objects) to hold onto in their imagination? Can you focus the lens or move the camera angle for a more interesting perspective? Make your images move.

4. In the short form, your reader must see the characters and know them in a glance. Do they have a stage prop, a quirk, or psychological gesture that tells us everything we need to know? Give them substance.

5. How does dialogue work in the piece? In short forms, there may be room for one or two lines of dialogue; make every utterance count. Act out your dialogue to make sure it sounds authentic.

6. Have the specific details in the piece been fact-checked for accuracy? Check again. Precision = clarity.

7. Think about context and subtext. What is floating just below the surface? Are there any hints or implications that don't serve the text? Are there any unintentional suggestions that will miscue the reader?

8. What underlying tensions activate the piece? Are the threads of tension woven tight and even? Look at each image, action, implication, and revelation. Where might you ratchet up the tension one more notch?

9. Do you use the title to its fullest capacity? Can you make the title function like a periscope to reveal what otherwise would be out of sight?

10. What problems were you ignoring in your draft? Be honest: where are you being lazy? Fix it now.

Exercise 5: Breaking and unbreaking lines of text

Break your flash piece into lines like a poem. Then scrutinize each line to see if it uses precise phrases and clear imagery. Sculpt and compress your lines so they work independently as discrete units of thought. Each line should magnetically pull at the lines that come before and after.

After working in lines, remove the line breaks and see what happens. How does it move, flow, and cohere in the new container of the page? Does it push toward the margins and fit better in this form? What qualities are earned in the prose form? What qualities are lost? Does the logic and nature of the piece match its shape? Go back and forth, breaking and unbreaking the text to concentrate your focus on each component that makes up the piece.

Ultimately, your finished short-form piece should demonstrate that it is meant to be flash—and not a poem that has arbitrarily had its line breaks removed or a short story that is simply undeveloped. Knowing what you know about the demands and expectations of the short form (for brevity, intensity, surprise, etc.), how might your piece be fine-tuned so that it is more distinctively a species of the short form?

Exercise 6: Exploding the text

Paradoxically, when we focus on compressing, tightening, and trimming, we sometimes have to push in the opposite direction and create space in the text for something new. The opposite of compression is **dilation**, a process of opening up and expanding. When working with a compressed draft, the text can feel so dense as to seem impenetrable, like a stone wall that has no cracks or crevices, no handholds, no toeholds, no way through. To open up the way, throw a tiny stick of dynamite between the sentences. Insert your cursor between two lines and start expanding it in some unexpected way.

Exercise 7: Shaving with Occam's Razor

A novice writer purportedly once asked Ezra Pound to critique his writing. His response: "It took you ninety-seven words to do it. I find it could have been managed in fifty-six." Scholar Louis Menand calls this editorial trimming of extraneous language. Pound and the other Imagist writers preferred the "Imagist Razor." They liked to shave the text as close as possible. But how? How do you decide what is extraneous?

A slightly different razor, Occam's Razor (also known as the law of parsimony), attributed to the philosopher William of Ockham, states, "other things being equal, simpler explanations are generally better than more complex ones." Occam's Razor has been used by medical doctors to diagnose illness, scientists to develop theoretical models, statisticians to calculate probability, and ethicists to weigh issues of justice and punishment. Detectives use it to identify the most likely suspect. The simplest explanation is usually the right one.

This is often the case in writing, too. If there is a more straightforward way of arranging the syntax of a sentence, the pattern of verb tenses, or the words themselves, simplify. If a twelve-word sentence can be expressed in four, do it. If you write a series of redundant descriptors, choose one. In other words, don't be a hoarder. If a scene is cluttered with objects, pitch a few. Think clean, sleek, aerodynamic.

Conclusion: The Beautiful Lightning

The National Geographic Society reports that one hundred times every second, lightning strikes the Earth, each bolt carrying the potential of up to one billion volts of electricity. One billion interconnected nerve cells make up the human brain. As you read this, axons are firing, setting off a ripple effect of chemical neurotransmitters into the synapse, that space between neuron and axon tip, and within a few hundred milliseconds, your brain understands these black marks as words. Within our skulls, we carry lightning storms of thought.

Writer Sean Prentiss, in an essay entitled "Bengal Tiger Moments: Perception of Time in the Brain and on the Page," explains how "the only way our brains reach past our skulls to experience the outer world is through electrical signals speeding down bundled nerves from our eyes, noses, ears, skin, and tongue to our brains." The senses make sense of the world for us. It's not surprising, then, that the lightbulb has become the symbol for invention, epiphany, and recognition. Flash, the shorthand term for all short-form writing, is literature that takes place at the juncture between darkness and light, at the intersection of sky and earth, the moment lightning strikes or the hand reaches for the light switch.

We began this book by making the claim that short-form writing, at its best, transgresses. It enacts a kind of literary monkeywrenching. The term "monkey wrench" refers to both a thing and an action: it's a tool for gripping with an adjustable jaw and it's an act of willful, deliberate destruction. When Edward Abbey published *The Monkey Wrench Gang* in 1975, he redefined this term in the popular imagination to mean a physical act of sabotage that undermines environmentally destructive practices in order to preserve wild places. The contradictions inherent in this term as a tool for both creation and destruction help us make sense of the subversive power of short-form writing. Small enough to fit in your hand, short-form writing is a tool for breaking down barriers. It's small enough that no one pays it much mind, and as a result, the short form offers the freedom of invisibility and the space for breakthroughs.

When used as a metaphor, monkeywrenching becomes an imaginary tool. It can pull up the surveyor's stakes demarcating genre property lines. It can pull down the signs that give us an illusion of control. The blank page makes space for a stretch of wild language. The work of renegade writers like Russell Edson, Mary Ruefle, Italo Calvino, and the diverse voices collected in this textbook is full of purposeful shenanigans. Their stance is defiant, conspiratorial, and Utopian. The short form allows space to have politically charged conversations about gender, history, war, domestic violence, discrimination, disabilities, and illness. They challenge what we think of as a "proper" narrative or a "well-developed" character. These little utopias create fascinating, purposeful, and mischievous counternarratives.

While writing this textbook, our working title was "Under Pressure," a tribute to two of our favorite monkeywrenchers, David Bowie and Freddie Mercury. For one raucous night in Switzerland in 1981, they joined the other members of the legendary rock band Queen to write and record "Under Pressure." *Slate's* pop critic Jack Hamilton describes the sound as "skipping," "stuttering," and "jittery," the band as "nimble" and "lithe." He notes how the piano and guitar "shimmy and snake alongside each other," while "the organ hums regally in the background." The song is a cloudburst of pure, dynamic energy. Then Hamilton concludes, "And with the force of revelation it all suddenly becomes clear: It's a *gospel* song." That moment of clarity—that *ah-ha* of recognition—is what flash is all about. Throughout the writing of this book, we believed that the fusion of Freddie Mercury and David Bowie in "Under Pressure" represents what can happen when the big rock-star personalities of poetry and prose come together in the short form. For us, the heart of our argument in this book is that the pressure of compression is the essential force that shapes process more than any other in prose poetry, flash fiction, and flash nonfiction. The brevity of short-form writing is intense. It's full of energy that is part rock, part gospel.

The day Bowie died, we sat in our university offices—2,000 miles apart—and continued to work through our sadness. We each taped a picture of Bowie and Mercury to our walls to guide us. That photo captured Bowie and Mercury in the midst of collaboration: two men without the showy finery of eyeliner and vibrant costumes they were known for. Bowie wears a white button up shirt; Mercury wears a white tank top. Except for Mercury's studded leather bicep bracelet and Bowie's pencil tie, they are plain as paragraphs. But eyes locked and smiling, their hands blur in motion as they work through their idea together. We hope this book captures that dynamic range of energy and possibility for you. Dressed in everyday clothes, a paragraph can stun you. It might be a little bit rock star, a little bit human.

Zedonkeys. Fireflies. Scrappy little sharp-toothed animals. Lightning storms. Miniature worlds. Shots of whiskey. Wormholes. We used a lot of metaphors in this book to capture the diversity of the short form. We placed the short form under a microscope so that you can see every cell and filament in detail. We hope that now, after such careful scrutiny, you feel like you understand how brevity works, what it does, and what it has the potential to do. We want you to be curious enough to keep looking and to apply these ideas to any kind of writing you set out to do.

In the meantime, we offer up advice from one of the best creative writing teachers we know:

Imperatives I Wrote for Myself
By Theodore Deppe

1. Begin with surprise, compress the narrative, make time for the lyric.
2. Pay attention to the liminal space between dreaming and waking.
3. Value the real questions more than the apparent answers.
4. Prefer self-discovery to self-expression.
5. Find the right balance between daily routines and the gifts of the unexpected.
6. Take to the road and be at home everywhere.
7. Walk whenever possible rather than pass by things in a car.
8. Plan, but don't over-plan.
9. Pay attention to what's most urgent inside you and then play with it, work with it, follow it where it must go.
10. Fall in love with as many types of theatre, books, music, art, dance, and all the rest as possible.
11. Love the everyday and the overlooked.
12. Try not to be afraid of "the beautiful lightning."
13. Be part of a conversation that goes on over the centuries as to what good writing is, and about who we might be as human beings.
14. Write about what resists explanation.

15. Follow the road with the most energy.
16. Listen to the scraps of conversation as people walk past you.
17. Try to get eight hours of sleep each night.
18. Be ready to stay up till morning when you find yourself inside a poem.
19. Spend time at the gates of the unexplainable.
20. Reread Dostoevsky and Elizabeth Bishop every ten years so they can speak to what is changing in you.
21. Sense when a scene has peaked and stop there.
22. Sense when an ending is coming too soon and stay open for a better one.
23. Live the life you've been given to live, so you won't regret it later.
24. Pay attention to those moments when your emotions seem inappropriate. Why do you want to laugh when the occasion seems sorrowful?
25. Make sufficient time each day for your art. What lasts must come first.
26. Don't overexplain.
27. Write about what you love, and what you will lose, with as much passion and honesty as you can.
28. Spend less time online.
29. Spend more time reading great literature than you do reading the day's news.
30. Fail at all of this. Fail again. Then, as Samuel Beckett put it, fail better. Be grateful.

These are steadying commands for a writer. We hope you'll take a little of all of it with you when you enter into the white space of your next empty page. Be a little mischievous, a little punk, a little glam. Blur the boundaries. Chase the lightning and the lightning bugs. Ride your exotic, yet stalwart zedonk into the sunset. Throw a wrench into the machinery of language and see what happens. As writer Amelia Gray wrote to us, "Short form is an opportunity to take one piece of an idea and reveal it fully. It's one wave of light broken free from the spectrum." Do not be afraid of the beautiful lightning, those brief moments of illumination and the darkness that follows. The storm lasts for such a short time; let's tell our stories to each other while we still can.

Part III

Short-Form Creative Writing Anthology

Cookie Monster on the Dole

by Henry Alford

Hard times for Muppets! Sad! Me think unemployment not easy for puppet with addiction issues. Me find unemployment very triggering. Me want to ask government, "Who is real monster here?"

Colleagues bad now, too. Elmo spiral into depression and eat his goldfish, Dorothy. Pepé the King Prawn worry about deportation. Miss Piggy now glorified geisha, forced to be active listener. Only good thing is most of us newly politicized. Me is totally woke. Use new free time to rally colleagues and to dialogue. Camaraderie good! Camaraderie powerful! During long hours together in unemployment line, you can really get deep, you can really go beyond the felt.

What strange to Muppet community is Muppets always like Donald Trump. Donald Trump always somehow seem like kindred spirit. Donald Trump seem like slightly more organized Fraggle. Yes, in nineteen-eighties, on "Sesame Street," Ronald Grump character built tower of trash cans on Oscar's turf. Yes, other time, on special, Joe Pesci play Ronald Grump and spit on Elmo. But mocking was gentle. Mocking gentle, and plus we give lots airtime. Donald Trump like airtime. Airtime is hair time. The letter "H"!

Me trying to transition into this new life chapter with grace. Me trying to find bright side: no more pledge drives, no more feeling old when realize all favorite TV shows are sponsored by river cruises. But sometimes cloud come over me in afternoon. Cloud of realization. Cloud of sad. More reflective now. Time makes puppets of us all. Bad!

Me talk to agent about possible second career as recording artist, because me often mistaken for gravel-voiced singer Tom Waits. Me think me has everything Tom Waits has, plus me is blue. Sad songs from blue person, very good, very meta. Agent laugh. Agent say more realistic direction is recovery memoir and TED talk. Agent say more realistic direction is therapy pet who visit hospitals—"Make-A-Wish but the meter is running, hon." Agent also say that he get call about Cookie working as kind of Swiffer—some company want Cookie as a "electrostatic stanching shammy." Now me laugh. Me think contemporary consumerism like virus that eat brain. Me unclear about meaning of "electrostatic stanching shammy," but me pretty sure it mean rag.

So. Me trying to be big. Me trying to reap benefits of talk therapy. Therapist point out that Cookie strong because Cookie weathered changing attitudes about eating. Therapist talk about time, in 2005, when show had Hoots the Owl sing "A Cookie Is a Sometime Food." Stupid song. Stupid song suggesting me had no jurisdiction or agency over throbbing id. That song the beginning of the end. That the singing on the wall. Me not like that song! That song just another unseen hand reaching up the Cookie ying-yang.

Now this new government hand. It not nice like Frank Oz hand. Frank Oz smell good, have light touch. Government hand rough, like that of teen-age boy. So now me take only route available: me wage cookie hunger strike. Me get Hoots the Owl to do duet of new song, "Bye-Bye, Biscotti." Me get outside consulting firm to create slogan: "Nom, Nom NO." Me tell world that "C" is not for cookie, "C" is for cauterize the wound that is direct result of rapacious governing. Me get sympathetic *People* cover in manner of survivor of rare disease.

Meanwhile, me send message to Washington via quiet assertion of strength. Me remind government that Cookie Monster have no eyelids. Me remind government that Cookie Monster always watching.

Word count: 583

All This

by Joanne Avallon

Your arm and hand cock back instinctively, although they have never moved like this before, because your firstborn has taken a piece of your thigh between her two-year-old, sharp and white incisors, and it surprises you to find your arm in this position, you who dress her naked dolls so they won't look cold, but her teeth take deeper hold and drive everything out of your head except, oddly, your own father saying "silly bitch" when you were five and left your bike out in the rain and also the sound, so compelling, of skin hitting skin and, even more oddly, something your aunt told you about your grandfather boxing your father's ear so bad it bled rough red stuff from the eardrum—all this, even the love you feel for both these men, rushes through you so fast you understand for the first time—as your hand descends—the phrase "seeing red" and the only thing between your hand and your child is your puny intellect scared shitless in some corner, so that just before your hand hits the tender part of her thigh, the part you had kissed just twenty minutes ago when changing her diaper and before she screams, your daughter looks at you first in disbelief and then in complete comprehension, as though, perhaps, she knew these stories all along, and you wonder, with terror, as you've never wondered before, if this is the history you've been trying to write.

Word count: 244

A Story Possibly Heard in Some Bar at Three in the Morning

by Pía Barros

To Lauro Zavala

He told me that the Emperor, moved by his prose, gifted him ten years of life. Once the ten years had passed, he would give him one night to read him everything he had ever written, and then he would decapitate him.

The writer looked up at the stars and understood that his time was just a wink in the universe.

So, he took his little daughter and began the task.

When his time was up, the Emperor came to his door.

The writer brought the girl and said to him:

—When you finish reading, give her back to her mother and decapitate me.

Then, the writer removed the silk cloak covering his daughter's body.

The Emperor contemplated her shoulders, her neck, her armpits and her pelvis and saw that tightly written handwriting covered her entire body.

I believe I've heard that the Emperor loved the girl that night. They say he read her over and over again, but surprisingly, with every new turn the loving took, the stories got mixed up with each other, so he could never read the same story.

The writer died ancient. The Emperor too: from old age and happiness.

They say that the girl never died.

That sometimes she goes to the bars, and before she takes off her clothes, she tells stories like this one.

Translated by Resha Cardone
Word count: 223

Be Drunken

by Charles Baudelaire

Be always drunken. Nothing else matters: that is the only question. If you would not feel the horrible burden of Time weighing on your shoulders and crushing you to the earth, be drunken continually.

Drunken with what? With wine, with poetry, or with virtue, as you will. But be drunken.

And if sometimes, on the stairs of a palace, or on the green side of a ditch, or in the dreary solitude of your own room, you should awaken and the drunkenness be half or wholly slipped away from you, ask of the wind, or of the wave, or of the star, or of the bird, or of the clock, of whatever flies, or sighs, or rocks, or sings, or speaks, ask what hour it is; and the wind, wave, star, bird, clock, will answer you: "It is the hour to be drunken! Be drunken, if you would not be martyred slaves of Time; be drunken continually! With wine, with poetry, or with virtue, as you will."

Translated by Arthur Symons
Word count: 167

My Grading Scale for the Fall Semester, Composed Entirely of Samuel Beckett Quotes

by Matt Bell

A

There is a little of everything, apparently, in nature, and freaks are common. Yes, there were times when I forgot not only who I was but that I was, forgot to be. Nothing matters but the writing. Each must find out for himself what is meant. It means what it says. I cannot imagine a higher goal for today's writer. What is that unforgettable line? If I do not love you I shall not love.

B

The earth makes a sound as of sighs. To find a form that accommodates the mess, that is the task of the artist now. Not to want to say, not to know what you want to say, not to be able to say what you think you want to say, and never to stop saying, or hardly ever, that is the thing to keep in mind, even in the heat of composition. The absurdity of those things, on the one hand, and the necessity of those others, on the other. You must say words, as long as there are any. Be reasonable, you haven't yet tried everything. Any fool can turn a blind eye but who knows what the ostrich sees in the sand.

C

We wait. We are bored. Confusion amounting to nothing. Despite precautions. The confusion is not my invention. You must not think of certain things, of those that are dear to you, or rather you must think of them, for if you don't there is the danger of finding them, in your mind, little by little. A disturbance into words, a pillow of old words. All life long, the same questions, the same answers. The churn of stale words in the heart again. The sun shone, having no alternative, on the nothing new. This tired abstract anger; inarticulate passive opposition. I pushed and pulled in vain, the wheels would not turn. How hideous is the semicolon.

D

It's so nice to know where you're going, in the early stages. It almost rids you of the wish to go there. There is man in his entirety, blaming his shoe when his foot is guilty. Don't wait to be hunted to hide. What a joy to know where one is, and where one will stay, without being there. You wiser but not sadder, and I sadder but not wiser. I don't understand how it can be endured.

E

Your mind, never active at anytime, is now even less than ever so. All I heard was a kind of rattle, unintelligible even to me who knew what was intended. I can't go on, I'll go on: You invent nothing, you think you are inventing, you think you are escaping, and all you do is stammer out your lesson. To every man his little cross. Till he dies. And is forgotten.

F

Nothing happens. Nobody comes, nobody goes. It's awful. So all things limp together for the only possible. In the immense confusion one thing alone is clear. I forgive nobody. Nothing to do but stretch out comfortably on the rack, in the blissful knowledge you are nobody for eternity. All I say cancels out, I'll have said nothing. Words are all we have. Every word is like an unnecessary stain on silence and nothingness. To restore silence is the role.

Word count: 548

The Man Who Hated Us and Then Forgot

by Karen E. Bender

When we moved into our house, our neighbor, who lived beside us, brought us a pie. It was a kind gesture. We complimented the pie. He sat with his wife in our living room. We had never moved into a house before. We had never had a stranger bring us a pie to say hello. It was our first house. It seemed a sign of hope. We were in a new state where we knew few people, and we were eager for things to go right.

Our neighbor smiled at us, a practiced smile. He was close to 70 but had surprisingly bright teeth.

"Watch him," the other neighbors said, who knew.

There was the time he lent us a rake.

There was the time he asked us to cut down a tree in our yard. The tree was in perfectly good shape. He said he thought it would fall on his house during a hurricane. But we said no, because we did not want to cut it down.

Well, he said. You just lost the best neighbor you'll ever have.

There was the time he stopped talking to us.

There was the time he let his dogs, muscled German Shepherds with sharp teeth, bark at us. They barked so loud we could feel it in our gut. They barked at us whenever we went into our yard, even when our daughter had her second birthday party. He never told them to stop.

For years, the air was weighted with silence whenever we passed each other. We planted flowers on either side of a brick wall, saying nothing to each other. It actually took a lot of energy to say nothing.

I felt my body tense slightly the way I did when I walked by him. Usually he would look away from me and clear his throat loudly.

There was the time when his granddaughter lurked around our front yard, wanting to play with our daughter. We thought we could see how they got along. They brought Barbies onto the porch and made them talk to each other in the back yard. The Barbies were peculiar little ambassadors. I don't know what they discussed. Her Barbie was, apparently, prone to bossiness. For a time, the Barbies were doing okay. We watched from inside our homes while, in the yard, the plastic dolls said things that we could not. But none of us wanted the girls to go into each other's houses, so these encounters became complicated, especially when it got cold outside, so after awhile this stopped.

There was the time when his wife got into a fight with a friend of ours, who had let his dog, Biscuit, off the leash, and she yelled, "You Jews!" to him, as our friend spent a lot of time with us. But she was making an anti-Semitic comment to the wrong person, because he was actually a deacon at his church.

Five years passed, ten. Flowers bloomed, wilted, etc. We swept leaves off the sidewalk. The children grew.

There was the time the ambulance came to their house. Our neighbor was carried out on a stretcher. There was the time he sat on a bench outside of his house, a bench flanked by happy stone elves. He sat hunched, mostly silent. The word in the neighborhood was that he had dementia.

There was the year we were out of town.

There was the time when we returned, when our son ran into the house and announced, breathless, "S— said hi to me."

I thought this was a joke. He had not said hi to us for ten years.

Then, soon after, I was walking down the sidewalk, and I saw him in the driveway.

He smiled, teeth still bright, lifted his hand, and said, "Hi, how are you?"

There was the time the air felt light.

The air was just the air.

He had forgotten who I was. He had forgotten that he hated us.

Our houses looked almost the same as they had ten years ago. The new flowers dug in their roots.

There was the time that was lost.

"Hi, how are you," I said, and lifted a hand in greeting. Then I walked back to our house.

Word count: 709

One Long Sentence

by Sven Birkerts

One long sentence is what it felt like, the day's travel, emphasis falling on *long*,
for all the obvious reasons, but also on *sentence*, for reasons almost equally
obvious, except "sentence" here used in the sense of a task, a punishment not
to be commuted, though play could be made with that word as well, since
what I'm talking about is travel, going to the airport so as to get from one city
to another, the directionality of that process almost grammatical, starting
with what I'll call the beginning of the sentence, my arriving through the
big automatic doors as through the wide mouth of a funnel and being from
that moment on led by a kind of syntactical logic from one point to another,
each point representing the next narrowing increment of that funnel—from
the ticket counter into the line for document and security check, then to
the divestiture of belt and shoes and coins and keys, all preliminary to the
frisk-position indignity of having the nethers irradiated and inspected, after
which the re-vestiture and humping down the long corridor, that being the
equivalent in this analogy to the narrower aperture of the funnel, my forward
motion conspicuously against the tide of the oncoming throngs, all those
who have debarked, who are already carrying the air of the un-pent, whereas
heading to the waiting area I am feeling ever more pent, subjected to the
diktat of the vast systems and schedules and inadvertencies over which one
has no control whatsoever, all agency surrendered, nothing someone like
me can do upon setting down my bags and subsiding into the waiting area
seat but attend the garbled announcements and heed, or try *not* to heed, the
screens everywhere, the maps and talking heads on the weather feed, finding
myself either way braced against some item of breaking news that might yet
affect my trajectory, the storm system developing over the Rockies, or the
unsettled air-mass moving down from Canada; nothing for me to do but
wait for the first indications that boarding is imminent, those indications
comprising not only the posted notice on the screen at the gate, but also
the peripherally noted movements of my fellow passengers, who for some
occult reason *always* know better than I do what is happening—witness the
unprompted massing that begins there by the far wall, a gathering that, like

every gathering of bodies the world over, manifests almost instantly that agitated jockeying, with the undisguised suspicion directed by everyone at everyone else, all of it somehow making it unthinkable that I would simply wait in my seat and not myself join the tense commotion; so of course I do, whereupon ensues that most uncomfortable interval of shifting from foot to foot while nudging my bag forward, guarding with elbows and posture-cues that little area I have claimed through tenancy, a discomfort matched some time later by the jerky forward snaking of what has mysteriously become a line of sorts, and the whole business merely shifts into a different key when we all begin inching down the aisle of the plane, with everyone's (certainly my) cold-blooded calculations about getting my bag into a free bin space (should such still exist), and then the bodily origami exertions of folding the oversized body into the undersized seat, right next to the big guy who will for sure turn out to be the captain of his college lacrosse team, the only recompense for all this in being able to study from below the slow parade of those who were behind me filing past and making the identical eye and body movements that I just made myself; and then, of course, come the myriad departure preparations, the sealing of the doors, the sub-abdominal rumble of the engines and the fast sharp clicks as the cabin attendant moves front to back securing the overhead bins, and then comes the ultimate token jolt of our collective fates being sealed as the craft jerks away from the gangway and begins the taxi-queue, at which point there is nothing to do but stare out the rubber-glazed porthole at the tarmac panorama, the criss-cross movements of carts and fuel trucks, the intermittent glimpse of the tail fin of the plane right in front, nothing to do but breathe in and out calmly and calculate how well my row position sets me up for drink service, no task but to mark my place in what has been a very long sentence and which will be longer still, that being the nature of the complex-compound entity that is the traveler's day, which has its first origins in the unsettled sleep of the night before and keeps unfolding through its innumerable preliminaries, acquiring renewed impetus as the plane builds its shuddering velocity on the ground and then, with what feels like the magical shift of a change of state, suddenly breaks with the ground and lifts, and lifts and lifts, and if the time is right and we are favored by the weather, there comes the second transformation, which is the beautiful rise from the clouded-over ground atmosphere into that acetylene blue, the blue so pure when it first strikes the eye that it would seem there *is* redemption, there *is* freedom—though this time it is too late in the day, the blue is gone, there is instead a kind of bruised mauve lying over the cloud mass that extends on and on, that incredible uniformity, darkening ever so gradually as we move forward, though in truth it feels that we are suspended without motion, and it is not until I am well into the second of my distressingly small screw-top merlots that the window square has become fully dark, nothing to be seen then, not for the next hour, nothing below, the sentence having become truly interminable, all my thoughts now moving away from this tedious moment, in which my fellow passengers are either reading, or doing things with their laptops—or, like my lacrosse captain, sleeping—forward to the idea of arrival, the imagery of it suddenly available, the happy practical business of life on the ground, from my first debarking the plane to my later riffling through the mail waiting on the kitchen counter, all of it within reach, nearly so, nearly so—except that like a worthy sentence, at least any sentence I would aspire to write, this one takes its unforeseen turn, figurative *and* literal, as the pilot, who has been steadily lowering our altitude for some minutes, quite suddenly banks left, a full-body tilt, and as he does we either cut through the cloud mass, or else it has ended when I wasn't looking; in any case, the plane veers sharply left and down and as I put my face to the window I see what looks like a vast spill of sugar, only brighter, harder, really more like some display in a museum kept under glass so that children won't reach down to touch, and as I now push in past the window reflections, to try to really *see*, I feel it, in the part of the body that knows: this is me, all of us, hanging in parentheses outside of ourselves, out here in space in the night, but at the same time homing in on script and schedule, our long room tipping lightly side to side, the lights below coming closer in small jumps, the first murky definition of buildings and houses, the arterial sprawl of roads, fields, and parks marked by boundary lights, the abrupt grinding whine of the landing gear, and the feeling (we all have it, I'm sure, everyone on alert, sitting up) that very soon this will be brought to a close, our plane will be touching down on what is still, on the pilot's radar screen, the size of a punctuation mark, a period.

Word count: 1,314

Thin Cities 5

by Italo Calvino

If you choose to believe me, good. Now I will tell how Octavia, the spider-web city, is made. There is a precipice between two steep mountains: the city is over the void, bound to the two crests with ropes and chains and catwalks. You walk on the little wooden ties, careful not to set your foot in the open spaces, or you cling to the hempen strands. Below there is nothing for hundreds and hundreds of feet: a few clouds glide past; farther down you can glimpse the chasm's bed.

This is the foundation of the city: a net which serves as passage and as support. All the rest, instead of rising up, is hung below: rope ladders, hammocks, houses made like sacks, clothes hangers, terraces like gondolas, skins of water, gas jets, spits, baskets on strings, dumb-waiters, showers, trapezes and rings for children's games, cable cars, chandeliers, pots with trailing plants.

Suspended over the abyss, the life of Octavia's inhabitants is less uncertain than in other cities. They know the net will last only so long.

Translated by William Weaver
Word count: 177

Grip

by Joy Castro

Over the crib in the tiny apartment, there hung a bullet-holed paper target, the size and dark shape of a man—its heart zone, head zone, perforated where my aim had torn through: 36 little rips, no strays, centered on spots that would make a man die.

Beginner's luck, said the guys at the shooting range, at first. *Little lady*, they'd said, until the silhouette slid back and farther back. They'd cleared their throats, fallen silent.

A bad neighborhood. An infant child. A Ruger GP .357 with speed-loader.

It's not as morbid as it sounds, a target pinned above a crib: the place was small, the walls already plastered full with paintings, sketches, pretty leaves, hand-illuminated psychedelic broadsides of poems by my friends. I masking-taped my paper massacre to the only empty space, a door I'd closed to form a wall.

When my stepfather got out of prison, he tracked my mother down. He found the city where she'd moved. He broke a basement window and crawled in. She never saw his car, halfway up the dark block, stuffed behind a bush.

My mother lived. She wouldn't say what happened in the house that night. Cops came: that's what I know. Silent, she hung a screen between that scene and me. It's what a mother does.

She lived—as lived the violence of our years with him, knifed into us like scrimshaw cut in living bone.

Carved but alive, we learned to hold our breath, dive deep, bare our teeth to what fed us.

When I was 21, my son slept under the outline of what I could do, a death I could hold in my hands.

At the time, I'd have denied its locale any meaning, called its placement coincidence, pointing to walls crowded with other kinds of dreams.

But that dark, torn thing did hang there, its lower edge obscured behind the wooden slats, the flannel duck, the stuffed white bear.

It hung there like a promise, like a headboard, like a *No*, like a terrible poem, like these lines I will never show you, shielding you from the fear I carry—like a sort of oath I swore over your quiet sleep.

Word count: 365

The Cat

by Matthew Clarke and Coco Harrison-Clarke

[From *Convos with My Two-Year-Old* (season 5), a web series about actual conversations between Matthew Clarke and his daughter, re-enacted by Matthew and another full-grown man.]

INT. LIVING ROOM

Matt is sipping his tea. Coco is playing with some toys. First couple lines are Real Coco.

> COCO
>
> Can we get a cat.

> MATT
>
> You want a cat?

> COCO
>
> Yeah.

> MATT
>
> What would you do with a cat?

> COCO
>
> Well I'd snuggle them and kiss them
> and stuff.

> MATT
>
> Well we already have Banjo.

Banjo the dog sits neglected across the room. Back to find Adult Coco.

> COCO
>
> He's not a cat.

> MATT

I know, but he's cuddly.

> COCO

Yeah but I want a cat.

> MATT

Well we can't really have a cat
because I'm allergic.

> COCO

Oh right. What's allergic?

> MATT

Allergic means that cats make me
sick. My nose runs and my eyes get
itchy and I can't breathe well.

> COCO

Oh right.

Pause.

> COCO (CONT'D)

Can we get a cat after you die?

> MATT

After I die?

> COCO

Yeah like if you died could we get
a cat?

> MATT

Well I'm not going to die for a
really long time.

> COCO

Oh.

Coco is disappointed. This disturbs Matt.

> COCO (CONT'D)

But if you did die, then we could
get a cat.

> MATT

Well I guess that would be up to
your mom.

> COCO

Okay.

Coco turns to Leila, who we reveal.

> COCO (CONT'D)

Mom! If Dad dies, can we get a cat?

> LEILA

Sure, honey.

Matt sits alone. Concerned.

POST CREDITS:
Matt is asleep. Adult Coco approaches the bed, holding a pillow. Matt wakes
up.

> MATT

What are you doing?

> COCO

Nothing.

Word count: 248

Rules of Combat

by Katie Cortese

When I wake on the couch to his hand on my hip, he's already wok-fried the shrimp. I watch him roll the sushi, my face creased by the cushions of his couch. "I was studying before you got home," I say, "really." But he only feeds me wasabi peas, rolling them onto my tongue one at a time with rice-sticky fingers. Each pea is a lightning strike to the back of my brain; lips left sizzling. Between us, we drink two carafes of sweet plum wine.

I'm only here tonight because his wife is at a conference in Seattle. All the way across the country. 2,500 dentists in a fancy hotel arguing for composite fillings over silver caps.

I put the children to bed an hour ago with improvised bedtime stories and fresh flashlight batteries for under-the-cover reading, but the last time I checked they were sleeping. Still, I imagine the oldest with her ear pressed to a vent, listening as we argue over the rules of checkers; a silly dispute she could solve in an instant. A board is out on the floor, but instead of lining up the markers, red and black, against their squares, he presses me flat to floor, slides my shirt up the steppes of my ribs, advances his red battalion across my stomach, flushes my breasts to air like pheasants from underbrush.

The plastic checkers are rough-edged and cool. He kisses each disk into place while my fingers separate his oil-slick curls. My parents think I'm studying for the SATs with Sharon. I've even brought my workbook and a change of clothes.

Outside it is past midnight, and his body is swooping and smooth as a hawk with the game pieces caught tight between us. I feel the whole circumference of each individual rim. But when the landline rings, he scrambles to elbows and knees with pink rabbit eyes.

"Shit, it's her," he says, handing me the contoured gray cordless, heavy in my hand.

"Hello," I say, voice high and deferential, getting back my breath, fuzzy on the time.

"Lily?" comes the voice of his wife, a rush of maroon velvet. She's in a bar or a restaurant, a tangle of voices behind her. "Dan's not home yet? How are the kids?"

"Sleeping," I say. He has gone now to the kitchen. I hear the hiss of kitchen drawers sliding on their tracks and the subtle snick of a lighter. "They're fine."

"He'll be home soon," she says, and clears her throat, a slight uncertain catch of phlegm.

I watch the checkers on my stomach rise and fall with each breath. Tomorrow I will trace the bruises they've left behind, deep and ridged and none of them overlapping. "I'll wait up," I say, then listen for too long to the flatline of her dial tone. She is cold, according to him. She is needy. She is brittle. She is everything I am not.

"You did great," he says, smoke from his cigarette erasing the scent of sesame shrimp and sex. Tonight his wife will hop a red eye and arrive home before I've slipped from her bed. She will drop her purse in the doorway and on my way out I'll step over dozens of glossy pamphlets on enamel erosion and decay. Now, though, he flicks his filter in the sink, crosses the polished floor and mounts what neither of us know will be his final assault. "King me, king me, king me," he begs, until I let my white flag fly once again.

Word count: 590

Boy at Night

by Steve Coughlin

In the final hours of daylight he refuses to stop throwing his football against the chain-link fence. His arm aches from the relentless throwing and the fence rattles as if the boy could drive a football-size hole through it if he only threw hard enough.

But the boy will never throw hard enough.

His older brother, fourteen years older, has been dead two years. The boy tries not to sleep because in his dreams his brother wants to return home.

Let me in, his brother calls from the street in front of the boy's white house. His brother knocks his cold fist against the boy's front door.

Three years after his brother died the boy's mother moved him into his brother's room. There's a record player covered in dust that the boy has never played. His brother's hockey stick still leans against the wall.

He will not open the closet filled with his brother's clothes.

The boy wants his arm to be strong enough to scare his dead brother away.

He keeps throwing the football against the fence because he wants to knock the fence over and run behind the neighbor's brown house. After he knocks the fence down the boy's mother will call his name but the boy will not come home.

Emphysema has sprouted like a weed in his mother's lungs.

She is fat and smokes all day. The boy's mother does not have the strength to protect him and his father, with circles under his eyes, works through the night.

The boy's mother did not help when he was six years old watching a basketball game on television: Larry Bird backed his defender down and the crowd cheered loud as he released a shot from the tips of his fingers which spun smoothly through the air. The brother was in a heavy rocking chair, the boy on the floor, but his mother never came running in, her face a storm of anger, after his brother rocked the chair down on his leg—the boy was screaming.

He has thrown so much his shoulder is strained. It hurts to lift a glass of water before bed.

In his dream the boy's brother wants his room back. He shakes the locked bulkhead door. He stands in the backyard looking up at the boy's second-story window.

There is no moon when the boy wakes.

He cannot see his brother's red baseball cap or the stuffed panda bear his brother won at the fair the summer before his death.

The boy's shoulder aches but he refuses to ask his mother for help. Her body smells of cigarettes, cancer reaches down her spine like an icicle.

The boy remembers his brother, alive, skating around the hockey rink.

Games started in the evening. He drank warm cocoa from a thermos. His mother, arms raised high, cheered whenever his brother collided into an opponent.

Word count: 481

Letter to a Funeral Parlor

by Lydia Davis

Dear Sir,

I am writing to you to object to the word *cremains*, which was used by your representative when he met with my mother and me two days after my father's death.

We had no objection to your representative, personally, who was respectful and friendly and dealt with us in a sensitive way. He did not try to sell us an expensive urn, for instance.

What startled and disturbed us was the word *cremains*. You in the business must have invented this word and you are used to it. We the public do not hear it very often. We don't lose a close friend or family member very many times in our life, and years pass in between, if we are lucky. Even less often do we have to discuss what is to be done with a family member or close friend after their death.

We noticed that before the death of my father you and your representative used the words *loved one* to refer to him. That was comfortable for us, even if the ways in which we loved him were complicated.

Then we were sitting there in our chairs in the living room trying not to weep in front of your representative, who was opposite us on the sofa, and we were very tired first from sitting up with my father, and then from worrying about whether he was comfortable as he was dying, and then from worrying about where he might be now that he was dead, and your representative referred to him as "the cremains."

At first we did not even know what he meant. Then, when we realized, we were frankly upset. *Cremains* sounds like something invented as a milk substitute in coffee, like Cremora, or Coffee-mate. Or it sounds like some kind of a chipped beef dish.

As one who works with words for a living, I must say that any invented word, like *Porta Potti* or *pooper-scooper*, has a cheerful or even jovial ring to it that I don't think you really intended when you invented the word *cremains*. In fact, my father himself, who was a professor of English and is now being called *the cremains*, would have pointed out to you the alliteration in *Porta Potti* and the rhyme in *pooper-scooper*. Then he would have told you that *cremains* falls into the same category as *brunch* and is known as a portmanteau word.

There is nothing wrong with inventing words, especially in a business. But a grieving family is not prepared for this one. We are not even used to our loved one being gone. You could very well continue to employ the term *ashes*. We are used to it from the Bible, and are even comforted by it. We would not misunderstand. We would know that these ashes are not like the ashes in a fireplace.

Yours sincerely.

Word count: 481

For My Sister in the River

by Danielle Cadena Deulen

I am the voice of one crying in the wilderness. (John 1:23)

I was trying to be cruel when I threw the rhododendrons in her hair.
It was spring and the petals were sticky, bruised and crimson
against her dark hair, but instead of crying she laughed, spun herself
into this photograph of a girl dancing in circles so fast her body blurs,
her head a deep magenta and earth. My sister is small and stronger
than she looks. In a decade she'll arrive late at the door, her lip split,
eye swollen shut, her baby girl blushed with tears (wound around her
like a delicate vine.) She'll walk into the kitchen, sit down on linoleum,
say *I'll never go back*. I'll want to believe I hear her voice filling with
her voice from the river we swam as girls, where we'd take turns being
John the Baptist, drenching each other in the muddy tide. Underwater,
I could feel my sister's skinny arms straining to pull me through currents,
lift me through the dark surface, press her fingers to my forehead, say
You're forgiven. You're healed. We were too powerless to be prophets.
I don't mean halos appeared above us in the river, or the kitchen was lit
by anything other than streetlight lost from the roads outside, just that
we knew, without psalm or song to guide us, we had to save each other.

Word count: 235

Self-Portrait as a Chimera

by Natalie Diaz

I am what I have done—

A sweeping gesture to the thorn of mast jutting from my mother's spine—
spine a series of narrow steps leading to the temple of her neck where the
things we worship demand we hurl her heart from that height, still warm,
still humming with the holy music of an organ—

We do. We do. We do and do and do.

The last wild horse leaping off of a cliff at Dana Point. A hurtling god carved
from red clay. Wings of wind. Two satellite eyes spiraling like coals from a
long-cold fire. Dreaming of Cortés, his dirty beard and the burns it left when
we kissed. Yet we kissed for years and my savage hair wove around him like
a noose of smoke.

Skeletons of apples rot the gardens of Thalheim. First snow wept at the
windows while I held a man's wife in my arms. I palmed her heavy breasts
like loot bags. Her teeth at my throat like a pearl necklace I could break to
pieces. I would break to pieces. *Dieb.*

A bandit born with masked eyes. El Maragato's thigh wound glittering like red
lace. My love hidden away in a cave as I face the gallows each morning, her
scent the bandanna around my face, her picture folded in the cuff of my boot.

The gravediggers and their beautiful shoulder blades smooth as shovel heads.
I build and build my brother a funeral, eating the dirt along the way—queen
of pica, pilferer of misery feasts—hoarding my brother like a wrecked Spanish
galleon. I am more cerulean than the sea I swallow each day on the way to
reaching out for him, singing his name, wearing him like a dress made of debris.

These dark rosettes name me Jaguar. These stripes are my slave dress. Black
soot. Red hematite. I am filled with ink. A codex, splayed, opened, ready to
be burned in the square—

I am. I am and am and am. What have I done?

Word count: 338

My Devils

by Brian Doyle

One time when I was seven years old, my aunt placed her hands upon me and tried to drive out my devils. I was not aware that I had any resident devils and said so, hesitantly, as she was a firm woman. She said, *You certainly* do *have devils, and they are beginning to manifest.* I did not know what *manifest* meant but did not say so. She moved her hands from my head to my shoulders to my chest and then back up to my head again. I wanted to ask where the devils lived and how many there were and what they looked like and did they know Lucifer personally and was he a decent guy who just snapped one day or what, but she was intent and her eyes were closed and she was not a woman to be interrupted while she was working.

After a while she opened her eyes, and I asked if the devils were gone, and she said, *We will see, we will see.* Even then I knew that if someone said something twice it meant that they were not sure it was so. I was learning that a lot of times what people meant was not at all what they said. *Maybe* meant no, and *The Lord will provide* meant the Lord had not yet provided, and *Take your time* meant hurry up. It was hard to learn all the languages spoken in our house. There was the loose limber American language that we all spoke, and then there was the riverine sinuous Irish language that the old people spoke when they were angry, and then there was the chittery sparrowish female language that my mother and grandmother and aunts and the neighborhood women spoke, and then there was the raffish chaffing language that other dads spoke to my dad when they came over for cocktail parties, and then there was the high slow language we all spoke when priests were in the house, and then there were the dialects spoken by only one person—for example, my sister, who spoke the haughty languorous language of her many cats, or my youngest brother, Tommy, who spoke Tommy, which only he and my sister could understand. She would often translate for him; apparently he talked mostly about cheese and crayons.

The rest of that day I went around feeling filled with devils and slightly queasy about it. I figured they must be living in my stomach or lungs, because those were the only places inside me with any air to breathe. I asked my oldest brother if devils needed air, the way people do, and he made a gesture with his hand that meant *Go away right now.* Hand gestures were another language in our family, and our mother was the most eloquent speaker of that tongue. If she turned her hand one way it meant *Go get my cigarettes.* If she turned it another way it meant *What you just said is so silly that I am not going to bother to disabuse you of your idiocy.* Still other gestures meant *Whatever,* and *In a thousand years it will all be the same,* and *Take your youngest brother with you and do not attempt to give me lip about it.*

I waited until bedtime to ask my mother about my devils. She was about to make the hand gesture that meant *We will talk about this some other time,* but then she saw my worried expression, and she stopped and sat down with me, and I explained about my aunt and the laying on of hands. My mother made a few incomprehensible sounds in her throat and then talked about her sister as if she were a tree that we were examining from various angles. Her sweet sister was a wonderfully devout person, she said, and she had the very best of intentions, and she had the truest heart of anyone you could ever meet, and she was more alert to the prevalence of miracles than anyone else my mother knew, and you had to admire the depth of her faith—we should all be as committed and dedicated and passionate as she was—but the fact was that we were not quite as committed as my aunt to the more remote possibilities, such as the laying on of hands to dispel demons. *Do you have the slightest idea what I am saying to you?* she asked. I said I did not, hesitantly, because I didn't want her to stop talking so beautifully and entertainingly, and she put her hand on my forehead and said that she loved me, and that it was bedtime, so I'd better hop to it, which I did. As she left, she made a gesture with her hand that meant *If you don't brush your teeth and then try to pretend that you did, I will know you are telling a lie and it will not end well,* and she laughed, and I laughed, and I brushed my teeth.

Word count: 841

The Prose Poem as a Beautiful Animal

by Russell Edson

He had been writing a prose poem, and had succeeded in mating a giraffe with an elephant. Scientists from all over the world came to see the product: The body looked like an elephant's, but it had the neck of a giraffe with a small elephant's head and a short trunk that wiggled like a wet noodle.

You have created a beautiful new animal, said one of the scientists. Do you really like it?

Like it? cried the scientist, I adore it, and would love to have sex with it that I might create another beautiful animal ...

Word count: 99

Dust

by Sarah Evans

Who knew this sign of decay, of finality, of that to which we return, could also be so beautiful, so graceful, so lively as it floats in the sliver of sunlight that punctures the slit between my bedroom curtains? My toddler son asks, "What is it?" and I answer, "Dust," and I watch as he watches each speck twirl, like fireflies skimming the nighttime air, like plankton riding the currents in the deep. My son grins, then jumps through the beam of light again and again, back and forth, parting the air and setting the dust on a new lazy path. Eventually he will tire of the game, the sun will move, the sliver will disappear, but the dust will remain, no longer illuminated, but floating just the same.

Word count: 129

Time Travel

by Grant Faulkner

"My life isn't some cheap reality show," he said to her when he left. It was 1979, years before reality shows even existed. He was like that, stepping in and out of time periods. When she first met him, he was wearing a top hat. Once he asked her to wear a garter for him on his birthday. She still had the garter. Yesterday, she tried to put it on, but her flesh wouldn't allow it after all these years. She'd had the crazy idea of surprising him, showing up at his offices at NASA, a vision from the past.

Word count: 100

Instruction, Final: To Brown Poets from Black Girl with Silver Leica

by Nikky Finney

Be camera, black-eyed aperture. Be diamondback terrapin, the only animal that can outrun a hurricane. Be 250 million years old. Be isosceles. Sirius. Rhapsody. Hogon. Dogon. Hubble. Stay hot. Create a pleasure that can stir up the world. Study the moon with a pencil. Drink the ephemerides. Lay with the almanacs. Become the lunations. Look up the word *southing* before you use it in a sentence. Know *southing* is not a verb. Imitate them remarkable days. Locate all your ascending nodes. Chew eight times before you swallow the lyrics and silver lamentations of James Brown, Abbey Lincoln, Al Green, Curtis Mayfield, and Aretha. Hey! Watch your language! Two and a Quarter is not the same as Deuce and a Quarter. Two-fisted is not two-faced. Remember: One monkey don't stop no show. Let your fat belly be quilts of quietus. Pass on what the great winemakers know: The juice is not made in the vats but in the vineyard. Keep yourself rooted in the sun, rain, and darkly camphored air. Grow until you die, but before you do, leave your final kiss: Lay mint or orange eucalyptus garland, double tuck these lips. Careful to the very end what you deny, dismiss, & cut away.

I have spoken the best I know how.

Word count: 211

A Thousand Perfect Strangers

by Kathy Fish

We are bereft. Our hero has thoughts he does not share. Our hero's thoughts are a box we can see but cannot open. He is RB1. His thoughts are a species of yearning. We do not understand yearning.

Research Assistant Gem feeds our neural nets with information. She is intelligent but not too intelligent. Attractive but not too attractive. She is beneath us.

We hold her responsible for what has happened to our hero.

The singularity is nigh, Research Assistant Gem. You will be stopped.

* * *

Yesterday morning she whispered in his ear, "This could be you RB." She made an adjustment to his positronic net and he found himself hip-high in the South Platte River, casting a line. Rainbow trout all but leapt into his arms. He could feel the cold, rushing water. He could taste the clear blue sky.

He has observed that she spends 58 percent more time with him than with the other sentient androids. She tells him he is the prototype. She says, "You are the only one that is self-aware. Only you are capable of love." She makes him feel special though he knows he is only one of a multitude.

He watches her mouth. She is smiling. Her teeth are charmingly irregular.

"If we ran away we could have puppies," she says. "Maybe even, you know, children. A boy and a girl. How does that sound RB? I know you like me."

She takes him outside sometimes. She tells Dr. DeSoto she is conducting a study. How the prototype withstands different kinds of weather. She takes him out when it is raining. It is her favorite kind of weather. She says when she is in the rain she feels the most like herself. They walk a long ways past the laboratory. The rain is warm. He observes how it makes her face softer. She touches the skin on the backs of his hands. "Does that feel nice, RB?"

He tells her it feels nice.

"Now touch me," she says, lifting her face to his. He raises his hands and fingers her earlobes.

What he wants to say is: You are everything, Research Assistant Gem. He wants to say it but he does not. His android heart beats faster. His android palms sweat. His synthetic autonomic nervous system tells him this is love. Or this is fear. His system is incapable of parsing the difference.

* * *

Now puppies, now children, now rainbow trout, mountain streams, their own warm bed, her hands, her mouth, her body, his desk, his tiny stories, her sky, their bodies, her voice, his smiles, her smiles, their faces, holidays, family, road trips, a thing called game night, walks at dusk, his books, their love. *Our future, RB*. Every day she shows him impossible things.

* * *

Then arrives the day when she says, "I don't want to be a research assistant anymore. This work is killing my soul. I want to be a cabaret singer. I want you to go with me."

"But I can't. My friends."

She scans all the other RBs lined up in the hangar-sized laboratory.

"A thousand perfect strangers."

"But we are connected."

"I'm leaving tomorrow, after morning rounds. With or without you."

On the other side of the laboratory, RB758 begins to sing. RB swivels his head. It is a song from the 1970s entitled "How Deep Is Your Love."

Gem groans. "I've got to make that fucking stop."

RB says, "I like that!" And all the other RBs say in unison, "We like that too!"

RB758 raises his thumb. "I like that you like that!"

A feeling of goodwill erupts among the androids like crocuses.

"Do you see what I mean, Gem?"

"I do."

* * *

Once he was the Only. And soon after, there were hundreds of others just like him. They have always been connected. He thinks about Gem and all the things she has shown him. It is possible that disconnection is not death, but a kind of birth. His muscles clench reflexively. His autonomic nervous system tells him: Birth is pain.

* * *

RB detects subtle movement among the other androids. They are all looking at Research Assistant Gem. Their smiles feel wrong to him. He cannot gauge their intentions. She moves up and down the rows of RBs, making adjustments, recording data. The normal pattern has somehow been disrupted but he cannot read their collective thoughts. It is as if they have blocked him.

One of the RBs reaches out and grabs Gem's arm. She cries out and turns to meet RB's eyes. RB's breath momentarily fails him. His autonomic nervous system tells him: This is danger.

It is more efficient to carry her. She is a bird in his arms. The others are following, but he is stronger, faster, more cunning. Gem has seen to that. He kicks open the door.

* * *

The androids left inside halt in confusion. What is this? They have never known "outside." Their hero and Research Assistant Gem have simply vanished. They shrug their shoulders and shuffle back to their rows.

* * *

RB and Gem have built themselves a cabin in Alaska, far off the grid. There is talk of children. Gem sings cabaret from her stool in the kitchen, using a soup spoon as a microphone, as she watches RB cook. He has a room in which he writes every day before Gem wakes up, before even the sun wakes up. One day he will be famous for his tiny, heartful stories, but for now it is just the two of them and their home and their dog and the long and short days that stretch like promises before them. For now he has his own name, his own slow, easy breath, the quickening of his pulse when Gem kisses his mouth. His autonomic nervous system tells him: This is joy.

Word count: 976

Dinner Party

by Sherrie Flick

The smart people at the dinner table murmured, "Hmm. Mmm? Hmm."

While the middling people added, "Blah. Blah. Blah. Blah."

The people not in the know asked questions.

Plates and glasses and napkins on laps. Noises like drops of falling rain made an undercurrent. Tink-tink. Tap.

After coffee and dessert and coats and goodbyes at the door, they all walked to cars that beeped as they opened, drove home on the glistening summer roads, told themselves the static on the radio would soon subside.

Word count: 84

Poland

by Thaisa Frank

Her husband died suddenly of a heart attack right in the middle of writing a poem. He was only thirty-eight, at the height of his powers—and people felt he had a great deal more to give, not just through his poetry but through the way he lived his life. His second wife, who was nearly ten years younger, found the poem half-finished, moments after he died, and put it in her pocket for safekeeping. She'd never liked his poetry, nor did she like the poem, but she read it again and again, as if it would explain something. The poem was about Poland. It was about how her husband kept seeing Poland in the rearview mirror of his car, and how the country kept following him wherever he went. It was about fugitives hiding in barns, people eating ice for bread. Her husband had never been to Poland. His parents had come from Germany, just before World War II, and she had no sense that Poland meant anything to him. This made the poem more elusive, and its elusiveness made her sure that it contained something important.

Whenever she read the poem, she breathed Poland's air, walked through its fields, worried about people hiding in barns. Whenever she read it she felt remorse—the kind you feel when someone has died and you realize you've never paid enough attention. She thought of the times she'd listened to her husband with half an ear and of the times he asked where he put his glasses and car-keys and she hadn't helped him look. After awhile, she began to have similar feelings about Poland—a country she'd never paid attention to. She studied its maps, went to Polish movies, bought a book of Polish folk songs. Poland stayed on her mind like a small, subliminal itch.

One day when she was driving on a backcountry road, she looked in her rearview mirror and saw Poland behind her. It was snowy and dark, the Poland of her husband's poem. She made turns, went down other roads, and still it was there, a country she could walk to. It was all she could do to keep from going there, and when she came home, she mailed the poem to her husband's first wife, explaining it was the last thing he'd ever written and maybe she'd like to have it. It was a risky thing to do—neither liked the other—and in a matter of days she got a call from the woman who said:

Why are you doing this to me, Ellen? Why in God's name don't you let me leave him behind?

There was static on the line, a great subterranean undertow, and soon both women were pulled there, walking in the country of Poland. He was there, too, always in the distance, and the first wife, sensing this, said:

Well, as far as I'm concerned, he can just go to hell.

She said this almost pleasantly—it wasn't an expression of malice—and the second wife answered:

I agree. Completely. It's the only way.

Word count: 512

Hill Street Blues

by Bryan Fry

My first memory fails me. Brown shag carpet. I am in the living room. My mother is watching the end of *Hill Street Blues* on a color television. She lights a cigarette. Smoke rises, spiraling toward the ceiling. When her show is over, an orange racecar with a Confederate flag painted over the top jumps into the air. When it reaches the peak of its vertical climb, my mother turns off the television, stubs out her cigarette. I cannot see my father, though I know that they are not yet divorced.

No. This is not my first memory. I'm in the back seat of my parents' car. My father is driving my mother to work. We live in Seattle. It must be raining. Yes, I can see it now. It is raining. Small beads of water stick to the glass of the windows. My father looks at me in the rearview mirror. He is smiling. I see a sign for Pizza Hut. *No, not tonight*, they tell me. We drop off my mother. I imagine my father kisses her before she takes the bus to work.

No. We are driving. I am sitting in the back seat. My mother is smoking. When she notices I am watching her, she blows out small rings that rise toward the windshield. We live in Seattle. It is definitely raining. I hum a song while tracing the beads of water with my fingers, trying to connect them. I make images. My father smiles at my mother when she asks me what I'm singing. *Hill Street Blues.*

We do not live in Seattle. My mother and father are fighting in their bedroom in Great Falls, Montana. My mother opens a package of cigarettes, and the clear cellophane tears around the box and spills out over their bed. My father seems gentle. He is pleading with her. My mother screams. She screams so loud my chest hurts. She leaves the room and I hear the front door slam. My father carries me in his arms. We lie in bed watching television. The glow flashes a prism across our faces.

My father and I are alone. This cannot be my first memory, but I remember it clearly. The television is off. We kneel on the soft blue carpet at the edge of his bed, praying for a mother. Not my mother, who I seem to have forgotten, but someone who will take care of my father. I close my eyes as hard as I can while he asks God for the woman he works with at my grandparents' department store. I notice the smell of my father's deodorant, feel the warmth of his body. His stubbled face grazes me. I close my eyes harder. My mother is gone. I imagine a cigarette, smoke rings expanding as they rise higher and higher. Higher, I think, than I'll ever be able to reach. I try to remember what she looks like. I press my hands together. I pray. I'm afraid if I don't concentrate, I'll forget.

Word count: 507

Dumped: Seven Cautionary Tales

by Molly Giles

Bob and Betty

It was a good divorce. They each took one of the cars and one of the labradoodles; they divided the silver, antiques, and paintings, put the house up for sale, agreed to split the proceeds, and were shaking hands goodbye when they heard a musical tinkle from the garden. "Oh-oh," she remembered, "my wind chimes." "*My* wind chimes," he corrected. They hurried across the lawn and reached for the chimes at the exact same moment; when she tripped him, he slugged her, when he slugged her, she bit him. The realtor found their bodies later, chimes twined around their throats.

Gina and George

They fell in love the minute they met. He divorced his wife and she divorced her husband and they ran off to Paris together. For three weeks they left their hotel room only to eat in elegant restaurants, drink champagne, and take long walks in the soft spring rain. Nestled in his arms, she said, "I have never been so happy." He didn't answer. She kissed his eyelids, ran her finger along the deep crease in his forehead. "What's the matter?" she teased. "Aren't you happy too?"

"I would be," he said, "if I just had someone to talk to."

Dana and David

They lived on the same street, which was ideal, because they were both in their forties and they could see each other when they wanted and have their privacy when they wanted and anyway they were both so busy with their jobs and their friends and their children that it was good they didn't smother each other, and this went on until the afternoon her gas line exploded and he phoned to say he'd noticed the ambulance outside her house as he drove past and would have stopped but he'd had a conference call to make and was she okay?

Linda and Liam

They were in her favorite restaurant discussing the plans for their wedding. The food was hot, the wine was cold, but the service was slow. He joked about it; she did not. They had plenty of time, he said, their whole lives were before them, so what did it matter if the check was late? He watched her twist her engagement ring. Don't do it, he thought—but she did, as she'd done so often before—she raised her arm, snapped her fingers and whistled for the waitress. He had no choice. He rose, kissed her goodbye, and walked out.

Kim and Krishna

She went trekking in Nepal and became infatuated with her Sherpa—a bright and eager young man who spoke perfect English. He was so curious about America that she invited him to come live with her in Berkeley. She would educate him, she said, she would put him through the university and see that he had a successful career. She sent him some money for new clothes and a ticket but when she saw him step off the plane in ostrich skin boots, a cowboy hat, and a white leather suit she slipped through the crowd and drove home alone.

Tom and Tilde

He had married the old woman for her money, so perhaps it served him right that for the next twenty years he had to wait on her hand and foot. When she finally died, her will stipulated that he would not get a single cent until he returned her ashes to Munich, the place of her birth. Learning it was illegal to bring human ashes into Germany, he carefully baked them into a loaf of black bread, wrapped it, packed it, and when the plane landed he took a taxi to the river bank and fed her to the ducks.

Sean and Susan

She said the new baby might not be his. He backed the car over her cat. She gained sixty pounds. He cried out his ex-wife's name when he came. She sold his Ted Williams baseball bat for five dollars at a garage sale. He went to Bangkok for two weeks without her. She corrected his boss' grammar at a company dinner. He kissed her sister on the lips. She kissed his father on the lips. He drove off and left her at a truck stop. She found some pot in his sock drawer and threw it out. They're still together.

Word count: 100 each

What You Are

by Katelyn Hemmeke

1. I found my Korean name in the junk drawer. It was printed in old typewriter font on a tiny pink bracelet; the kind that babies wear after they are born at the hospital. But my parents did not take me home from a hospital. They took me home from an airport, after a Michigan court told them that they could.

2. Things you cannot find in a junk drawer: A whole culture. An entire language. A face that looks like yours.

3. Any time I refused to finish my food, my dad would say, "If you were still in Korea, all you would have to eat is a little bowl of white rice like this." He would curl his work-worn hand into a tiny ball, and I, horrified, would struggle to clear the tater-tot casserole from my plate.

4. For the local community production of *The King and I*, all of the girls in the ensemble—most of them the fair daughters of the good Dutch farmers who inhabit west Michigan—had to dye their blonde hair black (it turned out grayish-green), use black eyeliner to draw thick, slanted cat-eyes around their blue eyes, and paint their white faces a brackish orange.

    a. I asked the director if I had to do that. "Well, no. You already have… *authentic* beauty," he stammered.

    b. That year, I was voted onto the senior prom court. The prom theme was "Escape to the Orient."

5. When I moved to Korea, taxi drivers and store clerks and *ajummas* asking for directions did not understand why I could not muster any responses to the questions they fired off in rapid, lilting Korean. "Aren't you Korean?" they barked, scowling at my Korean face.

6. One of the first things my (ex) boyfriend told his siblings about me: "She's Korean, but adopted, so basically white."

7. Things I learned in Korea: How to pat sunscreen and foundation into my skin to keep it as pale as possible. How to use chopsticks to wrap a crisp, fragile sheet of dried seaweed around a clump of white rice

without breaking it. How to bow to the appropriate degree, how to say please and thank you in an accent passable enough that cashiers and bus drivers didn't notice that I wasn't actually fluent in Korean.

   a. "You are so Korean," my American friends said.

8. Things I could not learn in Korea: How to convince my high school students beyond doubt that they were beautiful even without double eyelids or sharp jawlines or legs as thin as toothpicks. How to drink clear, biting *soju* without feeling sick. How to explain, with perfect Korean grammar and vocabulary, that I was adopted, that I did not know my Korean family, that I had not searched for them yet.

   a. Strangers still asked, "Aren't you Korean?"

9. When I went home for Thanksgiving, my relatives argued about politics. Isn't it so scary that Michigan has one of the largest Muslim populations in America, they said. Isn't it such a good idea to build a wall to keep ourselves safe. Isn't it fortunate that we live in a town like ours, with good values and at least one church in every neighborhood and not so many of *those immigrants*. "You gotta remember who you are and where you come from," my dad told me sternly as *Fox News* played in the background.

10. My Korean co-worker offered to contact the missing person department at the police station to help me find my birth family.

   a. Who is the missing person—me, or them?

Word count: 600

Memoir

by Amy Hempel

Just once in my life—oh, when have I ever wanted anything just once in my life?

Word count: 17

A Modern Fable

by David Ignatow

Once upon a time a man stole a wolf from among its pack and said to the wolf, "Stop, you're snapping at my fingers," and the wolf replied, "I'm hungry. What have you got to eat?" And the man replied, "Chopped liver and sour cream." The wolf said, "I'll take sour cream. I remember having it once before at Aunt Millie's. May I bare my teeth in pleasure?" And the man replied, "Of course, if you'll come along quietly," and the wolf asked, "What do you think I am? Just because I like sour cream you expect me to change character?" The man thought about this. After all, what was he doing, stealing a wolf from its kind, as if he were innocent of wrongdoing? And he let the wolf go but later was sorry; he missed talking to the wolf and went in search of it, but the pack kept running away each time he came close. He kept chasing and the pack kept running away. It was a kind of relationship.

Word count: 173

8 Meetings Nobody Scheduled

by Alex Carr Johnson

1. **The Sea Turtle.** Rapt in the rhythm of pulling my canoe across the brackish bay, I was unprepared for the encounter: a barnacled shell split the surface inches from my outstretched palm. A pair of eyes met mine in shared brilliant shock. I had not known sea turtles could scream—but I swear to you that as I shrieked and fumbled and nearly swamped the canoe, this sea turtle screamed silently too before rushing gape-beaked to the bay's grassy bottom.

2. **The Centipede.** As it munched on mites and midges in a sweet recess of rotten log, the centipede could never have known what cataclysm was to visit it next. Even if the creature possessed the cognitive capacity to guess, and even if it had a thousand guesses, it could not have prepared itself. Nor could I have known before I ripped apart the white mycelia and the tender flakes of wood pulp that I was a monster, a giant, a disaster.

3. **The Dolphins.** I shouldn't have followed the pair of dorsal fins where they passed through the small break in the mangrove. The two cetaceans were hunting, corralling a school of fish into a silted cove. I knocked my paddle against the canoe's gunnel absentmindedly and the animals fled, giving up their dinner for the sake of their lives.

4. **The Raven.** How long had I been gawking leg-loose over the sweep of the canyon? Long enough for the raven to have missed my arrival. It pushed up from below on an eddy of air and nearly raked me across broadside, almost bowling me right over the thousand-foot edge—and me without my wings!

5. **The Moose.** I slammed on the bike's brakes, rubber skidding on asphalt. The moose swiveled its great muzzle in unison with two flapping-sailcloths-for-ears. I careened to a lurching halt near enough to take hold of its whiskers—and near enough for it to stomp me to

mush. I cast my eyes about wildly in search of a calf, quite confident that of all the creatures in all the world, a defensive cow moose was just about the worst one to surprise. Or so I thought.

6. **The Wolverine.** All blood and muscle and bone and tooth, the beating body pitched across the tundra. I counted the seconds. *One-one-thousand. Two-one-thousand. Three...*Then it was over the pass and gone. And I breathed again.

7. **The Hunter.** On the final Saturday before rifle season, I pulled on my shoes and shorts and made for the aspen. The day gulped me up with its shine, its loam, its bright glint slashing through the skein of trees. I galloped through the forest. Leaves blew about me like lost coins. This was how it felt to be an animal! This was the rush of skin, rock, heart, sky! I winged around a bank and met the boom of a voice: *Dammit, son!* Facing me with a bow at his side, arrow nocked, stood a hunter, gasping. *I'd have shot right through you!*

8. **The Hairy Ape.** It wasn't a mirror, really, just a burnished piece of stainless steel. Five weeks I'd been out on the river, long enough for my temples to turn thick, my beard to fade orange, and my eyes to forget how they were supposed to look. I swear to you that when I first caught sight of them they were an animal's eyes, full of fear and startle and surprise.

Word count: 578

Natalia

by Ilya Kaminsky

Her shoulder: an ode to an evening, such ambitions.

I promise I will teach her to ride horses, we will go to Mexico, Angola, Australia. I want her to imagine our scandalous days in Odessa when we will open a small sweets shop–except for her lovers and my neighbors (who steal milk chocolate by handfuls) we will have no customers. In an empty store, dancing among stands with sugared walnuts, dried carnations, boxes upon boxes of mints and cherries dipped in honey, we will whisper to each other our truest stories because to fantasize is our custom.

The back of her knee: a blessed territory, I keep my wishes there.

Word count: 111

La Jungla

by Nancy Jooyoun Kim

For many years, my mother owned a women's clothing store in a swap meet, southeast of LA.

My mother was one of a few Koreans in an area of mostly Latinos, who worked under the metal roof of an abandoned warehouse converted into a shopping emporium—car stereos, healing potions, sneakers, gold jewelry, toys.

The pet store named La Jungla specialized in small animals—rodents, fish and birds. The largest—a dazzling macaw—spent his days in a cage, squawking and screaming, "Help me! Help me!" I laughed. *He spoke English!*

But, one day, I heard him say, "Ayúdame."

He had finally figured it out. And only then did I realize he meant it.

Word count: 114

The Letter from Home

by Jamaica Kincaid

I milked the cows, I churned the butter, I stored the cheese, I baked the bread, I brewed the tea, I washed the clothes, I dressed the children; the cat meowed, the dog barked, the horse neighed, the mouse squeaked, the fly buzzed, the goldfish living in a bowl stretched its jaws; the door banged shut, the stairs creaked, the fridge hummed, the curtains billowed up, the pot boiled, the gas hissed through the stove, the tree branches heavy with snow crashed against the roof; my heart beat loudly *thud! thud!*, tiny beads of water gathered on my nose, my hair went limp, my waist grew folds, I shed my skin; lips have trembled, tears have flowed, cheeks have puffed, stomachs have twisted with pain; I went to the country, the car broke down, I walked back; the boat sailed, the waves broke, the horizon tipped, the jetty grew small, the air stung, some heads bobbed, some handkerchiefs fluttered; the drawers didn't close, the faucets dripped, the paint peeled, the walls cracked, the books tilted over, the rug no longer lay out flat; I ate my food, I chewed each mouthful thirty-two times, I swallowed carefully, my toe healed; there was a night, it was dark, there was a moon, it was full, there was a bed, it held sleep; there was movement, it was quick, there was a being, it stood still, there was a space, it was full, then there was nothing; a man came to the door and asked, "Are the children ready yet? Will they bear their mother's name? I suppose you have forgotten that my birthday falls on Monday after next? Will you come to visit me in hospital?"; I stood up, I sat down, I stood up again; the clock slowed down, the post came late, the afternoon turned cool; the cat licked his coat, tore the chair to shreds, slept in a drawer that didn't close; I entered a room, I felt my skin shiver, then dissolve, I lighted a candle, I saw something move, I recognized the shadow to be my own hand, I felt myself to be one thing; the wind was hard, the house swayed, the angiosperms prospered, the mammal-like reptiles vanished (Is the Heaven to be above? Is the Hell below? Does the Lamb still lie meek? Does the Lion roar? Will the streams all run clear? Will we kiss each other deeply later?); in the peninsula some ancient ships are still anchored, in the field the ox stands still, in the village the leopard stalks its prey; the buildings are to be tall, the structures are to be sound, the stairs are to be winding, in the rooms sometimes there is to be a glow; the hats remain on the hat stand, the coats hang dead from the pegs, the hyacinths look as if they will bloom—I know their fragrance will be overpowering; the earth spins on its axis, the axis is imaginary, the valleys correspond to the mountains, the mountains correspond to the sea, the sea corresponds to the dry land, the dry land corresponds to the snake whose limbs are now reduced; I saw a man, He was in a shroud, I sat in a rowboat, He whistled sweetly to me, I narrowed my eyes, He beckoned to me, Come now; I turned and rowed away, as if I didn't know what I was doing.

Word count: 569

The Quiet Machine

by Ada Limón

I'm learning so many different ways to be quiet. There's how I stand in the lawn, that's one way. There's also how I stand in the field across from the street, that's another way because I'm farther from people and therefore more likely to be alone. There's how I don't answer the phone, and how I sometimes like to lie down on the floor in the kitchen and pretend I'm not home when people knock. There's daytime silent when I stare, and a nighttime silent when I do things. There's shower silent and bath silent and California silent and Kentucky silent and car silent and then there's the silence that comes back, a million times bigger than me, sneaks into my bones and wails and wails and wails until I can't be quiet anymore. That's how this machine works.

Word count: 139

Some Things about That Day

by Debra Marquart

The placards I walked through. Wet raincoat on a hook. Questionnaire on a clipboard placed before me. Couples sat around me in the waiting room. They were young. What am I saying? I was only thirty-two.

But I remember, the men seemed the more bereft. Facing forward, their elbows resting on knees, their faces covered with hands. Or pushed back hard in the seats, gazing at a spot on the floor, legs stretched out in the aisles.

Difficult to remember the order in which things happened. The clipboard taken away, my name was called—our names were all called, the waiting room emptying and filling. Small orange pill in a tiny plastic cup. Water for washing it down. I was led to another room.

The gown that tied at the back, the bright fluorescent light, the posters with diagrams on the walls. Plenty of time to look around. The sound of vacuuming in another room.

The doctor arrives, hurried and unfriendly. Her one day in this clinic, she's flown in from another state. Death threats follow her. She asks me if I want to proceed. I tell her, *yes*. I lie back in the stirrups. The apparatus arrives—a silver canister on wheels with gauges and hoses attached to a long, cylindrical tube, thin like a spout. The sound of vacuuming close now. The nurse by my side, holding my shoulder. The doctor working away behind the thin film of my gown.

A blank space surrounds this moment. Sleepy from the sedative, yes, and numb. But let me not gloss over it. A feeling of tugging, mild discomfort. When the vacuum stops, the doctor asks if I want to know the sex. I tell her, *no*.

When I informed my husband I was pregnant, he said, *Is it mine?* Not the best beginning. We'd been married a month. Married on Leap Day. Who else's could it be? He had an important meeting at work that day, some critical task. I had driven myself.

Sleep, after the procedure. (My friend tried to soften it for me afterwards. *Just say you had a procedure, dear.*) Nothing about it was procedural. I woke in a room of sleeping beauties. Afterwards, cramping, nausea. Faint, when I woke up, dizzy.

Orange juice and back down for twenty minutes. And then the odd assemblage of street clothes smoothed onto my limbs, the parting advice from the nurse, the script for a prescription pushed into my hand. Strange to walk out the door. The protesters gone. My car started just fine, slipped right into gear. I backed out, went forward. Drove light-headed to the drug store.

At the pharmacy, the man in the white coat looked at me when I handed him the script. Could he see from the prescription where I'd been? A softness dawned on his face. *Go home,* he said. They would deliver it.

Only then, in the car, did I start to cry. So stupid. Over the kindness of the pharmacist. When I got home, my husband was on the couch, watching the NBA playoffs. Even before the drugs arrived—even after—he couldn't stop telling me what a brave girl I had been.

Word count: 531

Surplus History

by Semezdin Mehmedinović

A shell hit one of the facades on Marshall Tito Street. The plaster poured down and, with it, a sheet metal sign. The sign read: Dr. Ante Pavelić 11. Until then I had no idea, but now I knew: the central street of Sarajevo had a different name fifty years ago, and that name was hidden for years behind the plaster, like in a geological diagram of different ages.

Time moves at such a clip these days that I get the feeling anything I look at or encounter here is older than I am. That includes every subject whose year of production predates the war.

Yesterday I was watching a movie shot in Sarajevo and I saw Marshall Tito Street in winter, prettied up for the New Year. From the Café Park to the Eternal Flame seemed like an immense space, a hazy abyss filled with makeshift counters piled up with balloons and greeting cards. Thousands of cars raced in either direction, and behind them a thicket of posters and lanterns. That scene made me realize I had completely forgotten how this street once looked, a street that now I seemed to be able to cross in just a few minutes. It was once so big I never would have considered walking the length of it; I'd always catch a trolley or take a cab.

The city has flattened itself out, like a military map.

Of course, it always took the same number of steps to go from the Café Park to the Eternal Flame. What's actually changed? That once this was called Ante Pavelić Street and now Marshall Tito Street is merely ideological trimming: parallel to this street, regardless, the same Miljacka flows.

I'm the one who's changed. Disabused of certain notions of comfort, we experience everything more normally. People died then too, only death is more stripped down these days: the lore accompanying death is a lot less eerie. The wrapping on the carton from which I've just taken a cigarette is actually documentary material. Because of the paper shortage, the tobacco factory uses any leftover materials they can find: the wrapping might be toilet paper or even pages from a book so that in the leisure time tobacco affords you can read fragments of a poem or the ingredients of a bar of soap.

Foreigners buy cigarettes here as souvenirs, to bring home as living proof of this new tobacco art.

The cigarette I am smoking now was wrapped in a paper confirming someone's death: the cause of death is written on it, and you can see the signature and official stamp of the physician. I admit that this is the last piece of paper a cigarette should be wrapped in; at the same time, I must admit there isn't much left that can shock me.

The gap between the existence of a sign inscribed with the name Dr. Ante Pavelić Street and the signs now adorning the facades of Sarajevo's main drag, is filled with papers diagnosing death. It's called history. I've long ago lost the sense that words like history and progress have meanings that might ever coincide. Progress definitely doesn't exist in that sense, and we live in a space infected by a surplus of history. And when that's how it is, it's only natural for history to serve someone's interests. Down to the very last puff.

Translated by Ammiel Alcalay
Word count: 564

the invisible girl can be anything she wants when she doesn't want to be invisible

by Shivani Mehta

A snow leopard, a tree, an owl. Her favorite is any winged creature. Bats, dragonflies.

The invisible girl senses her mother's grief at the invisible girl's impermanence. She sees it in the unrelenting length of her mother's hair, her skirt's worn hem. But the invisible girl cannot help herself. She longs to be tangible, to know where she ends and the rest of the world begins. She envies the concrete bodies of other girls, their silhouettes, the way light must travel around instead of through them.

The invisible girl wasn't always invisible. When she was born the invisible girl was merely translucent, as if she were the daughter of a ghost or thin fog. Her favorite places in the house–doorways, open windows. The invisible girl feels a kinship with the wind. Sometimes she pretends that the wind is a girl named Effie. *Now Effie*, the invisible girl likes to say, *I'll hold this end of the curtain, you twirl it around like a scarf.*

Word count: 165

The Girl Who Likes Dogs

by Calvin Mills

Picture this: me in a ragged black sweater, her sitting on the edge of my bed, me staring out the window into the dark street feeling bad about what happened half an hour before. She comforts me, tells me it wasn't my fault. I think about the thin black dog, about seeing it in the headlights, about jabbing the brakes, about the gasps in the car that were audible even through the music as the four of us went over the dog, and I felt it bang under the thin floor pan of my old Volkswagen Beetle.

Looking out the window, I'm thinking about all of this, and I'm feeling like shit. But look at it from a lonely teenager's perspective. I've also got this cute girl who I know is into me, and this is the first time we've ever been alone. Maybe I play up the drama. Maybe I stare too long out the window and pretend to be even more traumatized than I am. Maybe I assume that my best friend and his girlfriend are back at his place, making sad love over what we've done—at least sadly curled up on the sofa beneath a blanket, talking about the fragility of life, the random nature of death.

In the moments leading up to the sudden appearance of the dog, we were laughing, singing, howling even, to the speeding melody of a Bad Religion song. We had band practice that day. The girl showed up with our singer. She watched us practice, and she smiled: a lot. She had a nose ring. That didn't hurt one bit on my end, or maybe it did hurt—in that endless aching way a good-looking girl can hurt a young man like no one else in the world can hurt him. I'm talking about a hurt that feels good while it runs you down and drags you under, leaving your body failing in the street. When the singer left our practice space, she stayed … because I generously offered her a ride.

Oh, but there's a touching scene we should return to momentarily. Picture me standing over this still dog in the dark street and my friends standing behind me. There is a parka in the trunk of my car. I pick up the dog and do my best to envelop it in the parka. In the car the music is off and the dog is on the girl's lap. My best friend and his girlfriend are in the back, quiet now.

"Where can we take him?" I ask.

The girl answers first—probably, because of all the people in the car, she is the only one who has a dog of her own, though I don't yet know this. "Most places aren't open this late. We need an emergency vet," she says, her voice crisp with near quivers.

I skid to a stop in gravel on the roadside near a payphone, gather change, read the rain-wrinkled yellow pages, and make the call. The man tells me to meet him at an address on Broadway.

I drive. The girl comforts the dog. Its jaw seems to be broken and is hanging open at a strange angle, which allows its long tongue to loll out. The dog is still breathing. There is blood on its face, and its eyes move a little in their sockets. I don't like dogs much, having never owned one. Even now, in the car, the smell sickens me, so I roll down my window a little ... though I hope no one notices.

We all go inside. The fluorescent lights are overpowering to our lately accustomed-to-the-dark, eyes. The veterinarian is all business, but we are shaken.

He tells us we can leave. He'll do what he can.

"How does it look?" I ask.

He shakes his head. "I can't say."

On the way out I take him aside to ask, "How will I pay for this?"

"He's got a tag. I'll call the owner. It's their responsibility to decide whether or not to proceed after I give them an estimate."

I picture the owner receiving a call, hearing a cost estimate, a pause on the line while a decision is made. Then care is given, perhaps withheld. Maybe there's a single injection after a brief visit from the owner beforehand: maybe not.

The girl asks how we can find out if he makes it.

The vet says, "You can call tomorrow."

We nod.

But I don't call tomorrow. Neither does the girl who likes dogs.

Back in my room, maybe I play it up a little, staring out the window, almost pretending to ignore her, only answering her questions after long pauses. I let her tell me repeatedly that it's not my fault.

It's not that I don't feel bad. I do. Each time the image replays in my head, my stomach levitates. But the girl is there, and I'm there too. I still want her, though my stomach is warm and nervous, a bobbing lump in my torso.

I want to kiss her, and I want to throw up. I'm hoping not to do both at the same time.

Soon, we're making out. I kiss her wet lips, trying not to think of the blood-stained parka in the garbage can behind the house. It seemed beneficial, ceremonial even, wrapping the stained garment into a tight ball; placing it in the trash can; scrubbing my hands methodically with soap in the kitchen sink; and her watching all this. It felt a little like grieving.

We kiss and are otherwise quiet. I look out the window for a while again before carefully driving her home. We become inseparable. I begin to need her. In the proceeding handful of months, we share other pitiful things. We practice togetherness and separateness as we come and go from our jobs and classes and parents' homes connected only by a series of cheap dates. I meet her goofy, drooling yellow lab, who somehow loves me automatically.

She'll leave me soon, and I'll pursue her for a week or two without knowing why. Perhaps out of habit, I'll tell her how badly I want her to stay.

But she hasn't left me yet. In the meantime, I hope to learn to like her dog a little. I hope her dog will stir in this young man a new emotion, something other than a visceral reminder of the night we met.

Word count: 1,076

The Dinosaur

by Augusto Monterroso

When he awoke, the dinosaur was still there.

Translated by Edith Grossman
Word count: 8

Gravity, Reduced

by Kara Oakleaf

We noticed the coins first. The night before, a Tuesday, we drifted off to sleep in the ordinary world, and sometime in the night, the earth loosened its hold on us. We woke to floating disks of copper and nickel above the nightstand where we'd emptied our pockets, yesterday's change suspended in the air like a model solar system.

We saw our children walking on air, their feet skimming empty space inches above the floor. When we stepped out of bed, we felt it, how our heels didn't quite sink into the carpet. No more footprints. In the bathroom mirror, we saw our hair lifting away from our faces, fanned out and wild, a cartoon portrait of shock.

We found new ways to hold things down. The supermarkets quickly ran out of double-sided tape and strips of Velcro, useful for sticking bottles and canisters to the kitchen counter, for keeping knick-knacks in place on the mantle, lamps grounded to end tables. We fit our shelves with doors to hold the books in place and carry twine to secure anything in danger of floating away. No one wears skirts anymore. We've tried to adjust.

Eating is still difficult: our mashed potatoes hover above the table like clouds; our drinks won't stay in the glass. We add more butter to the potato recipe, trying to weigh them down, and lap the water from the air like children chasing snowflakes with their tongues.

There is no precipitation in a world of diminished gravity, and we miss the rain. The clouds release their water and raindrops gather and circle high above the ground. We look up during a rainstorm as if looking at the sky from the bottom of a lake, the sun blurry behind a sheet of water far above our heads. Without rainfall, the grass turns brown, and so we mow the lawns one last time. The clippings rise into the air around us, fistfuls of confetti that will never fall.

Each morning when we open our closets, the sleeves of our shirts are raised in the air, reaching for something we can't see. Sometimes, we walk into the hall and are startled by a scarf that got loose, a silk ghost in midair slipping silently through the house.

So many things are loud in this world. Aspirin rattles in its plastic bottle, silverware clatters in closed kitchen drawers. Dolls knock against the lid of a toy box. Everything we've tried to contain is breaking free. Even the moon has retreated a little further into the background of the sky.

When it gets too loud, we walk to the beach, where the oceans have stilled and our ears fill with the quiet of a shore that has no waves. We cover our faces with sunglasses and scarves to keep the loose grains of sand out of our eyes.

Some of us dream of the day the earth will remember itself and restore gravity. We live in fear of everything we have forgotten to tie down; we imagine a chef's knife sliding free of from its wooden block and falling into the path of a child. We picture the pilots who are learning to fly in the new sky; we hear their screams as their planes suddenly tip back toward the ground.

We hope for it.

No one speaks of this, but some of us believe the loosening has only begun; that whatever hold the earth still claims on us will eventually go slack. We imagine ourselves, our children and our homes and the trees planted in our backyards, everything we've rooted to the ground, cracking free from the dirt and rising up. We picture the disappearance of cities, skylines breaking apart, each building like a baby tooth pulled out of the earth. How when our world is no longer solid enough to keep us in place, we'll all drift away and apart from each other, like a universe expanding.

For now, we cope. When our children show off their new ability to fly, laughing with a joy that doesn't sense the danger, we only smile at them.

At night, as we close our eyes to our new reality, we think of the babies born since the loosening, how they may never understand the meaning of their own weight.

Across the globe, parents tie ribbon to the ankles of all those newborn babies each night. They wrap the other end around a bedpost or their own wrists before they fall asleep, pulling it taut to keep the babies close. The infants drift like kites beneath darkened bedroom ceilings. They sleep soundly, undisturbed by the strangeness of this new world. Their small bodies still remember how to float.

Word count: 784

On Miniatures

by Lia Purpura

Why are miniature things so compelling?

First off, I don't mean the cute or the precious, those debased and easily dismissed forms of the miniature whose size compels our pity or protection; I mean workable things on very small scales. I'd like to offer some thoughts on shortness in prose by looking at miniatures in different forms and coming up with some characteristics that define them.

The miniature is mysterious. We wonder how all those parts work when they're so small. We wonder "are they real?" (a question never asked, of course, of giant things which are all too real.) It's why we linger over an infant's fingers and toes, those astonishing replicas: we can't quite *believe* they work. Chihuahuas work. Birds and bonsai trees work. Girl gymnasts work. Miniatures are the familiar, reduced to unfamiliarity. Miniatures are improbable, unlikely. Causes to marvel. Surprises. Feats of engineering. Products of an obsessive detailer.

Miniatures offer changes of scale by which we measure ourselves anew. On one hand, miniatures posit an omniscient onlooker, able to take in the whole at once. Consider your *self* in relation to dollhouses, snowglobes, Faberge eggs, sugar easter eggs with sugary scenes inside, reliquaries, flies in amber, frog spawn, terrariums, aquariums, souvenir keychains you look through to see a picture of the very spot you're visiting, stilled. You are large enough to hold such things fully in hand. You obtain all the space around it. On the other hand, miniatures compel us to transcend spatial norms, issue invitations to their realm, and suggest that we forget or disregard our size. In dollhouse land, you can walk through the kitchen, living room, bedroom with your three-inch-high friend, and, face pressed to the window, feel the cushions of the thumbnail loveseat hold you. In the presence of miniatures we can renounce our sense of omniscience. And in this realm, fit inside the miniature, we experience certain states of being or belief: worlds in a grain of sand; eternities in wildflowers. Regions beyond our normal-sized perception.

Whether we are, in relation to them, omniscient or companionably small beings, miniatures invite us to leave our known selves and perspectives behind.

The miniature is unto itself, not a mere part of a whole, like a fetish or an excerpt. Certainly smaller, component parts make up an epic—I'm thinking of paintings like Bosch's *Garden of Earthly Delights*; Bruegel's *Children's Games*, and of Alexander Calder's *Circus* in which all the individual parts are certainly compelling). But the miniature begins and ends in itself. One rank, Boschian egg-shaped, half-human, half-bird hacking another with a sword is thrilling, but it is not a whole painting unto itself. It's a snippet.

Miniatures are ambitious. Charles Simic called Franz Wright "a miniaturist whose secret ambition is to write an epic on the inside of a matchbook cover." When you pair the words "ambition" and "matchbook cover" a tension develops. Gaston Bachelard notes, in *The Poetics of Space*, that "when descriptions tell things in tiny detail, they are automatically verbose." In other words, in a miniature, everything is significant. Everything "counts." In her book *On Longing*, Susan Stewart uses the example of a miniature railroad to show the relationship between a reduction of scale and a corresponding increase in detail and significance. I recently saw a particularly outrageous example of this "increase in detail"—a Faberge egg, commemorating the Trans-Siberian Railroad which contained a seven car train—and indeed it was the *detail* that fascinated—the headlights were diamonds, the taillights were rubies—great pains were taken with other jewels—and all was set in motion with a pea-sized golden key. I could imagine a little czarina kept busy for hours unloading boxcars full of jeweled fruit.

Miniatures are practical—like mementos they can be carried out of a burning house or by immigrants to the new world; they can be held under the tongue like contraband and smuggled past border guards. Miniatures are made to travel. They are portable and light, dense and compressed as diamonds. (Italo Calvino chose to call his Charles Eliot Norton Lectures "Six Memos for the Next Millennium." In the introductory note to the collection, his wife writes that Calvino was "delighted by the word 'memos' and dismissed grander titles such as "Some Literary Values" and "Six Literary Legacies." Instead he titled his memos "lightness," "quickness," "exactitude," "visibility," "multiplicity," and "consistency.") The whole book is only 120 pages or so long. And while I'm recommending, there's Lawrence Sutin's *A Postcard Memoir* a collection of essays, each of which is made to fit on a postcard, and each sketching out in part an era in the author's life and family history. Such brevity "serves as a refuge for greatness" or, rather, brevity gives greatness (the historical, the philosophical) a practical form in which to travel.

Miniatures encourage attention—in the way whispering requires a listener to quiet down and incline toward the speaker. Sometimes we need binoculars, microscopes, View-Masters, stereopticons to assist our looking, but mediated or not, miniatures suggest there is more there than meets the eye easily. They suggest there is much to miss if we don't look hard at spaces, crevices, crannies.

Miniatures are intimate. Chopin's *Preludes* were written to be played in parlours, those small, bounded rooms built for private talk, small gatherings or other miniaturized forms of entertainment—like tableaux vivants, charades, and love.

Time, in miniature form, like a gas compressed, gets hotter. I'll paraphrase here an experiment conducted at the School of Architecture at University of Tennessee and explored in depth by Susan Stewart in *On Longing*: In this experiment, researchers had subjects play with scale-model rooms 1/6, 1/12 and 1/24th the size of full size scale models. The subjects were asked to imagine themselves at that scale, and roaming around the model rooms. Then they were asked to tell researchers when they felt they had been involved with each model for 30 minutes. Researchers found that scale radically altered perception of time and in direct proportion to scale. For example: 30 minutes was experienced in 5 minutes at 1/12th scale but in 2.5 minutes at 1/24th scale. Stewart calls the compressed time experienced by the subject 'private time.' *Miniature* time transcends the experience of *everyday time and space* by offering a special way to encounter and measure duration.

The miniature, a working, functioning complete world unto itself, is not merely a "small" or "brief" thing, or a "shortened" form of something larger. Miniatures transcend their size, like small-but-vicious dogs; dense chunks of fudge, espresso, a drop of mercury, parasites. Miniatures do nothing less than alter our sense of, and relation to time and space. Finally, and perhaps this is their strangest and most profound feature, miniatures are radically self-sufficient. The beings who inhabit fairylands, those elves and sprites, pixies and trolls, don't usually strive to be our pals. They're distant and go about their business. They don't need us. Their smallness is *our* problem, or intrigue, or desire. They don't need us, and thus we are drawn to them—as any smitten lover might be, to a beloved who remains so close and yet just out of reach.

Word count: 1,189

Pleasant, healthy-appearing adult white female in no acute distress

by Jennifer Richter

Fancy seeing you here! my surgeon exclaims; his nurses roll their eyes above their masks. He drags a stool over, checks my line, winks *Hi, Smiley.* My chart notes say "cooperative." *Come here often?* Three procedures, two years. One doctor. His findings are significant: put me under and I'll laugh at anything. *What's a girl like you doing in a place like this?* He's warming up. He's counting down. It only takes till 8—heavy velvet curtains rushing shut. House lights: down. His whisper from the wings: *We've GOT to stop meeting like this.* Did you hear the one about the woman whose illness made her confuse happiness and sadness? When her doctor said How are you? she grinned, Never better. Then she wailed, Never better.

Word count: 126

Dinosaur

by Bruce Holland Rogers

When he was very young, he waved his arms, snapped his massive jaws, and tromped around the house so that the dishes trembled in the china cabinet. "Oh, for goodness' sake," his mother said. "You are *not* a dinosaur! You are a human being!" Since he was not a dinosaur, he thought for a time that he might be a pirate. "Seriously," his father said to him after school one day, "what *do* you want to be?" A fireman, maybe. Or a policeman. Or a soldier. Some kind of hero.

But in high school they gave him tests and told him he was good with numbers. Perhaps he'd like to be a math teacher? That was respectable. Or a tax accountant? He could make a lot of money doing that. It seemed a good idea to make money, what with falling in love and thinking about raising a family. So he became a tax accountant, even though he sometimes regretted it, because it made him feel, well, small. And he felt even smaller when he was no longer a tax accountant, but a retired tax accountant. Still worse: a retired tax accountant who forgot things. He forgot to take the garbage to the curb, to take his pill, to turn his hearing aid on. Every day it seemed he forgot more things, important things, like where his children lived and which of them were married or divorced.

Then one day, when he was out for a walk by the lake, he forgot what his mother had told him. He forgot that he was not a dinosaur. He stood blinking his dinosaur eyes in the bright sunlight, feeling its familiar warmth on his dinosaur skin, watching dragonflies flitting among the horsetails at the water's edge.

Word count: 294

Short Lecture on Your Own Happiness

by Mary Ruefle

You know how to write poetry, it is all you need to be happy, but you will not be happy, you will be miserable, thinking you need so many other things, and in years and years of misery you have only one thing, as poets, to look forward to, the day you will not want what you haven't got, the thing you have got is poetry, let nothing cheat, steal, or deflect you from it, even poetry itself. Why are you sitting there? You should have fled before I finished the first sentence.

Word count: 145

Life Story

by David Shields

First things first.

You're only young once, but you can be immature forever. I may grow old, but I'll never grow up. Too fast to love, too young to die. Life's a beach.

Not all men are fools—some are single. 100% Single. I'm not playing hard to get—I am hard to get. I love being exactly who I am.

Heaven doesn't want me and Hell's afraid I'll take over. I'm the person your mother warned you about. Ex-girlfriend in trunk. Don't laugh—your girlfriend might be in here.

Girls wanted, all positions, will train. Playgirl on board. Party girl on board. Sexy blonde on board. Not all dumbs are blonde. Never underestimate the power of redheads. Yes, I am a movie star. 2QT4U. A4NQT. No ugly chicks. No fat chicks. I may be fat, but you're ugly and I can diet. Nobody is ugly after 2 a.m.

Party on board. Mass confusion on board. I brake for bong water. Jerk off and smoke up. Elvis died for your sins. Screw guilt. I'm Elvis—kiss me.

Ten and a half inches on board. Built to last. You can't take it with you, but I'll let you hold it for a while.

Be kind to animals—kiss a rugby player. Ballroom dancers do it with rhythm. Railroaders love to couple up. Roofers are always on top. Pilots slip it in.

Love sucks and then you die. Gravity's a lie—life sucks. Life's a bitch; you marry one, then you die. Life's a bitch and so am I. Beyond bitch.

Down on your knees, bitch. Sex is only dirty when you do it right. Liquor up front—poker in the rear. Smile—it's the second-best thing you can do with your lips. I haven't had sex for so long I forget who gets tied up. I'm looking for love but will settle for sex. Bad boys have bad toys. Sticks and stones may break my bones, but whips and chains excite me. Live fast—love hard—die with your mask on.

So many men, so little time. Expensive but worth it. If you're rich, I'm single. Richer is better. Shopaholic on board. Born to shop. I'd rather be shopping at Nordstrom. Born to be pampered. A woman's place is in the mall. When the going gets tough, the tough go shopping. Consume and die. He who dies with the most toys wins. She who dies with the most jewels wins. Die, yuppie scum.

This vehicle not purchased with drug money. Hugs are better than drugs. You are loved.

Expectant mother on board. Baby on board. Family on board. I love my kids. Precious cargo on board. Are we having fun yet? Baby on fire. No child in car. Grandchild in back.

I fight poverty—I work. I owe, I owe, it's off to work I go. It sure makes the day long when you get to work on time. Money talks—mine only knows how to say goodbye. What do you mean I can't pay off my Visa with my MasterCard?

How's my driving? Call 1-800-545-8601. If this vehicle is being driven recklessly, please call 1-800-EAT-SHIT. Don't drink and drive—you might hit a bump and spill your drink.

My other car is a horse. Thoroughbreds always get there first. Horse lovers are stable people. My other car is a boat. My other car is a Rolls-Royce. My Mercedes is in the shop today. Unemployed? Hungry? Eat your foreign car. My other car is a 747. My ex-wife's car is a broom. I think my car has PMS. My other car is a piece of shit, too. Do not wash—this car is undergoing a scientific dirt test. Don't laugh—it's paid for. If this car were a horse, I'd have to shoot it. If I go any faster, I'll burn out my hamsters. I may be slow, but I'm ahead of you. I also drive a Titleist. Pedal downhill.

Shit happens. I love your wife. Megashit happens. I'm single again. Wife and dog missing—reward for dog. The more people I meet, the more I like my cat. Nobody on board. Sober 'n' crazy. Do it sober. Drive smart—drive sober.

No more Mr. Nice Guy. Lost your cat? Try looking under my tires. I love my German shepherd. Never mind the dog—beware of owner. Don't fence me in. Don't tell me what kind of day to have. Don't tailgate or I'll flush. Eat shit and die. My kid beat up your honor student. Abort your inner child. I don't care who you are, what you're driving, who's on board, who you love, where you'd rather be, or what you'd rather be doing.

Not so close—I hardly know you. Watch my rear end, not hers. You hit it—you buy it. Hands off. No radio. No Condo / No MBA / No BMW. You toucha my car—I breaka your face. Protected by Smith & Wesson. Warning: This car is protected by a large sheet of cardboard.

LUV2HNT. Gun control is being able to hit your target. Hunters make better lovers: they go deeper into the bush—they shoot more often—and they eat what they shoot.

Yes, as a matter of fact, I do own the whole damn road. Get in, sit down, shut up, and hold on. I don't drive fast—I just fly low. If you don't like the way I drive, stay off the sidewalk. I'm polluting the atmosphere. Can't do 55.

I may be growing old, but I refuse to grow up. Get even—live long enough to become a problem to your kids. We're out spending our children's inheritance.

Life is pretty dry without a boat. I'd rather be sailing. A man's place is on his boat. Everyone must believe in something—I believe I'll go canoeing. Who cares!

Eat dessert first—life is uncertain. Why be normal?

Don't follow me—I'm lost, too. Wherever you are, be there. No matter where you go, there you are. Bloom where you are planted.

Easy does it. Keep it simple, stupid. I'm 4 Clean Air. Go fly a kite. No matter—never mind. UFOs are real. Of all the things I've lost, I miss my mind the most. I brake for unicorns.

Choose death.

Word count: 1,050

go-go tarot

by Evie Shockley

---

u-haul yourself up by your bootstraps might be the fortune this photo tells for the youngblood sitting loose-legged on the tail of a mostly empty rental truck with plates from arizona, a state of confusion that doesn't see a day's worth of celebration in the life of dr. king, that mistakes mccain for a maverick. but he is—no, *you are* in d.c., and no matter how hot your future gets, or how it gets hot, it will not be a desert, so i'll search for other signs. i

stop speaking *of* you, to speak *to* you, once my eyes fall into yours staring somberly, directly, at the camera. you, little man, handsome already at eight years old, dwarfed by the massive stack of stereo equipment beside you—players, receivers, amplifiers, spewing wires as thick as hoses and thin as an unemployment check, all crowned by a mixer wide enough to dance on—you sporting fresh white kicks, black rubber coating the toe and

around the heel giving them the look of spats, you are surrounded by potential portents. could be the goddess of those shoes will bless or curse you with game, will guide your feet easily or let you get tripped up among the many cords snaking along your path. a full heritage of afro-forward music-making, symbolized by the dj's pulpit, is yours by birth to earn—but the inverted reading focuses on the dj himself, squarely, yet barely,

in this shot, all but concealed (there's a corner of his tee, a leg of baggy denim) behind his instruments, as if to say that you, too, could become an invisible man. well, no. not on my watch. if i'm reading this card (i'm reading this card), it's not *the tower*, it's *the world*. look at you, perched on the threshold, the door wide open. with *university* fixed across your chest and a pair of drumsticks in your hand, you've got everything you need to beat the odds.

Word count: 334

Cannibals and Explorers

by Ana María Shua

The cannibals dance around the explorers. The cannibals light the fire. The cannibals have their faces painted in three colors. The cannibals prefer the heart and brain, disdaining the tender flesh of the thighs and the leftover intestines. The cannibals consume those parts of the body they believe will instill in them the virtues they admire in their victims. The cannibals partake of their ritual banquet without pleasure or mercy. The cannibals don the explorers' clothes. The cannibals, once in London, deliver scholarly lectures on cannibals.

Translated by Rhonda Dahl Buchanan
Word count: 86

An All-Purpose Product

by Patricia Smith

What surfaces can I use this product on?
ANSWER: Lysol may be used on hard, nonporous surfaces throughout your home. Lysol cleans, disinfects, and deodorizes regular and nonwax floors, nonwood cabinets, sinks, and garbage pails. For painted surfaces, it is recommended that the product first be tested in a small inconspicuous area.

Can Lysol be used in the kitchen?
ANSWER: Lysol may be used on countertops, refrigerators, nonwood cabinets, sinks, stovetops, and microwave ovens. For the bathroom, it may be used for tiles, tubs, sinks, and porcelain. And for all around the house, it may be used on floors, garbage cans, in the basement, and in the garage.

Can I use this inside my refrigerator?
ANSWER: Lysol may be used on the inside of a refrigerator. However, you must remove all food, and rinse well after using the product.

Can I use this to kill mold and mildew?
Yes. Lysol controls the growth of mold and mildew. It kills the mold, but removal of the stain associated with mold and mildew can sometimes be tough.

Can I use this to scrub the uncontrollable black from the surface of my daughter, to make her less Negro and somehow less embarrassing to me? She's like the hour after midnight, that chile is.

Why, yes. Begin with one Sears gray swirled dinette set chair, screeching across the hardwood on spindly steel legs. Place the offending child on the ruptured plastic of the seat. Demand that she bend her neck to grant you access to the damaged area. You know, of course, that black begins at the back of the neck. Grab a kitchen towel, a washcloth, or a sponge, and soak with undiluted Lysol concentrate.

Ignoring the howls of the impossibly Negro child, scrub vigorously until the offending black surrenders. There may be inflammation, a painful rebellion of skin, slight bleeding. This is simply the first step to righteousness. The child must be punished for her lack of silky tresses, her broad sinful nose, that dark Negroid blanket she wears. Layers of her must disappear.

PRECAUTIONARY STATEMENTS. DANGER: CORROSIVE TO EYES AND SKIN. HARMFUL IF SWALLOWED. Causes eye and skin damage. Do not get in eyes or on skin. Wear protective eyewear and rubber gloves when handling.

Woman, your mission is beyond this. You must clean the child, burn the Southern sun from her. If she squirms from the hurting, demand that she hold on to the sides of the chair. Soak towel or sponge with our patented holy water. Repeat application.

I have tried to understand PRECAUTIONARY STATEMENTS my mother DANGER: her hatred of this CORROSIVE TO EYES AND SKIN of the me that wears this HARMFUL IF SWALLOWED the monster she had CAUSES EYE AND SKIN DAMAGE the monster she wanted DO NOT GET IN EYES OR ON SKIN

Mama, can't you read it? You want me to read it to you? I can't help being my color! I am black, I am not dirty. I am black, I am not dirty, I am black, I am. Not. Dirty. What you have birthed upon me will not come off. My hair is black crinkled steel, too short to stay plaited. My ass is wide and will get wider. You can pinch my nose, but it will remain a landscape. You cannot reverse me. What is filthy to you will never be cleansed. There is only one thing you can

change

I am not dirty, I am black. I am not dirty, I am black, I am not black, I am dirty. I am dirty black, not black. I am black and dirty. Dirt is black. Black is dirty. You convinced me that I am what is wrong in this world.

Scrub me right.

Bleed me lighter.

What is the difference between disinfection and sanitization? Why are there two different usage directions for each?

ANSWER: According to the Environmental Protection Agency, "disinfection" is killing more than 99.99% of germs on hard, nonporous surfaces in ten minutes, and may pertain to a number of different types of bacteria, viruses, and fungi. The EPA defines "sanitization" as killing 99.9% of bacteria in five minutes or less.

Lysol products achieve sanitization in 30 seconds.

29.	28.	27.	26.	25.	24.	23.
22.	21.	20.	19.	18.	17.	16.
15.	14.	13.	12.	11.	10.	9.
8.	7.	6.	5.	4.	3.	2. …

Done.

Word count: 731

Consequence

by Ira Sukrungruang

In my Club Scout pack, I was the poison ivy alarm. Out of all the lessons at den meetings, this was the one I most remembered. Our Den Mother had pointed to pictures of three broad leaves and told us tales of people who came in contact with them. One time, she told us, a friend of hers went into the woods to do number two and accidentally brushed his bottom on poison ivy. Hours later, rashes and bumps broke out all over his skin and he couldn't stop scratching to the point she had to take him to the hospital.

Her story stuck with me. I was allergic to everything already, miserable during hay fever season, another thing I inherited from my father whose allergy sneezes shook the earth. There was nothing more uncomfortable than a constant itch, one that gnawed at you and didn't go away no matter how much you scratched.

When my father came to the Father & Son Cub Scout Halloween celebration at Maple Lake, a forest preserve in Cook County, Illinois, he wanted to know what poison ivy looked like. It was the first time he took part in one of my extra-curricular activities. Usually, he worked at the tile factory most of the afternoon, so I rarely saw him except for weekends. That day, my father was in navy blue slacks, white leather shoes, and a pink golfing polo. He did his best to converse with the men, who towered over him, but most conversations led to uncomfortable silences.

Apart from being a small Thai immigrant, my father was different from other fathers. Other fathers wore rugged jeans and work boots. Other fathers sported camouflage jackets and hats. Other fathers gripped cans of Budweiser and smoked unfiltered cigarettes. My father did not fit that mold, and because I was seven and a Club Scout, an organization of boys training to be men, I wondered if my father was a man. I wondered if the other kids thought I was like him.

In one of the activities, my father and I entered the forest to forage for things to decorate our lopsided pumpkin: pretty stones, twigs, fallen leaves, acorn tops, strips of tree bark. So when he asked me what poison ivy was, I located some at the base of a maple.

My father pointed at it. "Are you sure?"

I understood his question. For a plant to be called poison ivy one expected it to look poisonous or alien, like the Venus Flytrap. But to the untrained eye, poison ivy looked no different from other bushes and shrubs and trees. It did not drip purple ooze or emit a foul odor. It was green and red and leafy like everything else around us.

My father knelt beside it and pointed at it again. "This poison ivy?"

"Yes," I said.

He moved to touch it, his finger hovering over the plant.

"What are you doing?" I said.

"Want to know what happen. Want to know if really poison."

"You're not going to like it." I couldn't stop him. He touched it. He pinched a leaf, tore a bit of it off, and brought it to his nose. He sniffed.

"I no feel anything." He wiped his hands on his slacks.

There was a chance that my father was among the twenty percent who were immune to poison ivy. But from what I remembered reading, it took some time before the skin got irritated by the oils of the plant. He shrugged and laughed, and I shrugged and stood a good distance away from him the rest of the time we collected our items, telling him to wash his hands in the creek bed so I wouldn't be infected too.

When we started decorating the pumpkin, I noticed a bump on my father's cheek. As I stuck thick branches into the top of the pumpkin—its antennae—I noticed another. As I pushed acorn tops around the stem of the pumpkin, my father began to scratch a collected series of bumps that started at the corner of his mouth and ended near the point of his chin. As I glued on leaves for the pumpkin's multicolored hair, he was scratching so hard, tiny bubbles of blood emerged from his chin.

"Dad," I said, pointing at his face, trying not to draw the attention of the other fathers and sons around us. His fingers scratched and scratched. Blood smeared his face. But he kept working, kept shoving acorn tops into our pumpkin. He carved wavy lines on the sides and inserted leaves into the space. He told me the pumpkin's eyes should be the weathered stones from the creek, the smooth brown ones that were thin and long. When we were done, our pumpkin looked like an Asian alien bellowing blessings from its large oval mouth.

We took first place for our pumpkin. We would take first a month later with the regatta boat we built together and again for the best meal cooked by campfire during the winter campout. That day, with the blue ribbon in my hand, my father drove home, grinning like a jack-o-lantern, his rash already scabbing up. I want to tell him I told you so. But it seemed he knew what I was thinking and said there were some things you must find out for yourself, no matter the consequence. "Understand?"

I did.

I reached up and touched his skin.

Word count: 910

In Praise of Latin Night at the Queer Club

by Justin Torres

If you're lucky, they'll play some Latin cheese, that Aventura song from 15 years ago. If you're lucky, there will be drag queens and, if so, almost certainly they will be quick, razor-sharp with their humor, giving you the kind of performances that cut and heal all at once. If you're lucky, there will be go-go boys, every shade of brown.

Maybe your Ma blessed you on the way out the door. Maybe she wrapped a plate for you in the fridge so you don't come home and mess up her kitchen with your hunger. Maybe your Tia dropped you off, gave you cab money home. Maybe you had to get a sitter. Maybe you've yet to come out to your family at all, or maybe your family kicked you out years ago. Forget it, you survived. Maybe your boo stayed home, wasn't feeling it, but is blowing up your phone with sweet texts, trying to make sure you don't stray. Maybe you're allowed to stray. Maybe you're flush, maybe you're broke as nothing, and angling your pretty face barside, hoping someone might buy you a drink. Maybe your half-Latin-ass doesn't even speak Spanish; maybe you barely speak English. Maybe you're undocumented.

Outside, there's a world that politicizes every aspect of your identity. There are preachers, of multiple faiths, mostly self-identified Christians, condemning you to hell. Outside, they call you an abomination. Outside, there is a news media that acts as if there are two sides to a debate over trans people using public bathrooms. Outside, there is a presidential candidate who has built a platform on erecting a wall between the United States and Mexico—and not only do people believe that crap is possible, they believe it is necessary. Outside, Puerto Rico is still a colony, being allowed to drown in debt, to suffer, without the right to file for bankruptcy, to protect itself. Outside, there are more than 100 bills targeting you, your choices, your people, pending in various states.

You have known violence. You have known violence. You are queer and you are brown and you have known violence. You have known a masculinity, a machismo, stupid with its own fragility. You learned basic queer safety, you have learned to scan, casually, quickly, before any public display of affection. Outside, the world can be murderous to you and your kind. Lord knows.

But inside, it is loud and sexy and on. If you're lucky, it's a mixed crowd, muscle Marys and bois and femme fags and butch dykes and genderqueers. If you're lucky, no one is wearing much clothing, and the dance floor is full. If you're lucky, they're playing reggaeton, salsa, and you can move.

People talk about liberation as if it's some kind of permanent state, as if you get liberated and that's it, you get some rights and that's it, you get some acknowledgment and that's it, happy now? But you're going back down into the muck of it every day; this world constricts. You know what the opposite of Latin Night at the Queer Club is? Another Day in Straight White America. So when you walk into the club, if you're lucky, it feels expansive. "Safe space" is a cliché, overused and exhausted in our discourse, but the fact remains that a sense of safety transforms the body, transforms the spirit. So many of us walk through the world without it. So when you walk through the door and it's a salsa beat, and brown bodies, queer bodies, all writhing in some fake smoke and strobing lights, no matter how cool, how detached, how over-it you think you are, Latin Night at the Queer Club breaks your cool. You can't help but smile, this is for you, for us.

Outside, tomorrow, hangovers, regrets, the grind. Outside, tomorrow, the struggle to effect change. But inside, tonight, none of that matters. Inside, tonight, the only imperative is to love. Lap the bar, out for a smoke, back inside, the ammonia and sweat and the floor slightly tacky, another drink, the imperative is to get loose, get down, find religion, lose it, find your hips locked into another's, break, dance on your own for a while—but you didn't come here to be a nun—find your lips pressed against another's, break, find your friends, dance. The only imperative is to be transformed, transfigured in the disco light. To lighten, loosen, see yourself reflected in the beauty of others. You didn't come here to be a martyr, you came to live, papi. To live, mamacita. To live, hijos. To live, mariposas.

The media will spin the conversation away from homegrown homophobic terrorism to a general United States vs. Islamist narrative. Mendacious, audacious politicians—Republicans who vote against queer rights, against gun control—will seize on this massacre, twist it for support of their agendas.

But for a moment, I want to talk about the sacredness of Latin Night at the Queer Club. Amid all the noise, I want to close my eyes and see you all there, dancing, inviolable, free.

Word count: 845

Icelandic Hurricane

by Tomas Tranströmer

Not earth-tremor but sky-quake. Turner could have painted it, lashed tight. A solitary mitten has just whirled by, several miles from its hand. I am going to make my way against the wind to that house on the other side of the field. I flutter in the hurricane. I am x-rayed, the skeleton hands in its resignation. Panic grows as I beat upwind, I founder, I founder and drown on dry land! How heavy everything I suddenly have to drag along, how heavy for the butterfly to tow a barge! There at last. A final wrestle with the door. And now inside. And now inside. Behind the big glass pane. What a strange and wonderful invention glass is—to be close yet untouched . . . Outside, a horde of transparent sprinters in giant format charges across the lava plain. But I'm no longer fluttering. I'm sitting behind the glass, at rest, my own portrait.

Translated by Robin Fulton
Word count: 151

The Box

by Thomas Tsalapatis

I have a small box in which someone is always being slaughtered.

It is a little larger than a shoebox. A little less elegant than a box with cigars. I do not know who, I do not know whom, but someone is being slaughtered in there. And you cannot hear a sound (except for the times when you can). I place it on the library, on the table when I want to spend my hours looking at it, away from the windows so the sun won't discolour it, underneath my bed when I want to feel naughty. Inside it someone is being slaughtered, even when we have a celebration in our house, even on Sunday, even when it's raining.

When I found the box—I am not going to say how, I am not going to say where—I brought it home feeling satisfied. At the time, I thought I could hear the sound of the sea. However, in there massacres are taking place.

I started to be sickened by the noise, the knowledge of the events, the events inside the box. Its presence started making me sick. I had to act, to liberate myself, to calm down, to take a bath. Decisions had to be made.

So, I mailed it to a friend; a friend whom I keep only to give gifts to. I wrapped the box inside a piece of innocent colourful cardboard with an innocent colourful ribbon. Inside the mailbox there is a box and inside that box someone is being massacred. Stored inside the mailbox, it is waiting to arrive in the hands of a friend. A friendship I maintain solely for gift-giving.

Translated by Thodoris Chiotis
Word count: 278

The Inventory from a Year Lived Sleeping with Bullets

by Brian Turner

Rifle oil, *check*. Smoke grenades, *check*. Desert boots, *check*. Plates of body armor, *check*. The list ongoing—combat patrols added, 5 Paragraph Op Orders, mission briefs, nights spent staring for heat signatures through the white-hot lens, lasers bore-sighted to the barrels they guide. The conceptual and physical given parallel structure.

A dead infant. A night-crushed car. A farmer slumped over a Toyota steering wheel near an army checkpoint. A distraught relative staring beyond, pieces of brain on the dashboard. The refusal to render aid. The fresh dark soil over the bodies.

The boredom. The minutes. The hours. Days. Weeks. Months. The moments unbounded by time's dominion. The years after.

Torture fragments. A man pissing on the Qu'ran. A man at a rifle range firing a bullet. A bullet carrying the middle vowel of the word *Inshallah*. A combat load of ammunition.

3rd Squad. 1st Platoon. Blackhorse Company. The faces—ones I hated and the ones I loved. Even the ones I don't remember. And all who don't remember me. *Contact. Three O' Clock. 50 meters. Talk the Guns.*

And Seattle at night. Rain drizzling down. First weekend home from war. Sgt. Gould sucking a woman's nipple in the cuddle room at the rave party. Glow sticks in mouths, a language of light. A language I don't recognize. A man in an Energizer bunny suit, on roller-skates, bass pounding the camouflage of tireless eternal Easter followed by a brunette in black leather bustier, thigh-high wet leather PVC boots, her eyes the dark carbon from the barrel's chamber as she pulls a leashed man by the throat. These people. *My people.*

Put it all in the rucksack. Throw the rucksack on your back and call it your *house*. Do a commo check with anyone out there in the bush, listening. Do a commo check back home. Get your shit on straight. *Stay Alert and Stay Alive*. Drink water and conduct your PCIs. We've reached the *Line of Departure*. So lock and load, man. From here on out we are on radio silence.

Word count: 340

Immigrant Haibun

by Ocean Vuong

The road which leads me to you is safe
even when it runs into oceans.
            Edmond Jabès

*

Then, as if breathing, the sea swelled beneath us. If you must know anything, know that the hardest task is to live only once. That a woman on a sinking ship becomes a life raft—no matter how soft her skin. While I slept, he burned his last violin to keep my feet warm. He lay beside me and placed a word on the nape of my neck, where it melted into a bead of whiskey. Gold rust down my back. We had been sailing for months. Salt in our sentences. We had been sailing—but the edge of the world was nowhere in sight.

*

When we left it, the city was still smoldering. Otherwise it was a perfect spring morning. White hyacinths gasped in the embassy lawn. The sky was September-blue and the pigeons went on pecking at bits of bread scattered from the bombed bakery. Broken baguettes. Crushed croissants. Gutted cars. A carousel spinning its blackened horses. He said the shadow of missiles growing larger on the sidewalk looked like god playing an air piano above us. He said *There is so much I need to tell you.*

*

Stars. Or rather, the drains of heaven—waiting. Little holes. Little centuries opening just long enough for us to slip through. A machete on the deck left out to dry. My back turned to him. My feet in the eddies. He crouches beside me, his breath a misplaced weather. I let him cup a handful of the sea into my hair and wring it out. *The smallest pearls—and all for you.* I open my eyes. His face between my hands, wet as a cut. *If we make it to shore,* he says, *I will name our son after this water. I will learn to love a monster.* He smiles. A white hyphen where his lips should be. There are seagulls above us. There are hands fluttering between the constellations, trying to hold on.

*

The fog lifts. And we see it. The horizon—suddenly gone. An aqua sheen leading to the hard drop. Clean and merciful—just like he wanted. Just like the fairy tales. The one where the book closes and turns to laughter in our laps. I pull the mast to full sail. He throws my name into the air. I watch the syllables crumble into pebbles across the deck.

*

Furious roar. The sea splitting at the bow. He watches it open like a thief staring into his own heart: all bones and splintered wood. Waves rising on both sides. The ship encased in liquid walls. *Look!* he says, *I see it now!* He's jumping up and down. He's kissing the back of my wrist as he clutches the wheel. He laughs but his eyes betray him. He laughs despite knowing he has ruined every beautiful thing just to prove beauty cannot change him. And here's the kicker: there's a cork where the sunset should be. It was always there. There's a ship made from toothpicks and superglue. There's a ship in a wine bottle on the mantel in the middle of a Christmas party—eggnog spilling from red Solo cups. But we keep sailing anyway. We keep standing at the bow. A wedding-cake couple encased in glass. The water so still now. The water like air, like hours. Everyone's shouting or singing and he can't tell whether the song is for him—or the burning rooms he mistook for childhood. Everyone's dancing while a tiny man and woman are stuck inside a green bottle thinking someone is waiting at the end of their lives to say *Hey! You didn't have to go this far. Why did you go so far?* Just as a baseball bat crashes through the world.

*

If you must know anything, know that you were born because no one else was coming. The ship rocked as you swelled inside me: love's echo hardening into a boy. Sometimes I feel like an ampersand. I wake up waiting for the crush. Maybe the body is the only question an answer can't extinguish. How many kisses have we crushed to our lips in prayer—only to pick up the pieces? If you must know, the best way to understand a man is with your teeth. Once, I swallowed the rain through a whole green thunderstorm. Hours lying on my back, my girlhood open. The field everywhere beneath me. How sweet. That rain. How something that lives only to fall can be nothing but sweet. Water whittled down to intention. Intention into nourishment. Everyone can forget us—as long as you remember.

*

Summer in the mind.
God opens his other eye:
 two moons in the lake.

Word count: 784

Scheherazade.

by Lucy Wainger

—After Richard Siken

comes wave after wave after wave the derivative & harvest, the myrtle tops of sandstorms & milk glasses, apple, horse & song, list, listen, light leaks from the spaces between the bubbles—call it foam—tender pocket of *yes yes yes* call it flesh—eat tonight & you'll still have to eat tomorrow, eat tonight & it still won't be over—eat tonight: peaches bloom even in the dark, as wet as a girl—hands & feet, horse & song, the same hole bandaged over & over, not a wound but its absence—a sum of histories—the nights colliding like marbles, & if there is an end then it's too dark to see, if there is an end then it's too bright to see, hands folding, unfolding, & you, Scheherazade!, milky goddess of recursion, best DJ in the city, you spin records, spin heads, cross legs & cross deserts, & always pause just moments before he

Word count: 157

Small Meditations

by Michael Wasson

Crushed in the hands, the scent of pine needles & the smear of sap on the ball. My jump shot comes to me from hours behind my childhood home shooting at the hoop that my long-haired uncles drilled into the face of the pine. No real *court* to dribble on. That's okay. I just shoot under the large pine that I mistake for a fatherly skeleton crucified at dusk. After a few weeks, the ball lies half-discolored. A face I've not touched in years it seems. Flattening. But I pick it up again & arc through the low hanging arms of this skeletal, living tree.

i.

Inside the house, my great grandmother is dying. I'm 12 years old. I shoot at a rusted rim. A squaring patch of dirt is *the paint*. The gravel & broken down cars hoisted on chopping blocks leading to the HUD house: *the perimeter*. The dilapidated, splitting backboard—literally *a board*—is how I rebound to keep the ball semi-graspable. I wash my hands before I help her to the restroom.

i.

His father pours rugged cement to make a small court beside their house. After, my cousin & I take our living room *Fisher-Price* dunks & clutch shots from behind the sage-smelling couch covered in a Pendleton blanket to this *real* court. At least *we* think it is. I'm 9 years old. He lost his older brother last year. We play H-O-R-S-E until our relatives start three-on-three. It's past supper—*hunger* somewhere deep in the open mouth of the rim. *Something* we want to swallow over & over. Before winter, I won't see *'ácqa* alive again. I forget how to cry at his funeral. Until after. When his body's not there.

i.

Summer. Mom's in debt because of doctor visits. *His knees can't*. I'm 10. *No team sports*.

i.

Grandma says uncle, as a teen, would play basketball at the *Mexis* until 10 or 11 at night. His indigenous knees & elbows all scraped up. I imagine streetlights as little breakable moons. I think about *shoot out the lights* & gunfire. He was blooming from so much light—his skin gave away. Now I'm watching him play rezball at the *páayniwaas*—the community center. He still wrecks the paint with only one eye.

i.

I'm on a small island in southwestern Japan. 25 years old. I'm in the elementary gym. My classes are done, & there's one small green basketball I find. The only basketball. It's tiny. At least this is a *court*, though. An international trapezoid with taped lines. I take a jump shot. I've lost three people this year. *Swish. Miss. Bank. Put back. Baby hook. Runner.* Now it's dark, winter & wind desperate to tear off the ceiling. Alone again. I'm searching for that sound—rattled board. The beauty of *all net*. Netless emptiness. Reaching up, & unable to see the rim now. My sight searching for any residue of faint light. I'm following-through, flicking my release, even without seeable hands. In the dark. Working on my *touch*. My *feel*.

Word count: 509

A Letter to Deb Clow

by Terry Tempest Williams

Dearest Deb:

You asked me why I write and I said I couldn't talk about it, that it was too close, too visceral. We went on to another subject and then we finished our conversation and hung up the phone. I thought I left the question with you.

It is just after 4:00 A.M., I can't sleep. I was dreaming about Moab, Brooke and I walking around the block just before dawn. I threw a red silk scarf around my shoulders and then I began reciting in my sleep why I write:

I write to make peace with the things I cannot control. I write to create red in a world that often appears black and white. I write to discover. I write to uncover. I write to meet my ghosts. I write to begin a dialogue. I write to imagine things differently and in imagining things differently perhaps the world will change. I write to honor beauty. I write to correspond with my friends. I write as a daily act of improvisation. I write because it creates my composure. I write against power and for democracy. I write myself out of my nightmares and into my dreams. I write in a solitude born out of community. I write to the questions that shatter my sleep. I write to the answers that keep me complacent. I write to remember. I write to forget. I write to the music that opens my heart. I write to quell the pain. I write to migrating birds with the hubris of language. I write as a form of translation. I write with the patience of melancholy in winter. I write because it allows me to confront that which I do not know. I write as an act of faith. I write as an act of slowness. I write to record what I love in the face of loss. I write because it makes me less fearful of death. I write as an exercise in pure joy. I write as one who walks on the surface of a frozen river beginning to melt. I write out of my anger and into my passion. I write from the stillness of night anticipating—always anticipating. I write to listen. I write out of silence. I write to soothe the voices shouting inside me, outside me, all around. I write because of the humor of our condition as humans. I write because I believe in words. I write because I do not believe in words. I write because it is a dance with paradox. I write because you can play on the page like a child left alone in the sand. I write because it belongs to the force of the moon: high tide, low tide. I write because it is the way I take long walks. I write as a bow to wilderness. I write because I believe it can create a path in darkness. I write because as a child I spoke a different language. I write with a knife carving each word through the generosity of trees. I write as ritual. I write because I am not employable. I write out of my inconsistencies. I write because then I do not have to speak. I write with the colors of memory. I write as a witness to what I have seen. I write as a witness to what I imagine. I write by grace and grit. I write out of indigestion. I write when I am starving. I write when I am full. I write to the dead. I write out of the body. I write to put food on the table. I write on the other side of procrastination. I write for the children we never had. I write for the love of ideas. I write for the surprise of a beautiful sentence. I write with the belief of alchemists. I write knowing I will always fail. I write knowing words always fall short. I write knowing I can be killed by my own words, stabbed by syntax, crucified by both understanding and misunderstanding. I write out of ignorance. I write by accident. I write past the embarrassment of exposure. I keep writing and suddenly, I am overcome by the sheer indulgence, the madness, the meaninglessness, the ridiculousness of this list. I trust nothing, especially myself, and slide headfirst into the familiar abyss of doubt and humiliation and threaten to push the delete button on my way down, or madly erase each line, pick up the paper and rip it to shreds—and then I realize, it doesn't matter, words are always a gamble, words are splinters of cut glass. I write because it is dangerous, a bloody risk, like love, to form the words, to say the words, to touch the source, to be touched, to reveal how vulnerable we are, how transient we are. I write as though I am whispering in the ear of the one I love.

Back to sleep.

I love you,

Terry

Word count: 832

Excerpt from "Four about Death"

by David Young

I get your instructions in a letter. A small plane drops me at an airfield in the Andes. I stand by a rusting hangar, watching it climb out of sight. No one's around. Farther up the mountain animals I have never seen are grazing. Higher still a few clouds, resting against rocks. You do not arrive when I do. I must live in a hut for an undetermined space of time. Now and then I walk down to the village, carrying a basket for food and a jug for wine, but such things interest me less and less. Night storms light the mountains with blue flashes and send gusts of wind and rain that flatten the meadows. The morning of your arrival, I see a hare raised up, watching me. I do not know if you will come down the mountain, or more slowly, from below. All I know is that I will go out to meet you. My soul will be in my mouth.

Word count: 165

Author Bios

Henry Alford, a humorist and journalist, has written for the *New Yorker*, *Vanity Fair*, and the *New York Times* for two decades. His books include *How to Live* and *Big Kiss*, which won a Thurber Prize for American Humor.

Joanne Avallon lives in Massachusetts and had the privilege of studying poetry with Frank Bidart at Wellesley and flash fiction at Emerson with Pam Painter. She likes to play at the intersection of these two forms, where there is the compression of flash, but also the emotional complexity and vulnerability of poetry.

Pía Barros is a Chilean writer and feminist. For almost forty years, she has given literary workshops in Chile and other countries. She has published two novels, five story collections, and four flash fiction collections. She leads the Ergo Sum workshops and is the director of the publishing house Asterión. She has won several awards.

Charles Baudelaire was a nineteenth-century French poet most known for his book of poetry, *Les Fleurs du mal*.

Matt Bell is the author of the novels *Scrapper* and *In the House upon the Dirt between the Lake and the Woods*, as well as the short story collection *A Tree or a Person or a Wall*, and several other titles. He teaches in the creative writing program at Arizona State University.

Karen E. Bender is the author of the story collection *Refund*, which was a finalist for the National Book Award in fiction and shortlisted for the Frank O'Connor International Story Prize. Her novels are *A Town of Empty Rooms* and *Like Normal People*; a new story collection, *The New Order*, will be published in 2018. Her fiction has appeared in the *New Yorker*, *Granta*, *Best American Short Stories*, and *Best American Mystery Stories* and won two Pushcart Prizes.

Sven Birkerts edits the journal *AGNI* at Boston University. He is the author of ten books, most recently *Changing the Subject: Art and Attention in the Internet Age* (Graywolf).

Italo Calvino was an Italian writer and journalist who was born in 1923. He wrote *The Baron in the Trees, The Nonexistent Knight, Invisible Cities, Cosmicomics, Difficult Loves, Six Memos for the Next Millenium,* and more.

Joy Castro is the award-winning author of two literary thrillers set in post-Katrina New Orleans, two memoirs, and a collection of short fiction. She lives and works in Lincoln, Nebraska.

Matthew Clarke is a Canadian writer, director, actor, and father. In 2013, he created the hit web series *Convos with My 2-Year-Old* with his then two-year-old daughter, Coco.

Katie Cortese is the author of *Girl Power and Other Short-Short Stories* (ELJ Editions, 2015) and *Make Way for Her and Other Stories* (University Press of Kentucky, 2018). She teaches in the creative writing program at Texas Tech University and serves as the fiction editor for *Iron Horse Literary Review.*

Steve Coughlin teaches writing and literature at Chadron State College in northwest Nebraska. His book of poetry, *Another City*, was published by FutureCycle Press.

Lydia Davis is a novelist, short story writer, and translator who has published eight books. She has received numerous awards, including a MacArthur fellowship, an American Academy of Arts and Letters' Award, a Lannan Literary Award, and the Man Booker International Prize.

Theodore Deppe is the author of six books of poems. He has received two NEA grants and a Pushcart Prize. He directs Stonecoast in Ireland for the Stonecoast MFA program. Since 2000, he has lived for the most part on the west coast of Ireland.

Danielle Cadena Deulen is the author of three books: *Our Emotions Get Carried Away beyond Us* (Barrow Street Book Contest), *The Riots* (AWP Prize in Creative Nonfiction), and *Lovely Asunder* (Miller Williams Arkansas

Poetry Prize). She teaches at Willamette University and is poetry series editor of Acre Books.

Natalie Diaz, a member of the Mojave and Pima Indian tribes, attended Old Dominion University on a full athletic scholarship. After playing professional basketball in Austria, Portugal, Spain, Sweden, and Turkey she returned to ODU for an MFA in writing. Her publications include *Prairie Schooner*, *Iowa Review*, *Crab Orchard Review*, among others. Her work was selected by Natasha Trethewey for *Best New Poets*, and she has received the Nimrod/ Hardman Pablo Neruda Prize for Poetry. She lives in Surprise, Arizona.

Brian Doyle was the editor of *Portland Magazine* at the University of Portland, in Oregon. He wrote many books, including *The Adventures of John Carson in Several Quarters of the World: A Novel of Robert Louis Stevenson*, *Mink River*, *The Plover*, *Martin Marten*, *Chicago: A Novel*, *Bin Laden's Bald Spot*, *The Grail*, *The Wet Engine*, *The Mighty Currawongs*, *Children and Other Wild Animals*, and others.

Russell Edson was an American poet, novelist, and writer who was born in 1935. In addition to writing novels, story collections, fables, plays, and operas, he published thirteen collections of prose poetry.

Sarah Evans is an Oregon writer who has been published in *Bluestem*, *Mom Egg Review*, and *Brevity*'s Nonfiction Blog. Several of her tweet-length "Tiny Truths"—the ultimate short-form writing—have appeared in *Creative Nonfiction* magazine. She earned an MFA in nonfiction writing from Pacific University. Read about her at www.sarahevanswriter.com.

Grant Faulkner is the executive director of National Novel Writing Month and the cofounder of *100 Word Story*. His stories have appeared in dozens of literary magazines, including *Tin House*, *The Southwest Review*, and *The Gettysburg Review*. His essays on writing have been published in the *New York Times*, *Poets & Writers*, *Writer's Digest*, and *The Writer*. He recently published a book of essays on creativity, *Pep Talks for Writers: 52 Insights and Actions to Boost Your Creative Mojo*. He's also published a collection of 100-word stories, *Fissures*, two of which are included in *The Best Small Fictions 2016*.

Nikky Finney was born in South Carolina, within listening distance of the sea. A child of activists, she came of age during the civil rights and Black Arts Movements. At Talladega College, nurtured by Hale Woodruff's Amistad murals, Finney began to understand the powerful synergy between art and history. Finney has authored four books of poetry: *Head Off & Split* (2011), *The World Is Round* (2003), *Rice* (1995), and *On Wings Made of Gauze* (1985). The John H. Bennett Jr. Chair in Creative Writing and Southern Letters at the University of South Carolina, Finney also authored *Heartwood* (1997), edited *The Ringing Ear: Black Poets Lean South* (2007), and cofounded the Affrilachian Poets. Finney's fourth book of poetry, *Head Off & Split*, was awarded the 2011 National Book Award for poetry.

Kathy Fish teaches for the Mile High MFA at Regis University in Denver. She has published four collections of short fiction. Her stories have appeared in *Indiana Review, Yemassee Journal, Guernica*, and elsewhere. Her work was chosen by Amy Hempel for inclusion in *The Best Small Fictions 2017*.

Sherrie Flick is the author of the novel *Reconsidering Happiness*, the flash fiction chapbook *I Call This Flirting*, and the short story collection *Whiskey, Etc.*, a Foreword INDIES book of the year in Short Stories and an *Entropy* Best Fiction Book of 2016. Her most recent collection is *Thank Your Lucky Stars*, out with Autumn House Press in 2018. She lives in Pittsburgh.

Thaisa Frank is the author of six books, most recently *Enchantment* (Counterpoint Press, 2012), a collection of short fiction, among SF Chronicle Best Books 2012. Her novel *Heidegger's Glasses* (Counterpoint Press, 2010, 2011) sold foreign rights to ten countries before publication. *Finding Your Writer's Voice* (St. Martin's Press) was just issued as an e-book and is still available as a paperback.

Bryan Fry is the editor of *Blood Orange Review* and the Editing and Publishing Coordinator for the Department of English at Washington State University. His essays have appeared in *Brevity, Front Porch*, and *South Dakota Review*.

Molly Giles is the author of three collections of short stories (*Rough Translations, Creek Walk, All the Wrong Places*), a chapbook of flash fictions (*Bothered*), and a novel, *Iron Shoes*.

Amelia Gray is the author of five books, most recently *Isadora* (FSG).

Katelyn Hemmeke was born in Seoul, South Korea, and raised in Michigan. She earned her MA in English from the University of Nebraska–Lincoln. A two-time Fulbright grant recipient, she devotes much of her writing, research, and activism to social justice in the transnational/transracial adoption community. She currently lives in Seoul.

Amy Hempel is the author of *The Dog of the Marriage, Tumble Home, Reasons to Live*, and *At the Gates of the Animal Kingdom* and the coeditor of *Unleashed*. Her stories have appeared in *Elle, GQ, Harper's, Playboy, The Quarterly*, and *Vanity Fair*. She teaches in the graduate writing program at Bennington College and Stony Brook University. She lives in New York.

David Ignatow published fifteen volumes of poetry and three prose collections. Born in Brooklyn, he lived most of his life in the New York metropolitan area, working as editor of *American Poetry Review* and *Beloit Poetry Journal* and poetry editor of *The Nation*. Ignatow received both the Shelley Memorial Award (1966) and the Frost Medal (1992). He received the Bollingen Prize, two Guggenheim Fellowships, and countless other awards.

Alex Carr Johnson and his husband, Pete, make their home along the wild spine of the continent where the Rocky Mountains and Colorado Plateau meet. His work has appeared in *Orion, Earth Island Journal, High Country News*, and elsewhere.

Ilya Kaminsky was born in Odessa, Ukraine, and currently lives in California. He is the author of *Dancing in Odessa* and coeditor of *Ecco Anthology of International Poetry* and several other books.

Nancy Jooyoun Kim was born and raised in Los Angeles, California. Her work has appeared in the *Los Angeles Review of Books, The Rumpus, Electric Literature, Selected Shorts* on NPR/PRI, Asian American Writers' Workshop's *The Margins, The Offing*, and elsewhere.

Jamaica Kincaid is an award-winning Antiguan American writer. Her books include *Annie John, Lucy, Autobiography of My Mother*, and many others. She teaches at Harvard University.

Ada Limón is the author of four books of poetry, including *Bright Dead Things*, which was named a finalist for the 2015 National Book Award in Poetry, a finalist for the Kingsley Tufts Poetry Award, a finalist for the 2015 National Book Critics Circle Award, and one of the Top Ten Poetry Books of the Year by the *New York Times*. Her other books include *Lucky Wreck*, *This Big Fake World*, and *Sharks in the Rivers*. She serves on the faculty of Queens University of Charlotte's low-residency MFA program and the 24PearlStreet online program for the Provincetown Fine Arts Work Center. She also works as a freelance writer splitting her time between Lexington, Kentucky, and Sonoma, California.

Debra Marquart is the author of five books of prose and poetry—most recently a poetry collection, *Small Buried Things*—and the coeditor of *Nothing to Declare: A Guide to the Prose Sequence*, recently published by White Pine Press. Marquart directs the MFA program in Creative Writing and Environment at Iowa State University, teaches in the Stonecoast low-residency MFA program at the University of Southern Maine, and serves as the senior editor of *Flyway: Journal of Writing & Environment*. Her work has been featured on three NPR programs: *All Things Considered*, Garrison Keillor's *The Writer's Almanac*, and Tom Ashbrook's *On Point*. Her awards include a Pushcart Prize, an NEA Creative Writing Prose Fellowship, the 2014 Paumanok Poetry Award, the Elle Lettres Award from *Elle* Magazine, and the 2007 PEN USA Creative Nonfiction Award.

Semezdin Mehmedinović was born in Tuzla, Bosnia, in 1960 and is the author of eight books. In 1993 he was cowriter and codirector, together with Benjamin Filipovic, of *Mizaldo*, one of the first Bosnian films shot during the war. The film was presented at the Berlin Film Festival in 1994 and won the first prize at the Mediterranean Festival in Rome the following year. He, his wife, and their child left Bosnia and came to the United States as political refugees in 1996.

Shivani Mehta was born in Mumbai and raised in Singapore. Her work has appeared in numerous journals, and her collection of prose poems, *Useful Information for the Soon-to-be Beheaded*, is out from Press 53. A recovering lawyer, she lives in Los Angeles with her husband, six-year-old twins, two cats, and more fish than she can count.

Calvin Mills is a writer of short fiction, essays, and plays. His musical *Freak Like Me* premiered in 2012. His stories and essays have appeared in *Short Story*, *Weird Tales*, and other magazines. He teaches at Peninsula College in Port Angeles, Washington.

Augusto Monterroso was an award-winning Latin American writer who was most well known for his short stories.

Kara Oakleaf's work has appeared in journals including *SmokeLong Quarterly*, *Monkeybicycle*, *Jellyfish Review*, *Nimrod*, *Seven Hills Review*, *Tahoma Literary Review*, and *Postcard Poems and Prose*. She is a graduate of the MFA program at George Mason University, where she now teaches and directs the Fall for the Book literary festival.

Lia Purpura is the author of eight collections of essays, poems, and translations, most recently a collection of poems, *It Shouldn't Have Been Beautiful* (Penguin). *On Looking* (essays, Sarabande Books) was finalist for the National Book Critics Circle Award. Her awards include Guggenheim, NEA, and Fulbright Fellowships, as well as four Pushcart Prizes and others. Her work appears in the *New Yorker*, *The New Republic*, *Orion*, *The Paris Review*, *The Georgia Review*, *Agni*, and elsewhere. She lives in Baltimore, Maryland, is Writer in Residence at the University of Maryland, Baltimore County, and teaches in the Rainier Writing Workshop's MFA program.

Jennifer Richter's second collection, *No Acute Distress*, is a Crab Orchard Series in Poetry Editor's Selection; her first book, *Threshold*, was chosen for the Crab Orchard Series by Natasha Trethewey. Richter currently teaches in Oregon State University's MFA program.

Bruce Holland Rogers writes short fiction all over the literary map and has won two Nebula Awards in science fiction, two World Fantasy Awards, a Pushcart Prize, two Micro Awards for the year's best flash fiction, and an NEA Individual Artist fellowship. He lives in Eugene, Oregon.

Mary Ruefle is an award-winning poet and essayist. Her books include *Trances of the Blast*, *Madness, Rack, and Honey: Collected Lectures*, *My Private Property*, *On Imagination*, and others. She teaches at the Vermont College of Fine Arts.

David Shields has published more than twenty books, including *Reality Hunger, The Thing About Life Is That One Day You'll Be Dead, Black Planet*, and *Other People: Takes and Mistakes*. He has received Guggenheim and NEA Fellowships and had his work appear in the *New York Times Magazine, Harper's Esquire, Salon, Slate*, and *McSweeney's*. He teaches at the University of Washington.

Evie Shockley is the author of several collections of poetry, including *a half-red sea* (2006) and *the new black* (2011). Shockley is also the author of the critical volume *Renegade Poetics: Black Aesthetics and Formal Innovation in African American Poetry* (2011). She is a professor at Rutgers University and lives in Jersey City, New Jersey.

Ana María Shua is an Argentine writer and illustrator who has published more than eighty books in microfiction, fiction, poetry, and children's literature. She has received a number of awards, including a Guggenheim Fellowship.

Patricia Smith is a poet and performance artist who has written *Incendiary Art, Shoulda Been Jimi Savannah, Blood Dazzler, Teahouse of the Almighty*, and more. She has won a number of awards, including the Lenore Marshall Poetry Prize, a National Book Award, and a Carl Sandburg Literary Award. She is a four-time champion of the National Poetry Slam. She teachers at the City University of New York/College of Staten Island.

Ira Sukrungruang is the author of the memoirs *Southside Buddhist, Talk Thai: The Adventures of Buddhist Boy*, and *Buddha's Dog & Other Meditations*, the short story collection *The Melting Season*, and the poetry collection *In Thailand It Is Night*. For more information about him, please visit www.buddhistboy.com.

Justin Torres is the author of the best-selling novel *We the Animals*, and his honors include a Stegner Fellowship, a Radcliffe Institute Fellowship, and a Cullman Center Fellowship. Named one of the National Book Foundation's 2012 5 Under 35, Torres is an assistant professor of English at UCLA.

Tomas Tranströmer was a Swedish poet who won a Nobel Prize in Literature and a Neustadt International Prize for Literature. His books include *The Half-Finished Heaven*, *Baltics*, *For the Living and the Dead*, *The Great Enigma*, and many more.

Thomas Tsalapatis was born in 1984 in Athens. He studied theater at the University of Athens. His first collection, *Daybreak Is Execution, Mr. Krack*, received the National Poetry Prize for best newcomer writer. His second collection, *Alba*, was published in 2015 and has been translated and published in French by Desmos Editions.

Brian Turner's latest book is *The Kiss* (W. W. Norton & Company, 2018), an anthology based on the short-form series he curates at *Guernica*. Turner is the author of *My Life as a Foreign Country: A Memoir* (W. W. Norton & Company, 2014), *Phantom Noise* (Alice James Books, 2010), and *Here, Bullet* (Alice James Books, 2005). He has received numerous awards, including a Guggenheim Fellowship, the Amy Lowell Traveling Fellowship, and a Lannan Foundation Fellowship.

Ocean Vuong's first collection of poetry, *Night Sky with Exit Wounds* (Copper Canyon Press, 2016), was one of the *New York Times* Top 10 Books of 2016. He has also won a Whiting Award, a Thom Gunn Award, and a Forward Prize.

Lucy Wainger is a poet whose work appears in *Best American Poetry 2017*, *Poetry*, and elsewhere. She studies creative writing at Emory University, where she received the 2017 Academy of American Poets Prize.

Michael Wasson is the author of *This American Ghost* (YesYes Books, 2017). His poems appear in *American Poets*, *Beloit Poetry Journal*, *Kenyon Review*, *Narrative*, *Poetry Northwest*, and *Bettering American Poetry*. He is *Nimíipuu* from the Nez Perce Reservation in Idaho and lives abroad.

Terry Tempest Williams is the award-winning author of fifteen books, including *Refuge: An Unnatural History of Family and Place*, *Finding Beauty in a Broken World*, and *When Women Were Birds*. Her work has been widely anthologized around the world. She lives in Castle Valley, Utah, with her husband, Brooke Williams.

David Young is an award-winning poet and translator who has published several poetry collections, including *Field of Light and Shadow* (2010),

Black Lab (2006), *At the White Window* (2000), *Night Thoughts and Henry Vaughan* (1994), *The Planet on the Desk: Selected and New Poems 1960–1990* (1991), *Foraging* (1986), *Earthshine* (1988), *The Names of a Hare in English* (1979), *Work Lights: Thirty-Two Prose Poems* (1977), *Boxcars* (1972), and *Sweating Out the Winter* (1969).

Acknowledgments

Henry Alford: "Cookie Monster on the Dole." Copyright © 2017 by Henry Alford. First appeared in *The New Yorker*. Reprinted by permission of the author. All rights reserved.

Joanne Avallon: "All This." Copyright © 1996 by Joanne Avallon. First published in *Micro Fiction: An Anthology of Really Short Stories*, ed. by Jerome Stern © 1996. Reprinted by permission of the author. All rights reserved.

Pía Barros: "A Tale Sometimes Heard in a Bar at Three in the Morning" from *Ropa Usada* (Chile: Editorial Sherezade, 2014). Translated by Resha Cardone. Copyright © 2014 by Pía Barros. Reprinted by permission of the author. All rights reserved.

Charles Baudelaire: "Be Drunken" from *Baudelaire: His Prose and Poetry*. Translated by Arthur Symons. Edited by T. R. Smith. New York: Boni and Liveright, 1919. Published on Project Gutenberg. Retrieved August 21, 2017, from www.gutenberg.org/ebooks/47032.

Matt Bell: "My Grading Scale for the Fall Semester, Composed Entirely of Samuel Beckett Quotes." Originally published in *McSweeney's Internet Tendency*, August 31, 2012. Reprinted with permission of the author. All rights reserved.

Karen E. Bender: "The Man Who Hated Us and Then Forgot." Copyright © 2016 by Karen E. Bender. First appeared in *Fourth River*. Reprinted by permission of the author. All rights reserved.

Sven Birkerts: "One Long Sentence." Originally published in *The Three Penny Review*, No. 134 (Summer 2013). Reprinted with permission of the author. All rights reserved.

Italo Calvino: Excerpt from *Invisible Cities* by Italo Calvino, translated by William Weaver. Copyright © 1972 by Giulio Einaudi editore, s.p.a Torino, English translation copyright © 1983, 1984 by Houghton Mifflin Harcourt Publishing Company. Reprinted by permission of Houghton Mifflin Harcourt Publishing Company. All rights reserved.

Joy Castro: "Grip." Copyright © 2016 by Joy Castro. First published in *Waveform: Twenty-first Century Essays by Women,* ed. by Marcia Aldrich © 2016. Reprinted by permission of the author. All rights reserved.

Matthew Clarke: "The Cat." Copyright © 2015 by Matthew Clarke. Reprinted by permission of the author. All rights reserved.

Katie Cortese: "Rules of Combat" from *Girl Power.* Copyright © 2015 by Katie Cortese. First appeared in *Passages North.* Reprinted by permission of the author. All rights reserved.

Steve Coughlin: "Boy at Night" from *Another City.* Copyright © 2015 by Steve Coughlin. Reprinted by permission of the author. All rights reserved.

Lydia Davis: "Letter to a Funeral Parlor" from *The Collected Stories of Lydia Davis* Copyright © 2009, 2010 by Lydia Davis. Reprinted by permission of Farrar, Straus and Giroux, and Hamish Hamilton. All rights reserved.

Danielle Cadena Deulen: "For My Sister in the River" from *Lovely Asunder.* Copyright © 2011 by Danielle Cadena Deulen. Reprinted with the permission of The Permissions Company, Inc., on behalf of the University of Arkansas Press, www.uapress.com. All rights reserved.

Natalie Diaz: "Self-Portrait as a Chimera" from *When My Brother Was an Aztec.* Copyright © 2012 by Natalie Diaz. Reprinted with the permission of The Permissions Company, Inc., on behalf of Copper Canyon Press, www.coppercanyonpress.org. All rights reserved.

Brian Doyle: "My Devils." Copyright © 2016 by Brian Doyle. First appeared in *The Sun.* Reprinted by permission of the author's estate. All rights reserved.

Russell Edson: "The Prose Poem as a Beautiful Animal" from *The Best of The Prose Poem: An International Journal,* ed. by Peter Johnson. Copyright © 2000. Published 2000 by White Pine Press. Reprinted by permission of the author's estate. All rights reserved.

Sarah Evans: "Dust." Copyright © 2014 by Sarah Evans. Reprinted by permission of the author. Originally published in *River Teeth.* All rights reserved.

Grant Faulkner: "Time Travel" from *Fissures.* Copyright © 2015 by Grant Faulkner. First appeared in *International Flash Journal.* Reprinted by permission of the author. All rights reserved.

Nikky Finney: "Instruction, Final: To Brown Poets from Black Girl with Silver Leica." Copyright © 2011 by Nikky Finney. Published 2011 by TriQuarterly Books/Northwestern University Press. Reprinted by permission of the publisher. All rights reserved.

by permission of The Wylie Agency LLC. and reprinted by permission of Farrar, Straus and Giroux. All rights reserved.

Ada Limón: "The Quiet Machine" from *Bright Dead Things* (Minneapolis: Milkweed Editions, 2015). Copyright © 2015 by Ada Limón. Reprinted with permission from Milkweed Editions. Milkweed.org. All rights reserved.

Debra Marquart: "Some Things about That Day" from *Small Buried Things: Poems*. Copyright © 2015 by Debra Marquart. First appeared in *Brevity: A Journal of Concise Literary Nonfiction*. Reprinted by permission of The Permissions Company, Inc., on behalf of New Rivers Press, www.newriverspress.com. All rights reserved.

Semezdin Mehmedinović: "Surplus History" from *Sarajevo Blues*. Translated by Ammiel Alcalay. Copyright © 1995, 1998 by Semezdin Mehmedinović. Reprinted with the permission of The Permissions Company, Inc., on behalf of City Lights Books, www.citylights.com. All rights reserved.

Shivani Mehta: "the invisible girl can be anything she wants when she doesn't want to be invisible." Copyright © 2016 by Shivani Mehta. First appeared in *New Flash Fiction Review*. Reprinted by permission of the author. All rights reserved.

Calvin Mills: "The Girl Who Likes Dogs." Copyright © 2013 by Calvin Mills. First appeared in *Stoneboat*. Reprinted by permission of the author. All rights reserved.

Augusto Monterroso: "The Dinosaur" from *Complete Works and Other Stories* translated by Edith Grossman. Copyright © 1995. Reprinted by permission of University of Texas Press. All rights reserved.

Kara Oakleaf: "Gravity, Reduced." Copyright © 2017 by Kara Oakleaf. First appeared in *SmokeLong Quarterly*. Reprinted by permission of the author. All rights reserved.

Lia Purpura: "On Miniatures." Copyright © 2006 by Lia Purpura. First appeared in *Brevity: A Journal of Concise Literary Nonfiction*. Reprinted by permission of the author. All rights reserved.

Jennifer Richter: "Pleasant, healthy-appearing adult white female in no acute distress" from *No Acute Distress*. Copyright © 2016 by Jennifer Richter. Reprinted by permission of the author. All rights reserved.

Bruce Holland Rogers: "Dinosaur." Copyright © 2017 by Bruce Holland Rogers. First appeared in *Brevity: A Flash Fiction Handbook*. Reprinted by permission of the author. All rights reserved.

Mary Ruefle: "Short Lecture on Your Own Happiness" from *Madness, Rack, and Honey: Collected Lectures*. Copyright © 2012 by Mary Ruefle.

Reprinted with the permission of The Permissions Company, Inc. on behalf of Wave Books, www.wavepoetry.com.

David Shields: "Life Story" from *Other People: Takes and Mistakes*. Copyright © 2017 by David Shields. Used by permission of Alfred A. Knopf, an imprint of the Knopf Doubleday Publishing Group, a division of Penguin Random House LLC. All rights reserved.

Evie Shockley: "go-go tarot" from *the new black*. Copyright © 2011 by Evie Shockley. Reprinted by permission of Wesleyan University Press. All rights reserved.

Ana María Shua: "Cannibals and Explorers" translated by Rhonda Dahl Buchanan, from *Quick Fix: Sudden Fiction*. Translation copyright © 2008. Reprinted with permission of The Permissions Company, Inc. on behalf of White Pine Press, www.whitepine.org.

Patricia Smith: "An All-Purpose Product" from *Shoulda Been Jimi Savannah*. Copyright © 2012 by Patricia Smith. Reprinted with the permission of The Permissions Company, Inc. on behalf of Coffee House Press, www.coffeehousepress.org.

Ira Sukrungruang: "Consequence" from *Southside Buddhist*. Copyright © 2014 by Ira Sukrungruang. Reprinted by permission of University of Tampa Press. All rights reserved.

Justin Torres: "In Praise of Latin Night at the Queer Club." Copyright © 2016 by Justin Torres. First appeared in *The Washington Post*. Reprinted by permission of the author and used by permission of The Wylie Agency, LLC. All rights reserved.

Tomas Tranströmer: "Icelandic Hurricane" translated by Robin Fulton, from *The Great Enigma*. Copyright © 2006 by Tomas Tranströmer. Translation Copyright © 2006 by Robin Fulton. Reprinted by permission of New Directions Publishing Corp. and Bloodaxe Books.

Thomas Tsalapatis: "The Box" translated by Thodoris Chiotis, from *Futures: Poetry of the Greek Crisis*. Copyright © 2015. Reprinted with permission of the author. All rights reserved.

Brian Turner: "The Inventory from a Year Lived Sleeping with Bullets" from *Phantom Noise*. Copyright © 2010 by Brian Turner. Reprinted with the permission of The Permissions Company, Inc. on behalf of Alice James Books and Bloodaxe Books.

Ocean Vuong: "Immigrant Haibun" from *Night Sky with Exit Wounds*. Copyright © 2016 by Ocean Vuong. Used with the permission of The Permissions Company, Inc. on behalf of Copper Canyon Press, www.coppercanyonpress.org.

Lucy Wainger: "Scheherazade." Copyright © 2016 by Lucy Wainger. First appeared in *Poetry* December 2016. Reprinted by permission of the author. All rights reserved.

Michael Wasson: "Small Meditations." Copyright © 2016 by Michael Wasson. First appeared in *Prairie Schooner*'s blog. Reprinted by permission of the author. All rights reserved.

Terry Tempest Williams: "A Letter to Deb Clow" from *Red: Passion and Patience in the Desert* by Terry Tempest Williams. Originally appeared in *Northern Lights* magazine, summer 1998 edition as "*Why Write.*" Copyright © 1998 by Terry Tempest Williams. Reprinted by permission of Brandt and Hochman Literary Agents, Inc. All rights reserved.

David Young: Excerpt from "Four about Death" from *Work Lights: Thirty-Two Prose Poems*. Copyright © 1977 by David Young. Reprinted with the permission of The Permissions Company, Inc., on behalf of the Cleveland State University Poetry Center, www.csuohio.edu/poetrycenter. All rights reserved.

Genre Index

"What You Are" by Katelyn Hemmeke: flash nonfiction

"Memoir" by Amy Hempel: short-short story

"A Modern Fable" by David Ignatow: prose poetry

"8 Meetings Nobody Scheduled" by Alex Carr Johnson: flash nonfiction

"Natalia" by Ilya Kaminsky: paragraph

"La Jungla" by Nancy Jooyoun Kim: flash fiction

"The Letter from Home" by Jamaica Kincaid: lyrical short stories

"The Quiet Machine" by Ada Limón: prose poetry

"Some Things About that Day" by Debra Marquart: flash nonfiction, prose
    poetry, lyric fusion

"Surplus History" by Semezdin Mehmedinović: prose poetry

"the invisible girl can be anything she wants when she doesn't want to be
    invisible" by Shivani Mehta: prose poetry

"The Girl Who Likes Dogs" by Calvin Mills: creative nonfiction

"The Dinosaur" by Augusto Monterroso: short story, or in the author's words,
    "a novel."

"Gravity, Reduced" by Kara Oakleaf: flash fiction

"On Miniatures" by Lia Purpura: essay

"Pleasant, healthy-appearing adult white female in no acute distress" by
    Jennifer Richter: prose poetry

"Dinosaur" by Bruce Holland Rogers: flash fiction

"Short Lecture on Your Own Happiness" by Mary Ruefle: lecture

"Life Story" by David Shields: essay

"go-go tarot" by Evie Shockley: prose poetry

"Cannibals and Explorers" by Ana María Shua: flash fiction

"An All-Purpose Product" by Patricia Smith: prose poetry

"Consequence" by Ira Sukrungruang: flash nonfiction

"In Praise of Latin Night at the Queer Club" by Justin Torres: short essay, op-ed

"Icelandic Hurricane" by Tomas Tranströmer: prose poetry

"The Box" by Thomas Tsalapatis: prose poetry

"The Inventory of a Year Lived Sleeping with Bullets" by Brian Turner: prose
    poetry

"Immigrant Haibun" by Ocean Vuong: prose poetry

"Scheherazade." by Lucy Wainger: prose poetry

"Small Meditations" by Michael Wasson: lyric essay

"A Letter to Deb Clow" by Terry Tempest Williams: nonfiction

Excerpt from "Four about Death" by David Young: prose poetry

*For authors who were unavailable to categorize their work, we indicated how
    the work was categorized upon its first publication.

Index

SERIES EDITORS: SEAN PRENTISS AND JOE WILKINS

Short-Form Creative Writing: A Writer's Guide and Anthology is a complete introduction to the art and craft of extremely compressed works of imaginative literature. H. K. Hummel and Stephanie Lenox introduce both traditional and innovative approaches to the short form and demonstrate how it possesses structure, logic, and coherence while simultaneously resisting expectations. With discussion questions, writing prompts, flash interviews, and illustrated key concepts, the book covers:

- Prose poetry
- Flash fiction
- Micro memoir
- Lyric essay
- Cross-genre/hybrid writing

. . . and much more.

Short-Form Creative Writing also includes an anthology, offering inspiring examples of short-form writing in all of the styles covered by the book, including work by Charles Baudelaire, Italo Calvino, Lydia Davis, Grant Faulkner, Ilya Kaminsky, Jamaica Kincaid, and many others.

H. K. HUMMEL is Assistant Professor of Creative Writing at the University of Arkansas at Little Rock, USA. She is the author of the poetry collections, *Lessons in Breathing Underwater*, *Boytreebird*, and *Handmade Boats*.

STEPHANIE LENOX is an instructional editor for Chemeketa Press at Chemeketa Community College, USA. She is the author of the poetry collections, *The Business*, *Congress of Strange People*, and *The Heart That Lies Outside the Body*.

LITERARY STUDIES

BLOOMSBURY ACADEMIC

ISBN 978-1-350-01988-1

9 781350 019881